HOCKEY
IN
DAYTON

Front Cover: Dayton Gems goalie Pat Rupp blocks shots during a pregame warm-up at Hara Arena in this undated photograph. (Courtesy of Kathy Rupp.)

Cover Background: This photograph was taken by Max Surikov during the national anthem before a Dayton Bombers game against the Johnstown Chiefs at the Nutter Center on April 5, 2008. (Courtesy of Max Surikov.)

Back Cover: Troy Bruins forward Bill Murphy attacks the Chatham Maroons goal in a contest at Hobart Arena on November 4, 1951. (Courtesy of Bill Murphy.)

HOCKEY IN DAYTON

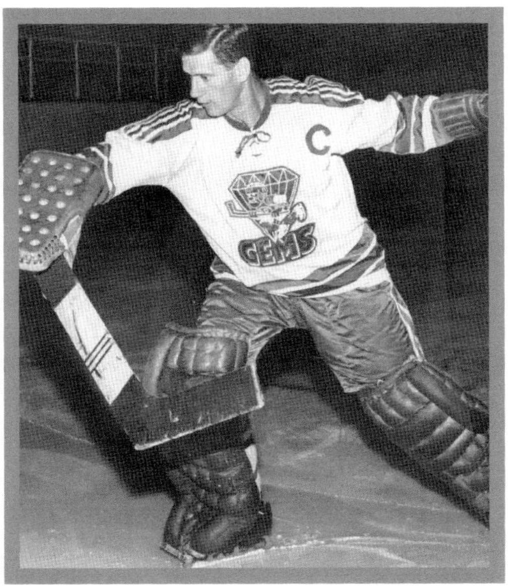

Chuck Gabringer

ARCADIA PUBLISHING

ISBN 978-1-4671-1432-5

Published by Arcadia Publishing
Charleston, South Carolina

Printed in the United States of America

Library of Congress Control Number: 2015930361

For all general information, please contact Arcadia Publishing:
Telephone 843-853-2070
Fax 843-853-0044
E-mail sales@arcadiapublishing.com
For customer service and orders:
Toll-Free 1-888-313-2665

Visit us on the Internet at www.arcadiapublishing.com

This book is dedicated to my son Joe and to my family for sharing many happy moments in our lives watching and talking about hockey.

CONTENTS

FOREWORD

My father took me to my first ice hockey game when I was 11 years old. It was in 1950, at the newly built Hobart Arena in Troy, where the home team was the Miami Valley Bruins. The club played an independent schedule for one season before changing its name to the Troy Bruins and joining the International Hockey League.

At that time, few people in the Dayton area knew much about hockey. The nearest cities with minor-league teams were Toledo and Cincinnati. The Bruins, with 14 players averaging 22 years of age, played at home every Sunday afternoon at 3:00. The sport grabbed my interest immediately. My dad loved it, too, so we began attending games regularly.

I started listening to Bob Elson's broadcasts of the Chicago Blackhawks at night with a transistor radio buried in my pillow. I can still hear Elson saying, "And now, while the puck is iced, why don't you ice up to a bottle of smootherized Old Crown Ale?"

The Bruins lasted nine years before closing shop in 1959, because it was not financially feasible to continue. Hockey would not return to the Dayton area until five years later, in 1964, when Ed "Lefty" McFadden established the Dayton Gems, who played in a new facility called Hara Arena.

The Gems were very popular for several years, winning the IHL's Turner Cup in 1969 and 1970. But the arrival of the Cincinnati Bengals in 1968 eroded the Gems' corporate revenue, and the formation of the World Hockey Association in 1972 reduced their access to veteran players.

Although the team won another Turner Cup in 1976, it folded after the next season. A succession of franchises followed, but none enjoyed the attention given the Bruins and the Gems.

Those two teams, along with the Dayton Bombers, are the primary focus of this book, which reflects the dedication of longtime hockey fan Chuck Gabringer, who succeeded in obtaining some seldom-seen photographs that illustrate the Miami Valley's hockey history. One of my favorites is that of Hobart Arena's homemade ice-resurfacing machine, which was attached to an Army-style Willys Jeep. The machines that Frank Zamboni introduced in 1949 were not yet produced in large numbers.

I hope you enjoy this pictorial history of ice hockey's journey in the Miami Valley as much as I did.

—Bucky Albers
former Dayton *Journal Herald* sportswriter
and Dayton Gems general manager

ACKNOWLEDGMENTS

This book would not have been possible without the help and contribution of dozens of great people who lent a hand in some way along the journey and whom I would like to thank. I could not have gotten this done without them.

First, I wish to thank the people who provided the photographs. For the Troy Bruins: Ken Siler at Hobart Arena, Kevin Anderson, Bill and Betty Murphy, Jeff Wilson, Patrick Kennedy and the Troy Historical Society, Chris Barno, and Bob Speck. For the Dayton Gems: Kathy Rupp, Rick Bragnalo, Steve Self, Bucky Albers, Jerry Dowling, Tim Ampleford, Barb Brigner, Jim Pettie, Marc Katz, and the McFadden family. For the Dayton Bombers: Melissia Morris-Taziar, Gregg Wurtzler, Nikki Jahns, and Max Surikov. Dr. Michael Hamilton, Doug Brown, Chris Arnold, and Mike Clare also provided images.

A special thanks goes to Gino Pasi and Chris Wydman at the Wright State University Special Collections and Archives for providing many of the photographs in this book, often on short notice.

Many, many people were interviewed for this book, some of whom provided images. But there are others who happily provided some time for me to talk about their involvement with Dayton hockey: Jim Playfair, Claude Noel, Warren Back, Ed Gingher, Lyle Stieg, Marty Szturm, Rich Szturm, Bill Kirby, Patti McAtee-Haren, John Siehl, and Jamie Ling.

A special mention goes to those with whom I spent time and are no longer with us: Lefty McFadden, Pat Rupp, Moe Benoit, Guy Trottier, and Bud Gingher.

Lastly, I would like to thank my editor, John Woods; Liz Gurley at Arcadia Publishing, for her patience; my legal counsel, Jim Dennis; and my friends and family, who encouraged me to finally get this done after 20 years so they won't have to hear me talk about writing it anymore.

I am grateful to have been able to work with so many people who were so enthusiastic in helping out and wanting to contribute to this project. Thank you all.

INTRODUCTION

Six teams were in the National Hockey League (NHL) in 1950. Many people in the Dayton and Miami Valley region probably could not have named the "original six," let alone the most prominent stars of hockey at the time. Hockey, a Canadian sport, was relegated to cities in more northern and eastern areas of the United States. Gordie Howe was not yet a big star, and Bobby Hull and Bobby Orr were still years away from prominence.

In Ohio, minor-league hockey had been in a few cities, most notably Cleveland, where the Barons had been playing in the American Hockey League (AHL) since 1937. In Cincinnati, the Mohawks, coached by the famous "King" Clancy, had a short run in the AHL (1949–1952), playing in the newly constructed Cincinnati Gardens. Toledo, too, had a new building, the Toledo Sports Arena. Hockey took up residence there in 1947, when the Mercurys joined the new International Hockey League (IHL).

As for the Dayton area, hockey was not on the sports map in 1950, except for the occasional small story or score in the *Dayton Daily News* or *The Journal Herald*. Sports interest in Dayton in 1950 was limited to Cincinnati Reds baseball, Ohio State Buckeyes football, and University of Dayton football and basketball. The University of Dayton Fieldhouse, home to UD basketball before the UD Arena was built, opened in 1950.

Nevertheless, the absence of hockey and the lack of knowledge of hockey did not deter Ken Wilson from bringing the sport to the area in 1950, when Hobart Arena opened in Troy. Wilson's gamble was that the combination of the novelty of hockey and the speed and excitement of the sport would attract enough of a following to give it a foothold in the area and make it a success. The fact that the Miami Valley Bruins, and later the Troy Bruins, would play in a brand-new building would not hurt hockey's chances of being a hit.

So, the puck was officially dropped for hockey in the Dayton area in October 1950. Though Troy and the area did not take to the sport or new team immediately, the community slowly warmed up to hockey over time. Eventually, crowds of more than 3,000 were attending Bruins games. During the 1952–1953 season, nearly half of all Bruins home games drew more than 3,000 fans—in a town with a population of just 10,000.

The hockey was good, too. Because the NHL was limited to six teams, and the minor leagues were few, the pool of talented players for teams to draw from was bigger. Troy fans witnessed some great players at Hobart Arena, including Bruins players Steve Gaber, Bill Tibbs, Max Szturm, and Brian Kilrea, who scored the first goal for the Los Angeles Kings when the team entered the NHL in 1967. Gilles Villemure, who won a Vezina Trophy in 1971 as the NHL's best goaltender, played three games for the Bruins in December 1958.

Attendance waned in the late 1950s for the Bruins. Though the team left Troy in 1959, the seed was planted for hockey to make a bigger run. One person who traveled from Dayton to Troy to watch the Bruins was Ed "Lefty" McFadden. While a writer for the *Dayton Daily News*, he would sometimes cover the team for the paper. When he was tapped to run the IHL expansion Dayton Gems in 1964, McFadden later admitted, "I didn't know a lot about hockey, but I liked the rough stuff."

As the Gems were getting off the ground, fans were doubtful the team would find much success. "We're not going to be the Mets," McFadden declared, referring to the record-breaking futility of the 1961 New York Mets when they entered major-league baseball's National League. The Gems, in fact, were worse than the Mets in the first part of their first year. One night in early December 1964, at a time when the Gems were losing most every game, McFadden looked out his Hara Arena office windows at a sparsely filled parking lot and wondered, "Where are the cars?"

Slowly, the team turned it around. McFadden and coach Warren Back added skilled players to the team, including Guy Trottier, Pat Rupp, Pat Donnelly, and NHL veteran Bob Bailey. The Gems got better, and the fans began to show up at Hara. In only its second year, the Gems were in the Turner Cup playoff finals—the first of five appearances. By their third year, home attendance exceeded 4,000 a game. By the Gems' fifth year, when they won their first Turner Cup playoff championship, attendance swelled to over 4,500 a game. Sunday-afternoon game tickets were almost impossible to get.

Though hockey expanded and became more popular in the early 1970s, the Gems had peaked. A poor economy and inflation took its toll on the Dayton area. In this industrial town, layoffs at Delco, Chrysler, NCR, and Frigidaire devastated the business climate. The job losses hurt the team at the turnstiles. By 1974, the beginning of the end had started. Lefty McFadden exited for a job with the NHL's Washington Capitals. Even though the Gems put one of the best IHL teams on the ice in 1975–1976, the team struggled financially. After the next season, the team suspended operations. The Gems' IHL rival Columbus Owls moved in and quickly left. The Gems returned for a season in 1979 and then called it quits, permanently, in the spring of 1980.

Many people were skeptics when Bud Gingher and Arnie Johnson considered locating an East Coast Hockey League franchise in Dayton in 1991. Though 11 years had passed, the Gems' failure was still fresh in the minds of Dayton hockey fans. But they were ready for hockey. The Bombers averaged 4,000 fans a game their first year at Hara Arena—something it took the Gems three years to do. And the team averaged 4,000 or more in attendance its first four years at Hara. During the 1992–1993 season, the Bombers sold out the "Hara Hockey Hangar" 12 times. But, while the team drew better than the Gems for a while, the Bombers never won a championship, which could have propelled the team to a higher level of popularity in the Dayton area.

Seeking to expand the fan base and grow the sport, Gingher and Johnson moved the team across town to the E.J. Nutter Center at Wright State University, in Greene County, east of Dayton. The fans on the north side of town felt betrayed by the move and stayed to watch the Dayton Ice Bandits for a season at Hara Arena before that franchise went out of business. The move never gained the traction the owners had hoped, and the team lost money, mostly due to the expense of putting ice in the Nutter Center. In 2000, the wildly successful Dayton Dragons baseball team arrived, and competition for entertainment and corporate dollars became fierce. New owners came and went for the Bombers. The team went out of business in 2009. An incarnation of the Gems, which existed after the Bombers in 2009, lasted three years. In 2012, the Dayton Demonz moved into Hara Arena taking the place of the Gems.

The year 2015 marks 65 years since Ken Wilson brought an unknown sport to Dayton. The area has seen six decades of action (with a few gaps), hundreds of players, thousands of games, and millions of fans. Throw in a rubber chicken or two, a few cowbells, and some missing teeth—and that is Hockey in Dayton.

1

In the Beginning

The Troy Bruins

The story of hockey in the Miami Valley ended almost as quickly as it began.

The general manager of the Miami Valley Bruins, Ken Wilson, had to be encouraged about the prospect for the success of his new hockey team. After all, 5,000 people had attended the first hockey game at Hobart Arena between the Cleveland Barons and Indianapolis Capitals on October 7, 1950. But, when the Bruins played St. Paul in their first game in Troy on October 11, only around 1,000 people showed up to watch. The next three home contests did not fare much better, drawing a total of 5,000 fans. By early November, newspaper articles began reporting that the fledgling hockey team might move or be disbanded due to lack of interest.

Determined not to fail, Wilson put together the Bruins Booster Club to drum up fan support for the team. The club drew immediate interest from the community, and its members went about the work of increasing the attendance numbers needed to keep the team in Troy. The first game the booster club helped promote drew 3,500 fans to Hobart Arena. Not long after, the team drew another 3,000 for a home game. For a home game versus Windsor on December 10, 1950, some 4,000 fans watched the Bruins win 11-1.

The team played in front of several more crowds in excess of 4,000 during the remainder of the season, including 4,500 versus the Cincinnati Mohawks in January 1951. By season's end, fan support was such that the Bruins applied for, and gained, entrance into the International Hockey League (IHL), where they remained for eight years. The team did not fold. Hockey in the Miami Valley got off the ground—but not without a few bumps along the way.

When they eventually left Troy in 1959, the Bruins were one of only two teams remaining from the six that had competed in the 1951–1952 IHL season. The Bruins outlasted nearly a dozen other IHL franchises in that time, including teams in Cincinnati, Milwaukee, Louisville, and Detroit. And, while the Bruins almost did not get through their first few months, Ken Wilson, the Bruins Booster Club, and the hockey fans of Troy made sure that hockey would succeed and become a part of the Miami Valley sports landscape for decades to come.

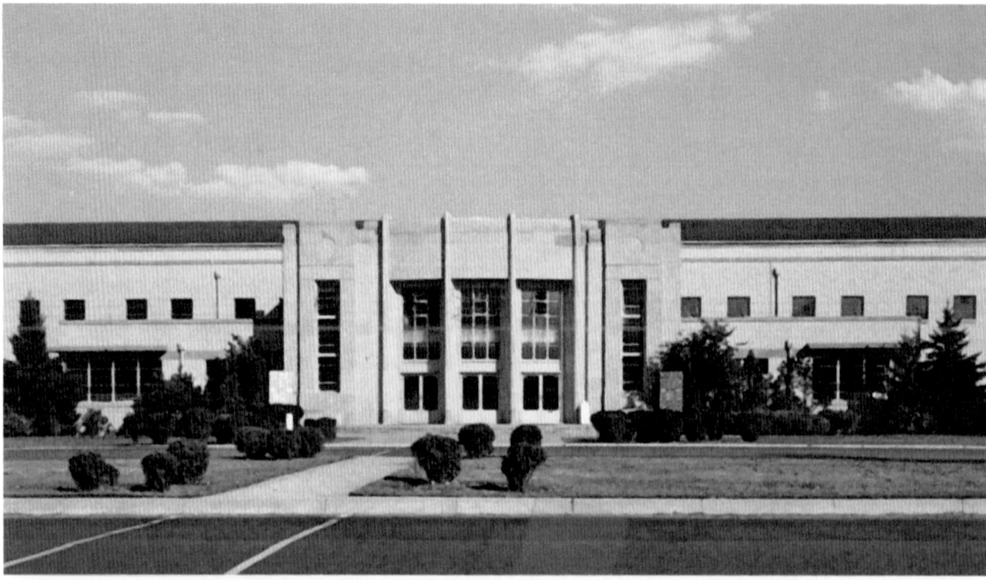

In 1946, Edward and William Hobart of the Hobart Corporation proposed the development of a new sports and recreation area across the Miami River from downtown Troy. The Hobarts proposed that if the residents approved a bond issue funding a new golf course and football stadium, the C.C. Hobart Foundation would, in turn, build a million-dollar sports arena with ice-making capabilities. The envisioned facility would be named Hobart Arena. (Courtesy of Hobart Arena.)

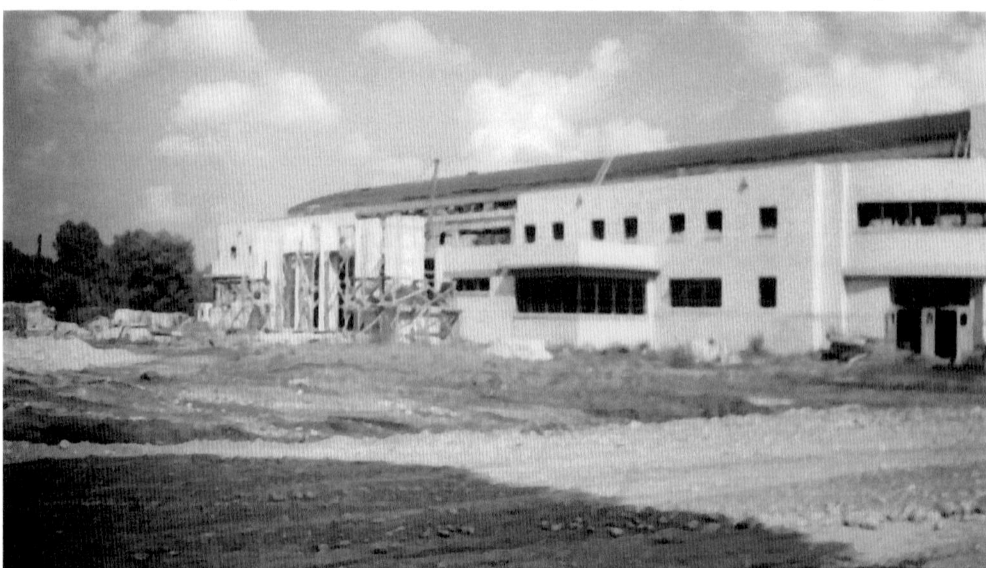

The voters of Troy approved the building of the stadium and golf course, and both were dedicated in 1949. Construction of the arena began in 1948 and continued for two years. When completed, it had 4,500 permanent seats (according to the Bruins hockey program) and was able to accommodate 6,000 fans, with temporary seating and standing-room areas. It was the only arena of its kind in the region. (Courtesy of Hobart Arena.)

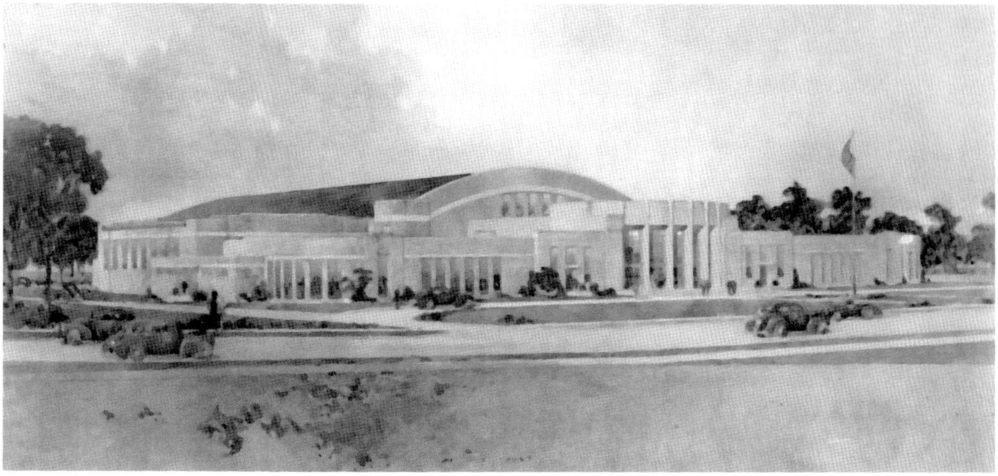

In the original artist rendering of Hobart Arena, the main arena was positioned in an east-west direction, with an extended and much larger front structure for the lobby and arena offices. When the building was finished, the main arena faced north-south and had a much smaller front lobby. The arena offices were located on the second floor. (Courtesy of Hobart Arena.)

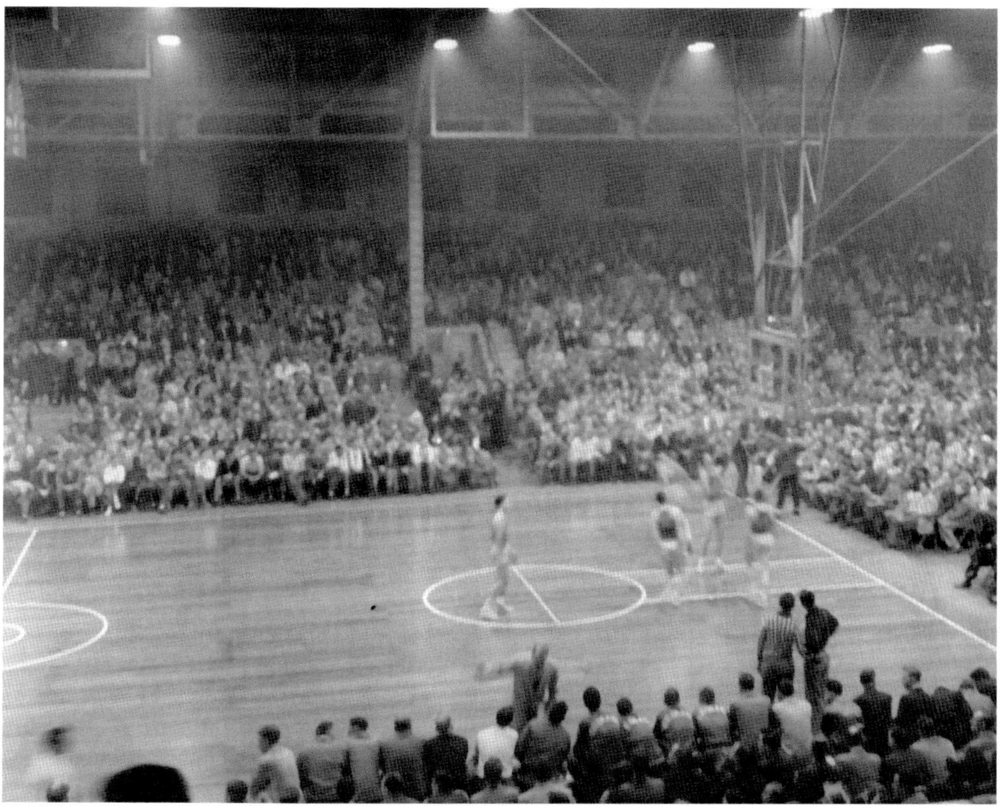

The first event at Hobart Arena was held on Friday, February 10, 1950, when 6,000 people jammed into the new building to watch Troy meet Kettering Fairmont in a high school basketball game. Troy won by a score of 36-30. (Courtesy of Hobart Arena.)

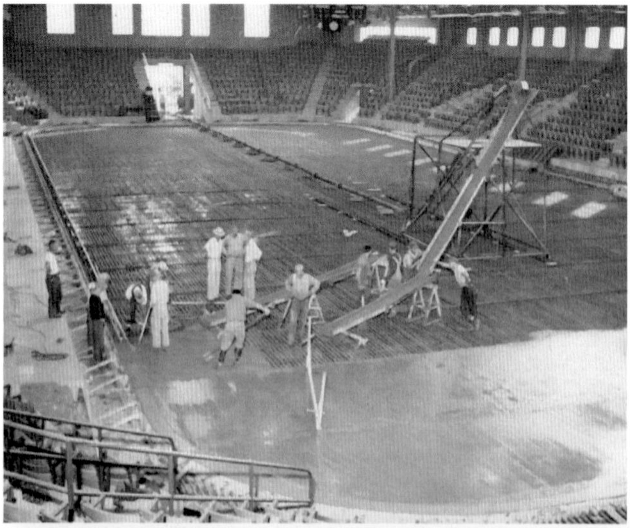

Installation of the piping and refrigeration unit into the floor of Hobart Arena began in February 1950, after the high school and college basketball seasons had ended. Workers would lay 11 miles of pipe to support the ice surface, which measured 190 feet long by 85 feet wide, slightly smaller than a regulation hockey rink. The work ended with the pouring of the concrete in July. (Courtesy of Hobart Arena.)

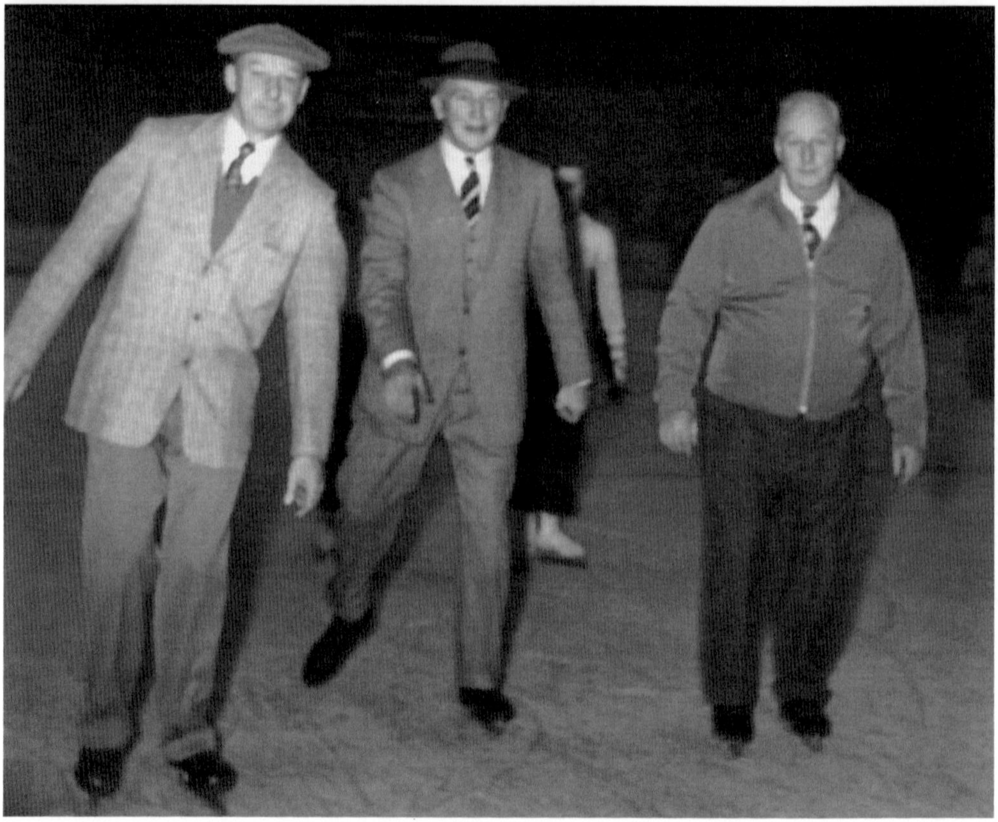

The official opening of Hobart Arena occurred on September 7, 1950, with the Hobart brothers taking a skate around the new ice. The first hockey game at the rink took place on Saturday, October 7, 1950, when a packed crowd of 5,000 watched the Cleveland Barons beat the Indianapolis Capitals 6-3. A few nights later, on October 9, in a second exhibition game, St. Paul beat Toledo 5-1. (Courtesy of Hobart Arena.)

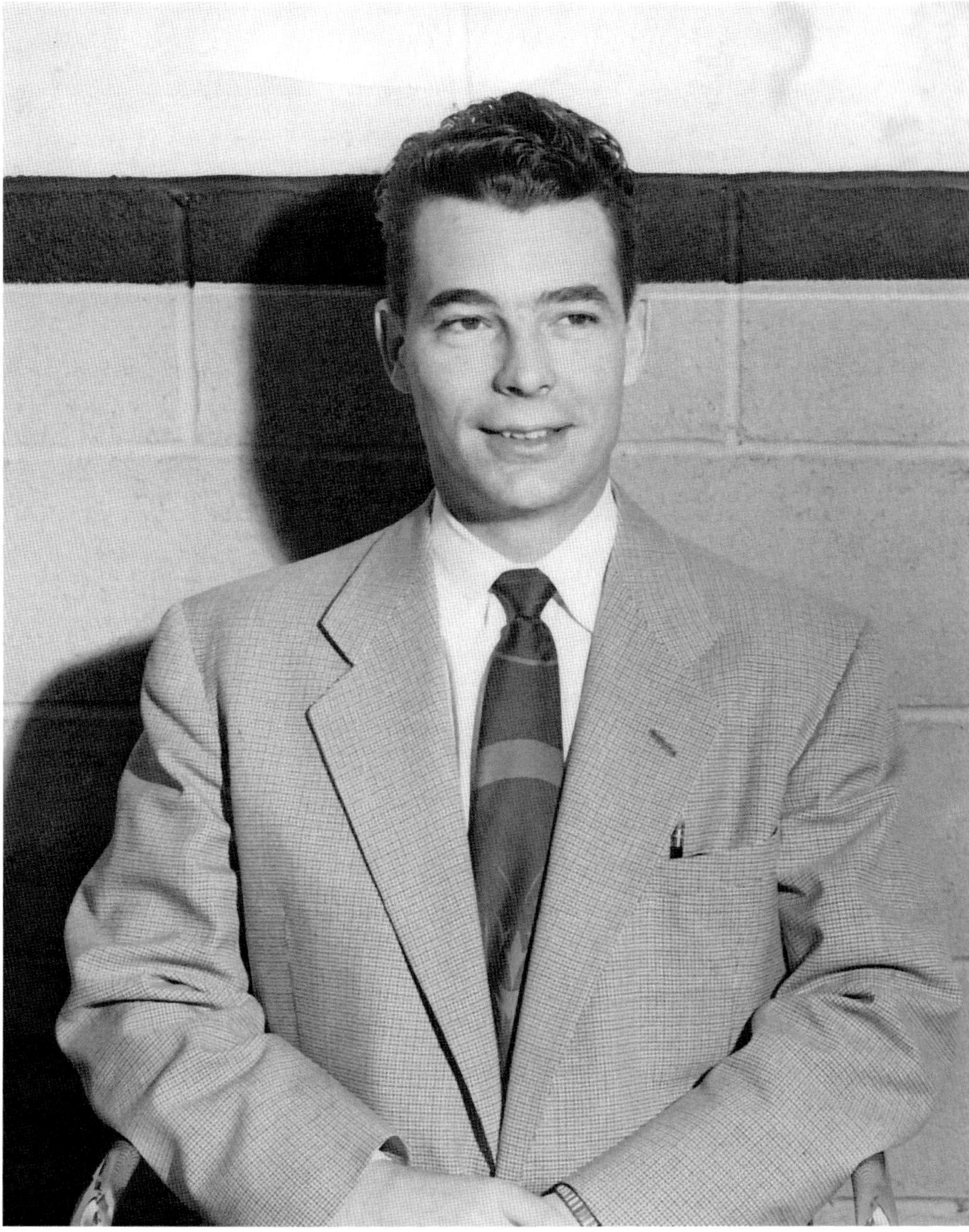

A native of Saskatchewan, Ken Wilson was already a hockey veteran when he took the position of general manager of Hobart Arena in 1950. Managing a brand-new arena with a rink in place, Wilson began making plans for bringing hockey to Troy. His first choice was to seek membership in the International Hockey League, a fledgling league formed in 1945 based mostly in the Detroit area. When he was told it was too late to join the loop for the 1950–1951 season, he and arena director Pat Thurkettle discussed the idea of forming a new league. Instead, Wilson decided to put an independent team on the ice and apply for the IHL after the upcoming season. He then went about selling hockey in a town where many had never seen a game. (Courtesy of Jeff Wilson.)

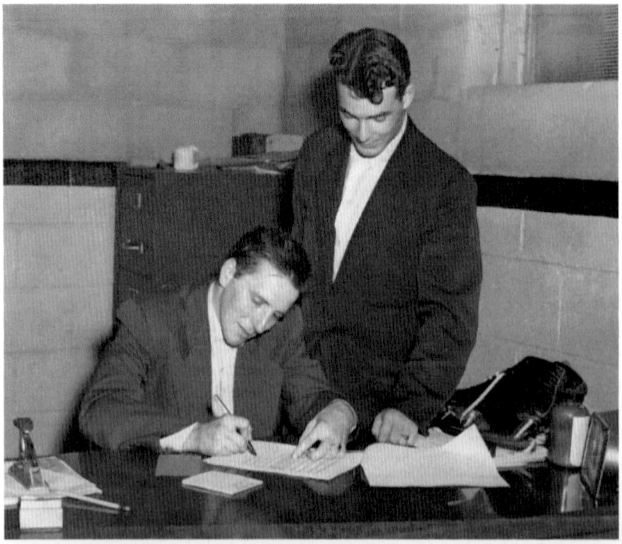

Ken Wilson watches as goaltender Don Dougall becomes the first player to sign a contract to play with the new Troy hockey team in September 1950. The name of the squad would be the Miami Valley Bruins, taking the name of the NHL's Boston franchise. Dougall was in goal for the Bruins' first game against the St. Paul Saints on October 11, 1950, which the Saints won 11-3. (Courtesy of Bill Murphy.)

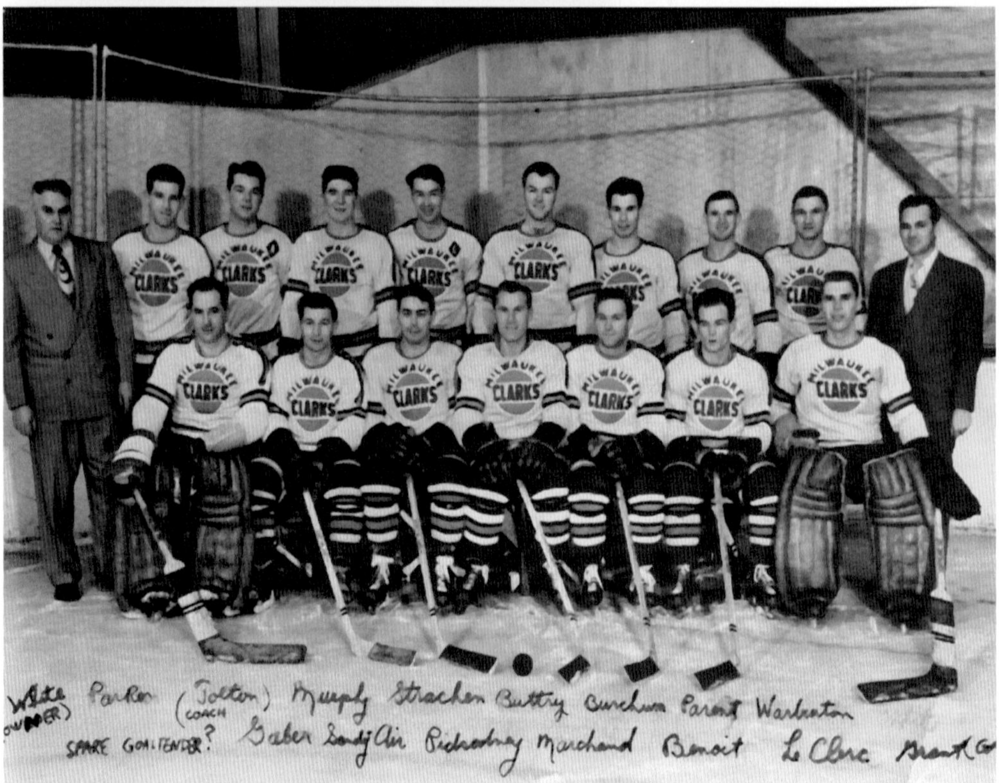

The Milwaukee Clarks played in the Eastern Hockey League (EHL) during the 1949–1950 season. When Milwaukee coach Keith Tolton was selected by Ken Wilson to lead the new hockey team at Hobart Arena, Tolton brought along from Milwaukee Steve Gaber, Gordon Buttrey, and Bill Murphy to play in Troy. Late in the Miami Valley Bruins 1950–1951 season, goalie Guy LeClerc (first row, far right) joined the team. (Courtesy of Bill Murphy.)

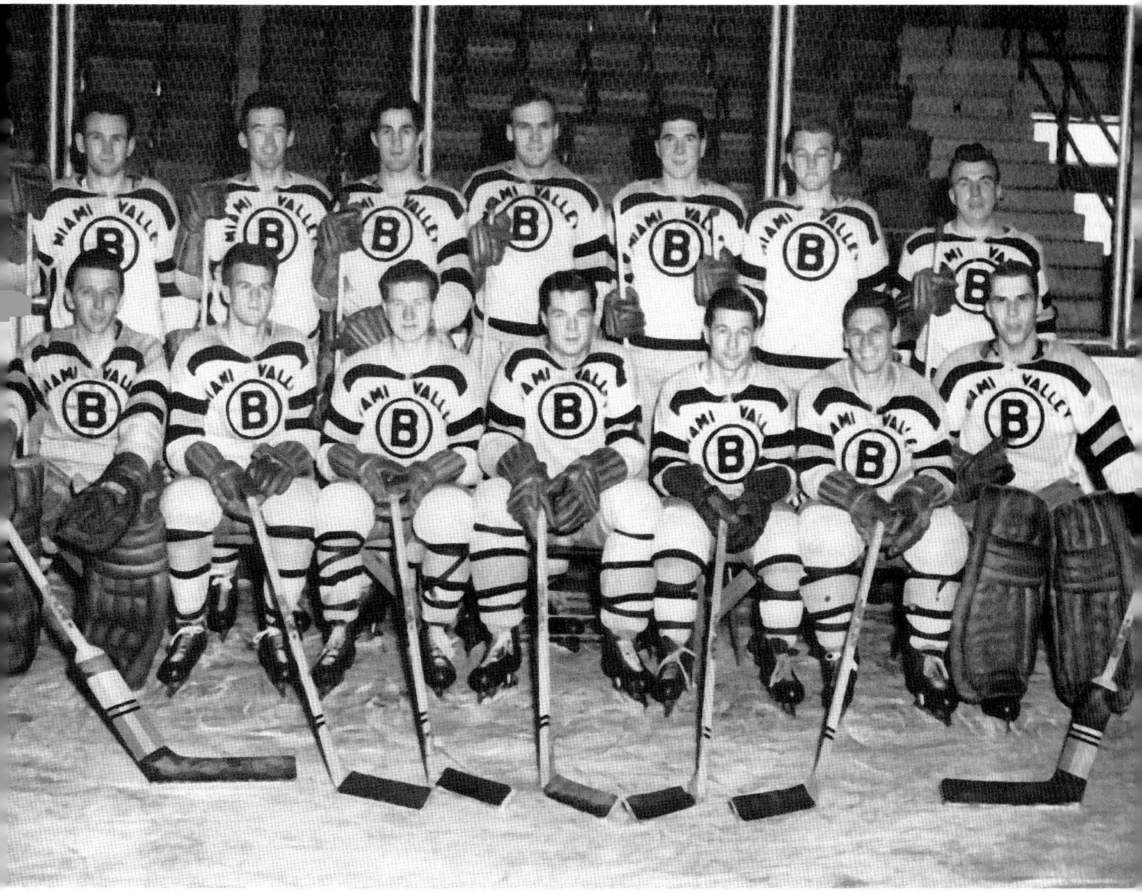

The Miami Valley Bruins were the Dayton area's first hockey team. Not affiliated with a league for the 1950–1951 season, the team played opponents from the IHL and EHL as well as club teams from the United States and Canada. Most of the games were played at Hobart Arena, though the team played a few games on the road. While attendance at Hobart was poor at the start of the season, home crowds picked up, with some games drawing over 4,000 later in the year. The team finished with a record of 22-11-4, losing to the Toledo Mercurys in the finals of the US Senior Open Hockey Championships. Steve Gaber scored 63 goals for the Bruins that season. (Courtesy of Bill Murphy.)

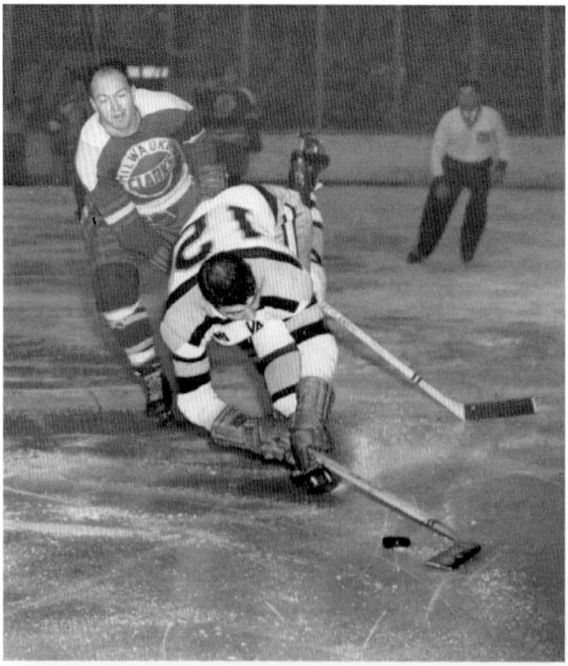

Bill Murphy takes a spill in a Miami Valley Bruins game on December 17, 1950, against the Toledo Mercurys. In this game, the Mercurys played in Milwaukee Clarks jerseys, as their uniforms were lost. A crowd of 2,500 saw the Bruins lose to Toledo 8-5. (Courtesy of Bill Murphy.)

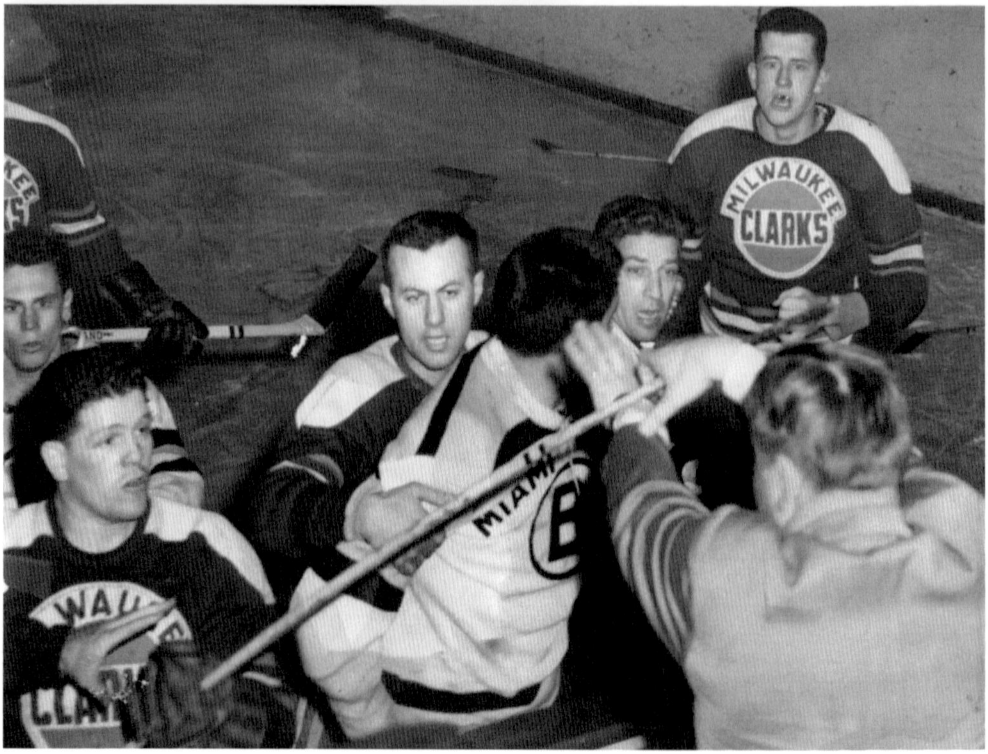

Fans were close to the action at Hobart Arena, which included roughhousing. This melee took place during a game between the Bruins and Mercurys on December 17, 1950. (Courtesy of Bill Murphy.)

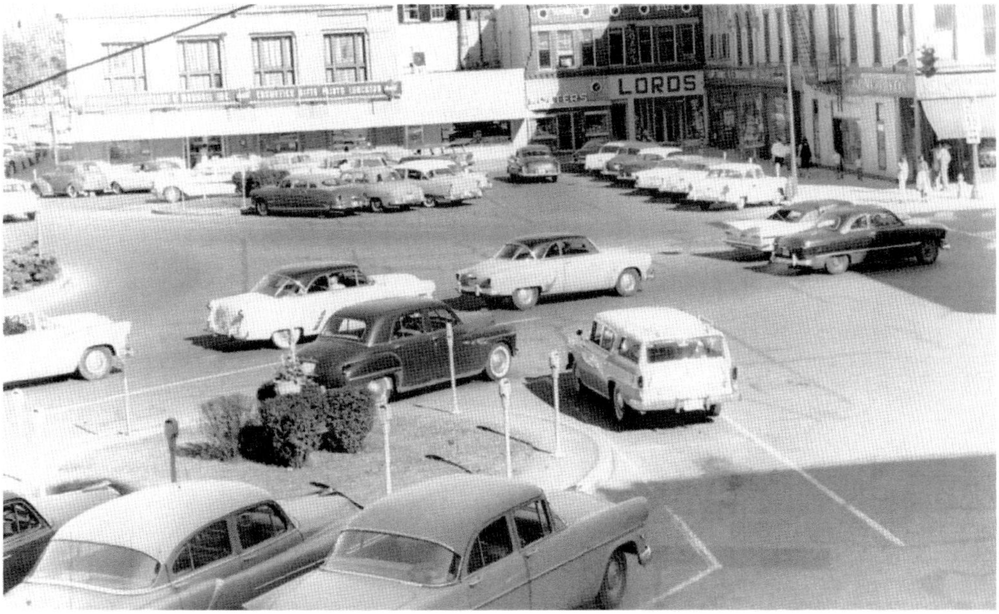

Downtown Troy is seen here in 1949. On April 27, 1951, Troy was admitted as a member of the IHL. The club would be called the Troy Bruins, dropping the Miami Valley name. When Troy entered the IHL in 1951, the city's population was just over 10,000, easily the smallest in the league, which also had teams in Detroit, Grand Rapids, Toledo, and Chatham, Ontario. (Courtesy of Troy Historical Library.)

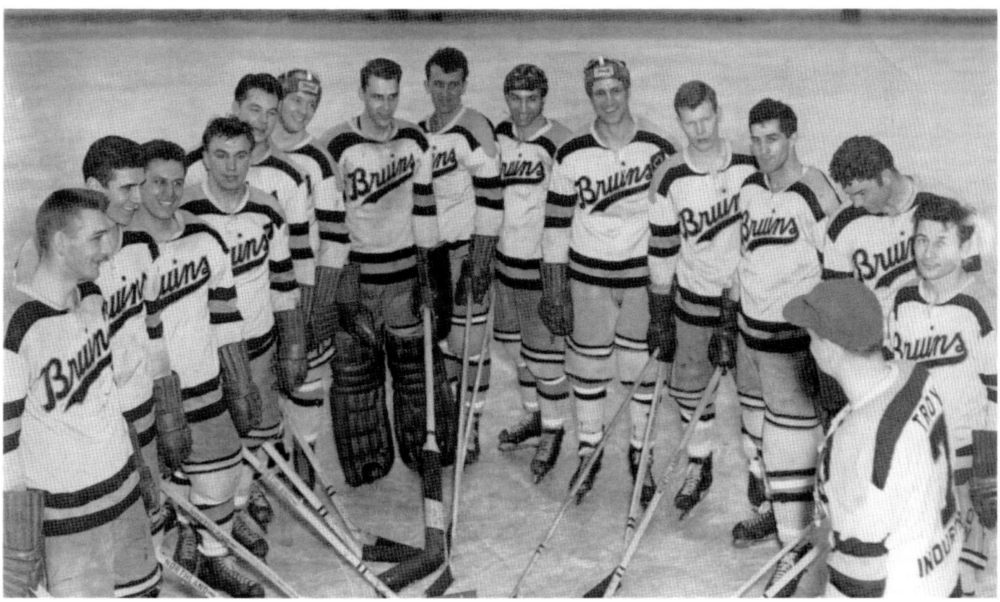

A total of eight players, including Bill Murphy, Steve Gaber, Johnny Myke, and Julius Swick, returned from the previous season to play for the 1951–1952 Troy Bruins. They were coached by NHL veteran Norm McAtee. The team fared well in its first season in the IHL, with a record of 23-19-6. Julius Swick led the team in scoring with 32 goals and 61 points. (Courtesy of Bill Murphy.)

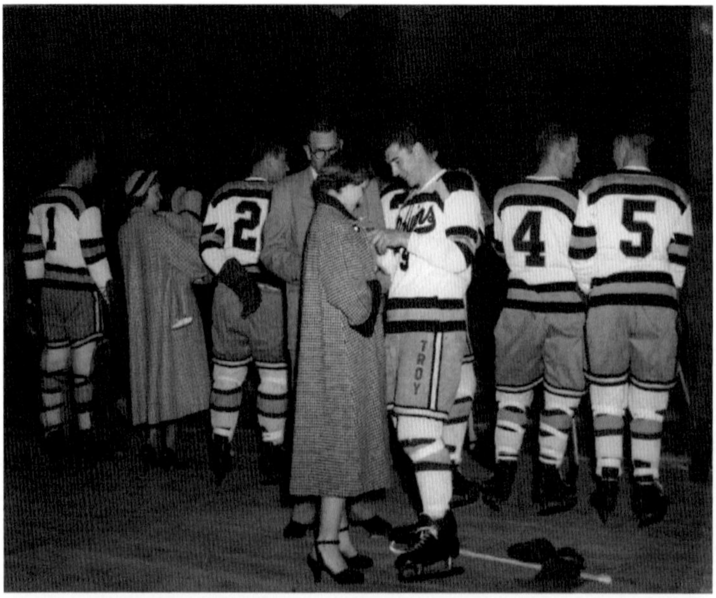

On November 1, 1951, the night after losing 4-0 on the road in their IHL debut to the Chatham Maroons, the Bruins hosted an open house at Hobart Arena, attended by 3,000 fans. The evening featured an introduction of the players and their wives to those in attendance, as well as a talk on the sport of hockey. (Courtesy of Bill Murphy.)

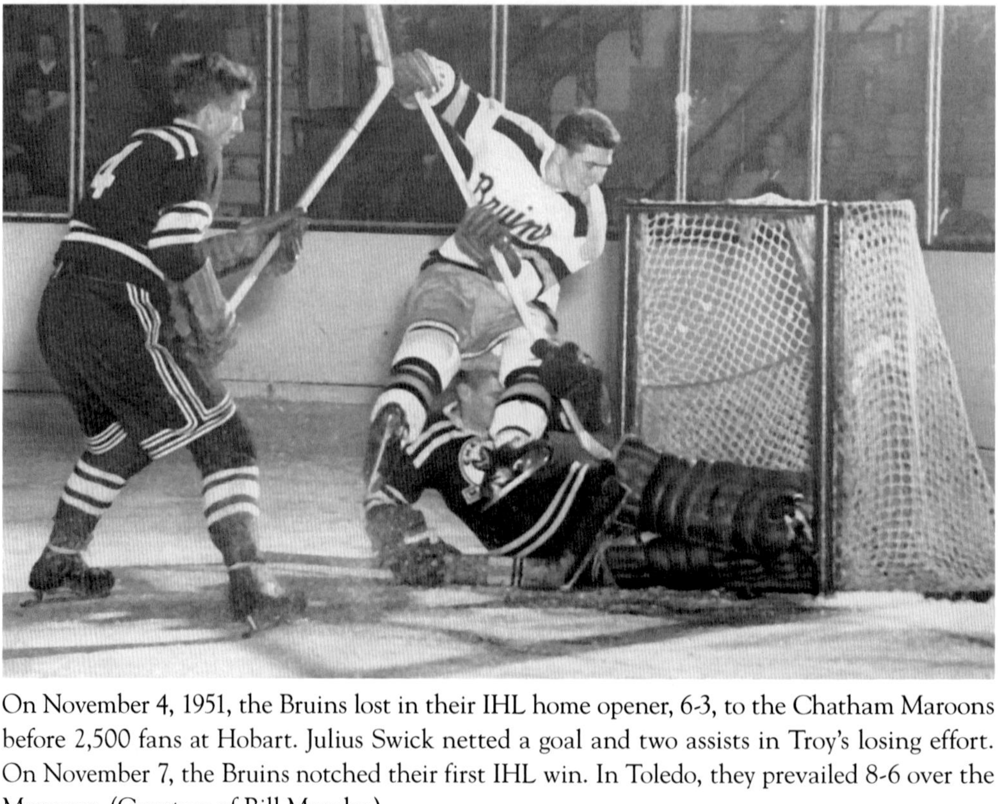

On November 4, 1951, the Bruins lost in their IHL home opener, 6-3, to the Chatham Maroons before 2,500 fans at Hobart. Julius Swick netted a goal and two assists in Troy's losing effort. On November 7, the Bruins notched their first IHL win. In Toledo, they prevailed 8-6 over the Mercurys. (Courtesy of Bill Murphy.)

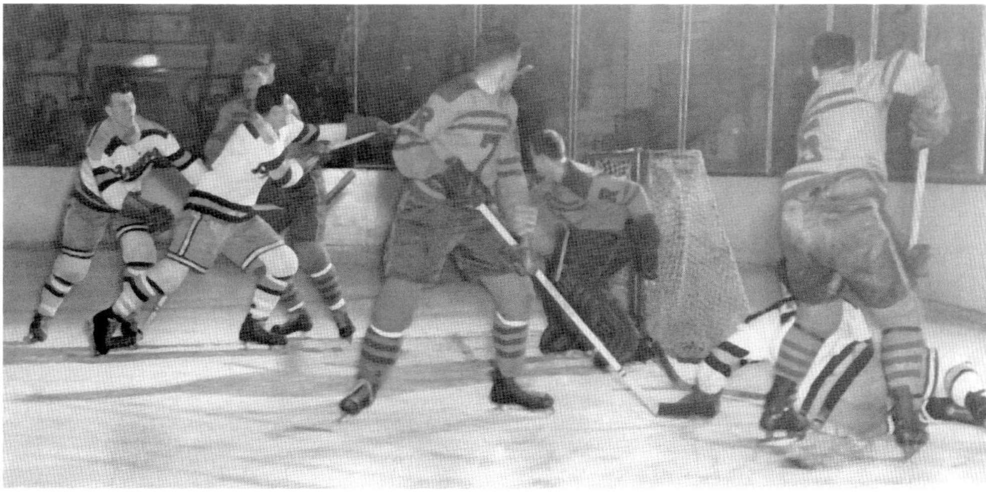

The Bruins made the playoffs in their first year. In the 1952 playoffs, the Bruins took on Grand Rapids in the first round, but lost to the Rockets in seven games. The Bruins would make the playoffs their first five years in the IHL. (Courtesy of Bill Murphy.)

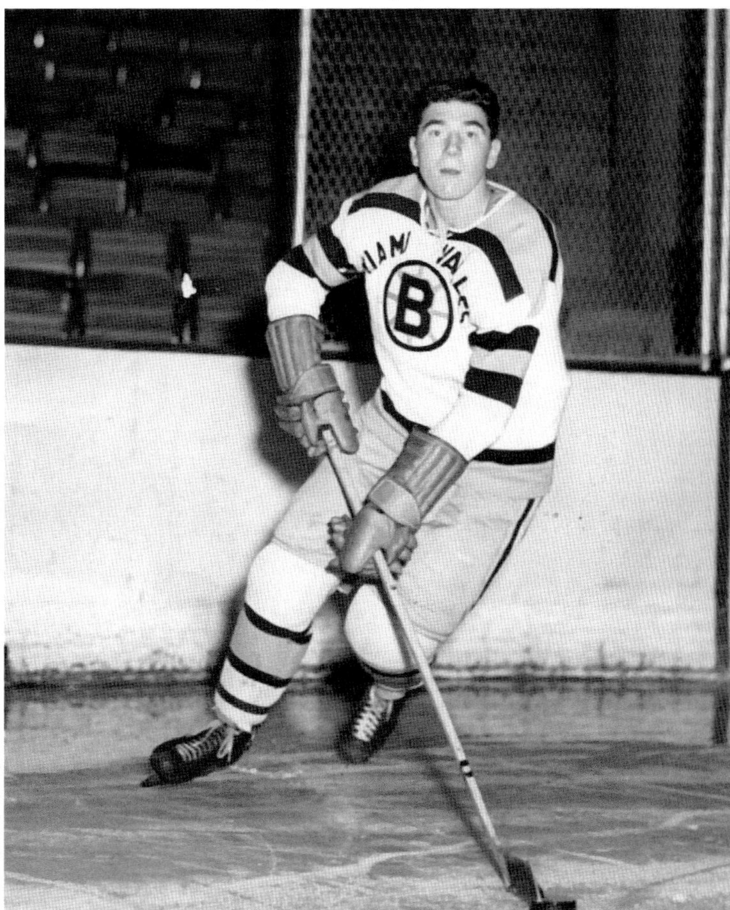

One of the first stars of the Bruins was Bill Murphy. The likable and easygoing "Murph" was a fan favorite. He played with both the Miami Valley and Troy Bruins. In two seasons with the IHL, Murphy scored 39 goals and 78 points. After his playing career, he worked as an IHL linesman at Dayton Gems games at Hara Arena. (Courtesy of Bill Murphy.)

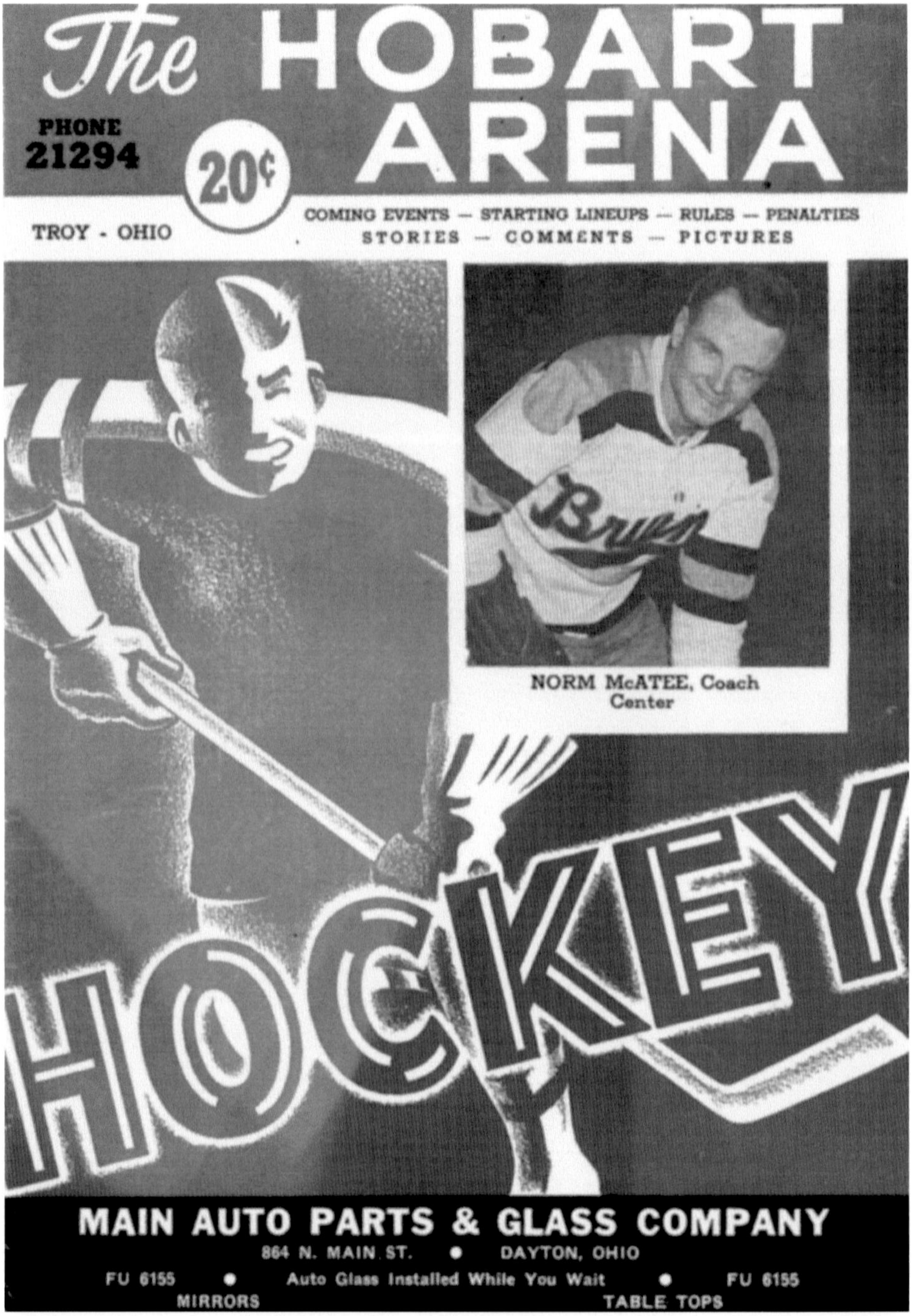

This 1952–1953 program has player-coach Norm McAtee on the cover. He led the Bruins in their first three seasons, finishing second in the IHL during the 1952–1953 season and going to the playoffs each year. As a player, McAtee scored 60 goals in three years. He played briefly with the Boston Bruins during the 1946–1947 season, which featured the famous "Kraut Line" of Milt Schmidt, Bobby Bauer, and Woody Dumart. (Courtesy of Hobart Arena.)

Bill Murphy's brother, Ron Murphy, had a long NHL career, playing on many of the "original six" teams. Ron was a member of the 1961 Stanley Cup champion Chicago Blackhawks. He finished his career with the Boston Bruins, playing on a line with Phil Esposito and Ken Hodge. (Courtesy of Bill Murphy.)

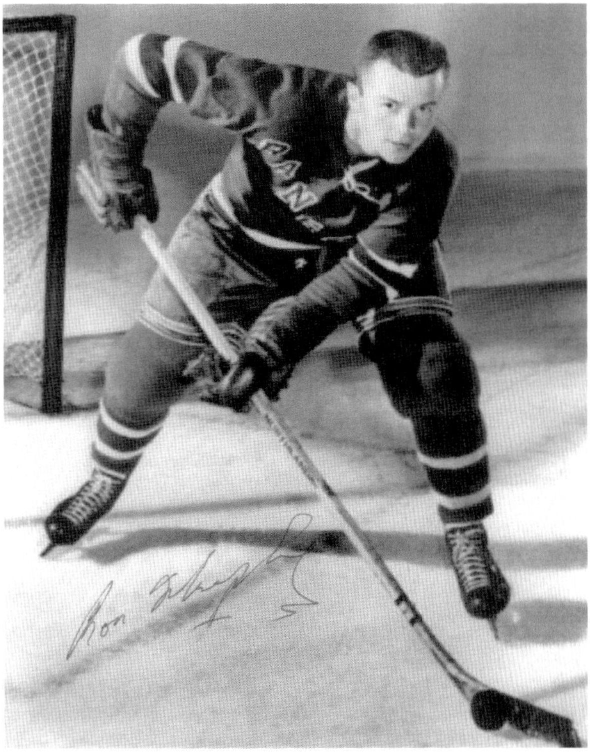

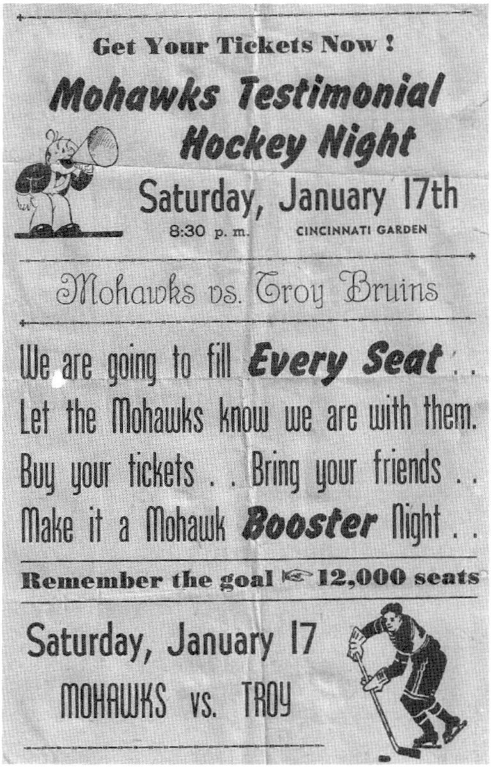

This newspaper advertisement promotes the January 17, 1953, game between the Troy Bruins and Cincinnati Mohawks at the Cincinnati Gardens. That evening, a crowd of 10,497 watched as the Mohawks and Bruins played to a 4-4 tie. (Courtesy of Kevin Anderson.)

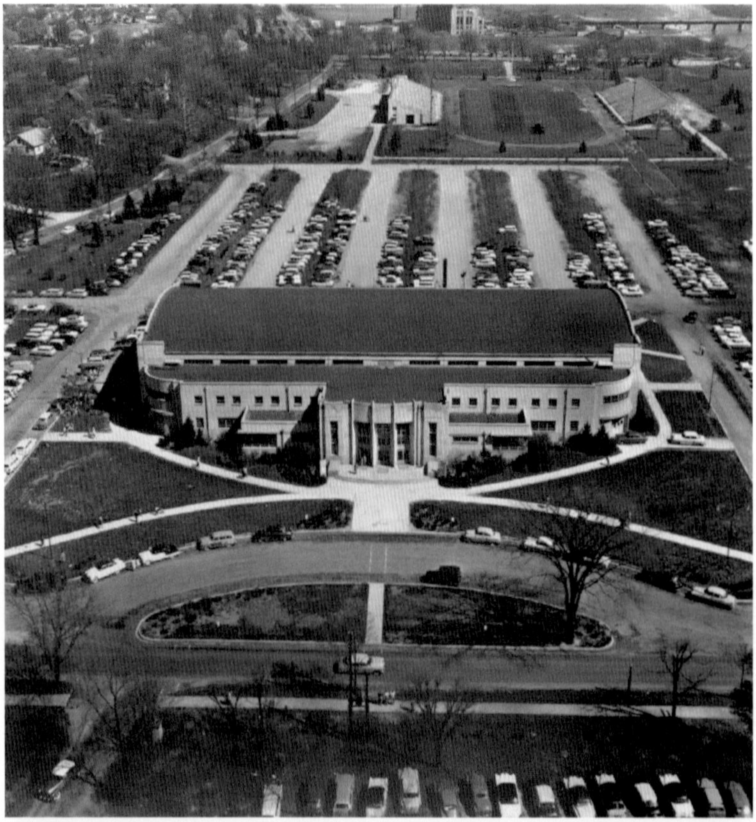

With a few exceptions, Bruins home games on the weekends were played at 3:00 on Sunday afternoons. The matinee starting times were bigger draws than the weeknight games, often drawing crowds over 4,000 to Hobart Arena. During the 1952–1953 season, the Bruins averaged nearly 3,200 on Sundays and 1,800 on other nights. (Courtesy of Hobart Arena.)

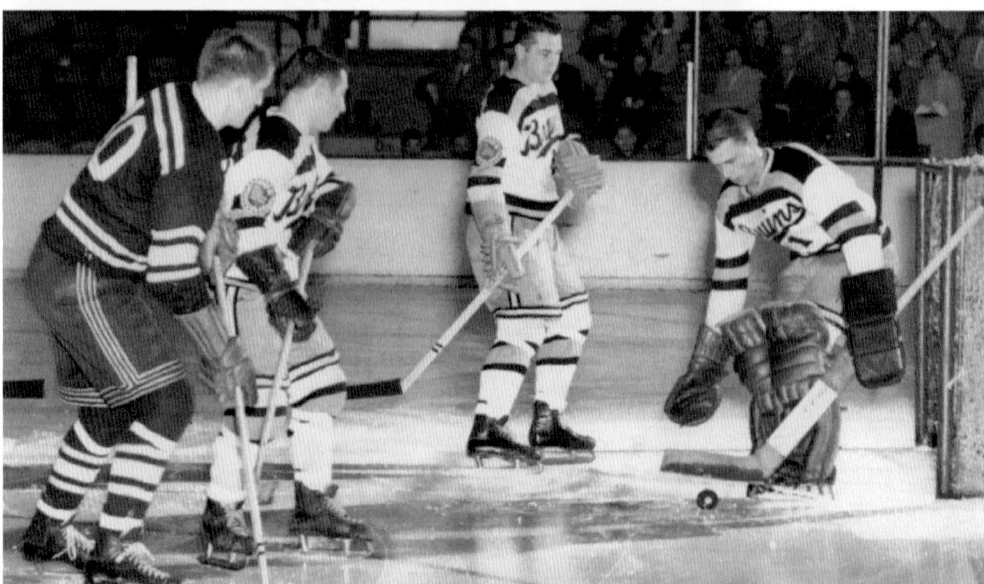

Guy LeClerc makes a stop against the Fort Wayne Komets on December 21, 1952. The Komets beat the Bruins 4-2 that day, snapping Troy's seven-game unbeaten streak. This was the longest winning streak they would have until 1956. (Courtesy of Bill Murphy.)

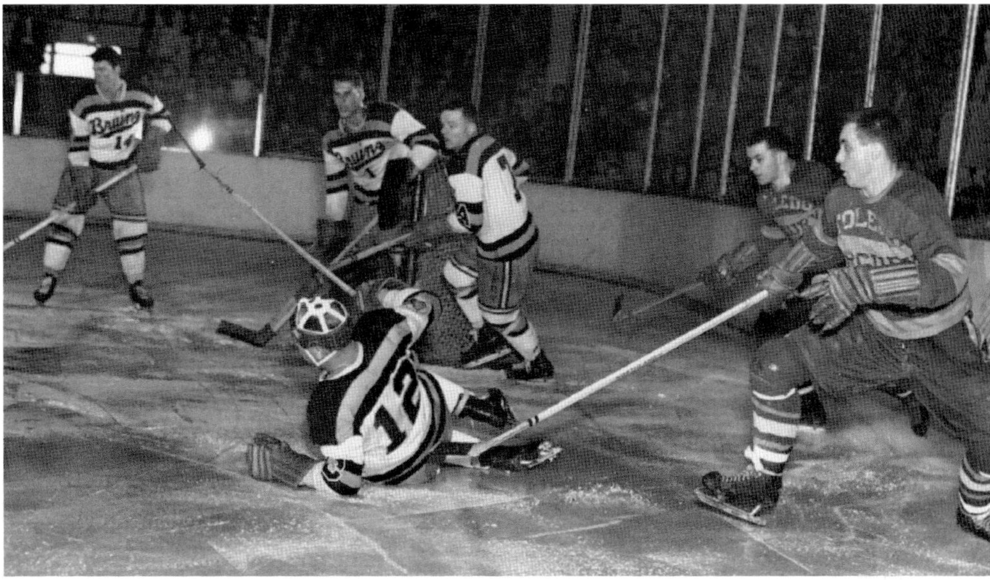

Troy blanked the Toledo Mercurys 1-0 at Hobart Arena on February 1, 1953. It was the fifth shutout of the season for goaltender Guy LeClerc (pictured), which set an IHL record for most shutouts in a season. LeClerc would hold the mark for three years. (Courtesy of Bill Murphy.)

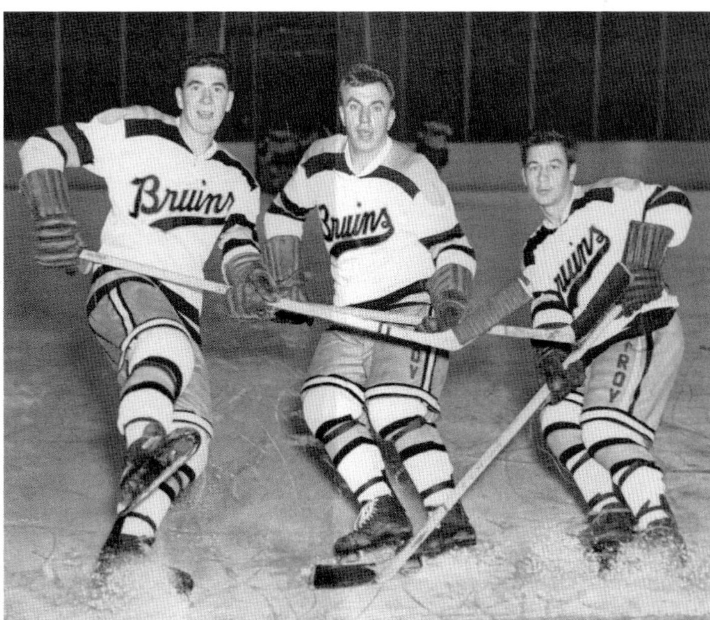

They called him "Little" Stevie Gaber, as well as "Pinocchio." But the five-foot, four-inch right winger (far right) put up big numbers for the Bruins. In his five-plus season with the Bruins, Gaber scored 177 goals, including 50 during the 1952–1953 season. He is the team's all-time leader in goals, points, and games played. (Courtesy of Bill Murphy.)

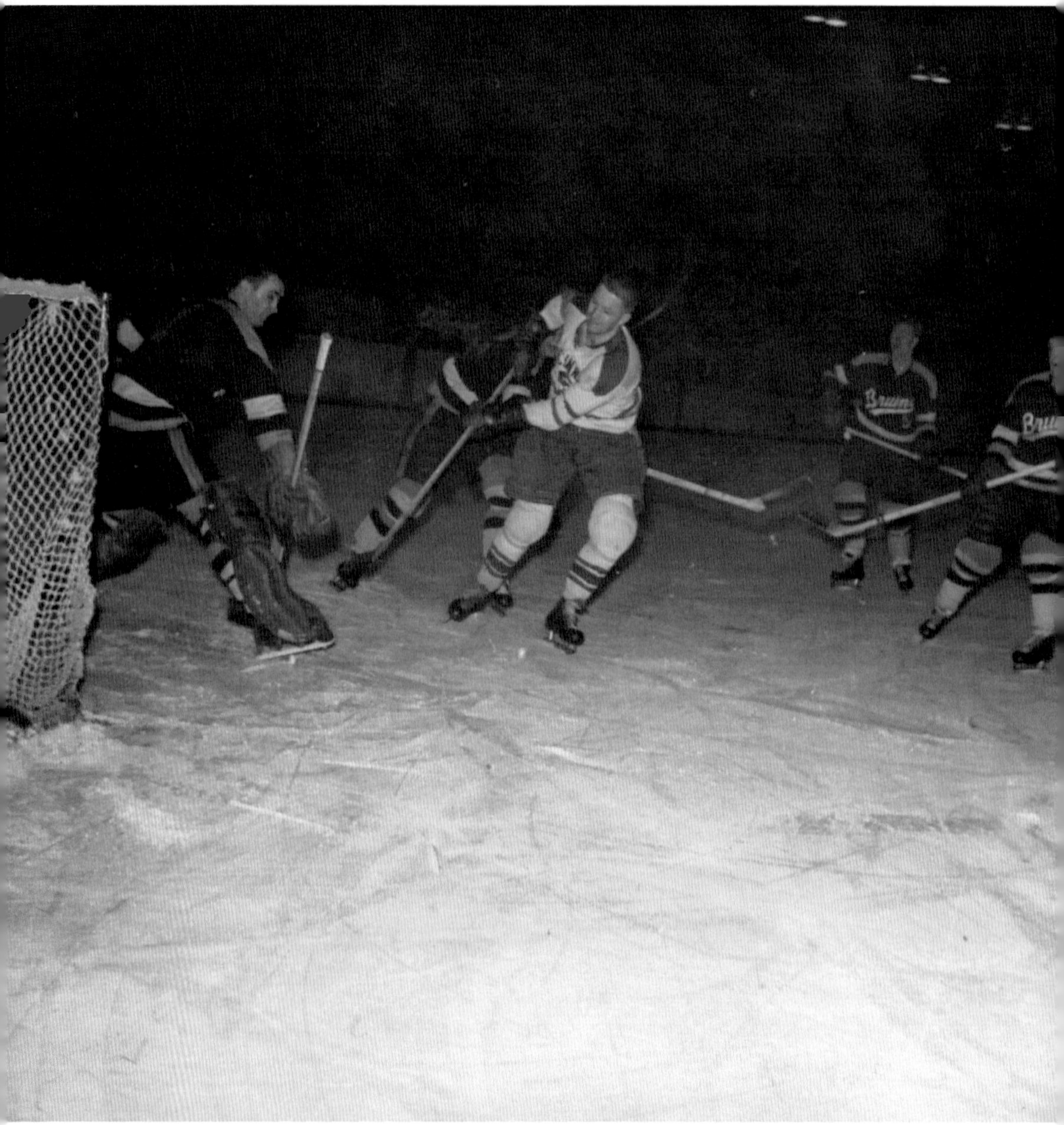

Due to a snow storm, Troy was unable to make the trip to Cincinnati to play the Mohawks for their game on November 29, 1952. The Mohawks demanded Troy pay the $400 Cincinnati Gardens rental fee for not showing up. Over the next several weeks, Ken Wilson collected pennies from fans to pay the fee. On January 25, 1953, the two teams played the only known hockey doubleheader. In the regularly scheduled game at Hobart Arena at 3:00 p.m., the Bruins defeated the Mohawks 3-0 before 4,716 fans. The two teams then made the trip to Cincinnati for the makeup game that night. Before the game, Wilson paid the fine by dumping 40,000 pennies onto a tarp laid out on the Cincinnati Gardens ice, to the delight of the Cincinnati crowd. The Mohawks won the second game 2-1. (Courtesy of Kevin Anderson.)

This advertisement from the *Troy Daily News* promotes "White Villa Night," December 11, 1952, pitting the Troy Bruins against the Cincinnati Mohawks at Hobart Arena. A crowd of 3,151 turned out that night to watch the two teams play to a 5-5 tie. White Villa was a local grocery chain and food brand. (Courtesy of Troy Historical Library.)

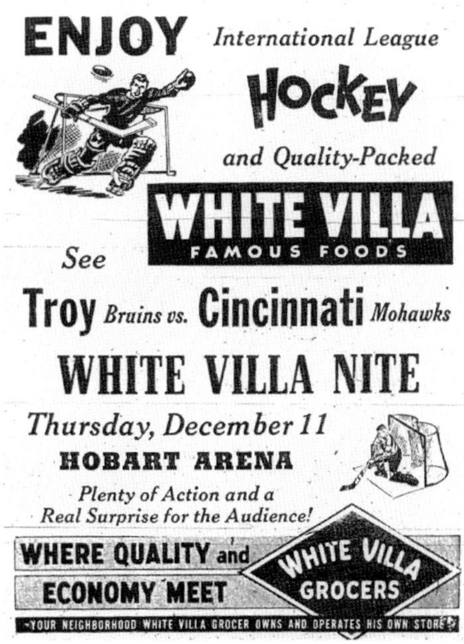

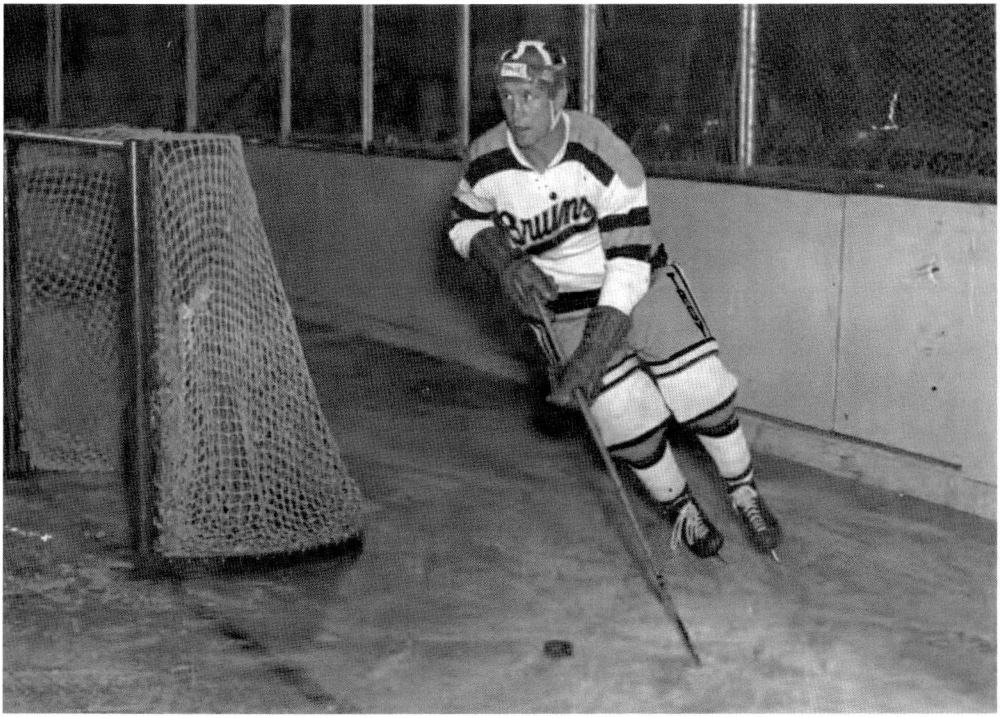

Julian Sawchuk got the nickname "Dad" for being the oldest player, at 31 years of age, on the Bruins their first year. Sawchuk was a tough defenseman who wore a modified helmet—rare for a 1950s player—as a result of a serious head injury. Sawchuk was Player of the Year for the 1951–1952 season and was a first-team IHL all-star for 1952–1953. Sawchuk owned and operated Dad's Carry Out on the south side of Troy for many years. (Courtesy of Chris Barno.)

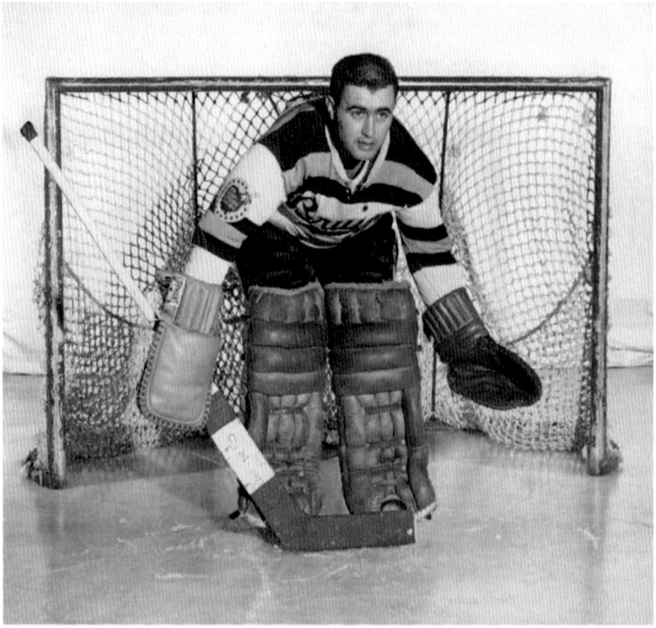

Bill Tibbs was already the best IHL goalie when he came to Troy in 1954. In two seasons (1954–1956), Tibbs posted 12 shutouts, including eight during the 1955–1956 campaign. He also set an IHL record for most consecutive shutout minutes by a goaltender, 197:54. He was the IHL's 1955–1956 First Team All-Star goalie and first recipient of the James Norris Trophy as the league's top goalie. (Courtesy of Bill Murphy.)

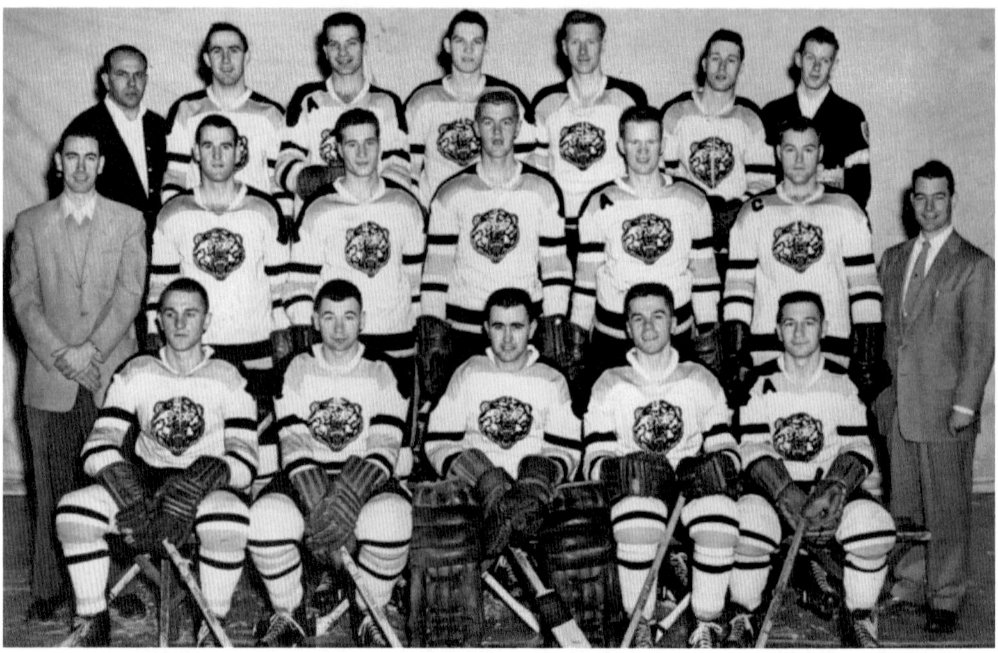

The 1954–1955 Bruins under new head coach Nellie Podolski won eight of its last 11 games to finish second for the regular season. After beating Grand Rapids in round one of the playoffs, the Bruins met the Cincinnati Mohawks in the Turner Cup finals. Down three games to one, the Bruins won games five and six to force a game seven, which the Mohawks won 7-0. It was Troy's only trip to the Turner Cup finals. (Courtesy of Bob Speck.)

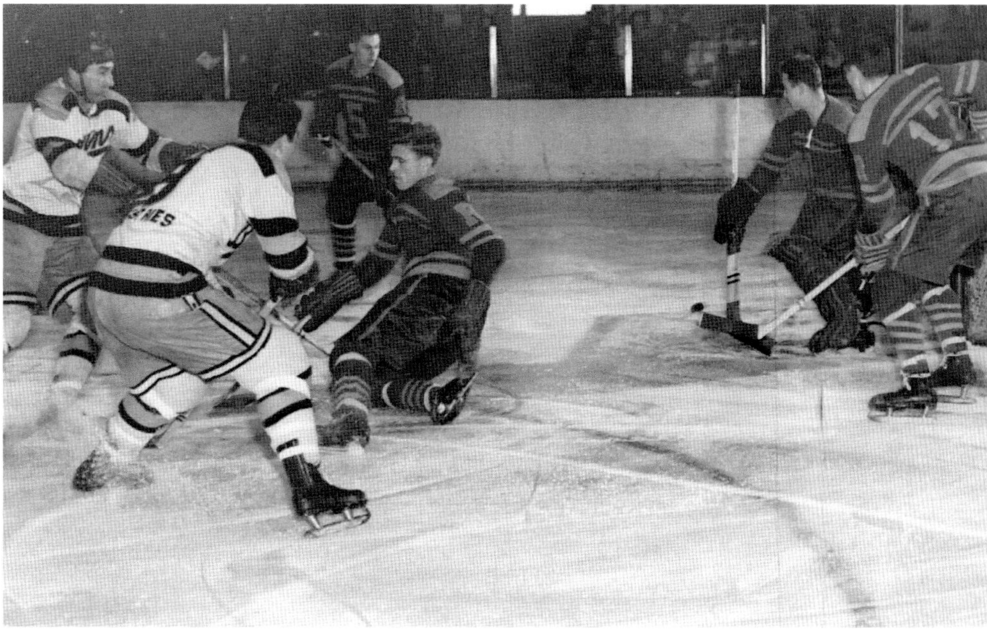

In the 1950s, long before the Internet, cable, and cell phones, fans usually had to wait for the next day's newspaper to get the results of an away game. During the 1955 playoffs, Ken Wilson kept the Hobart Arena box office open late so fans could call in for the score of Bruins road contests. (Courtesy of Bill Murphy.)

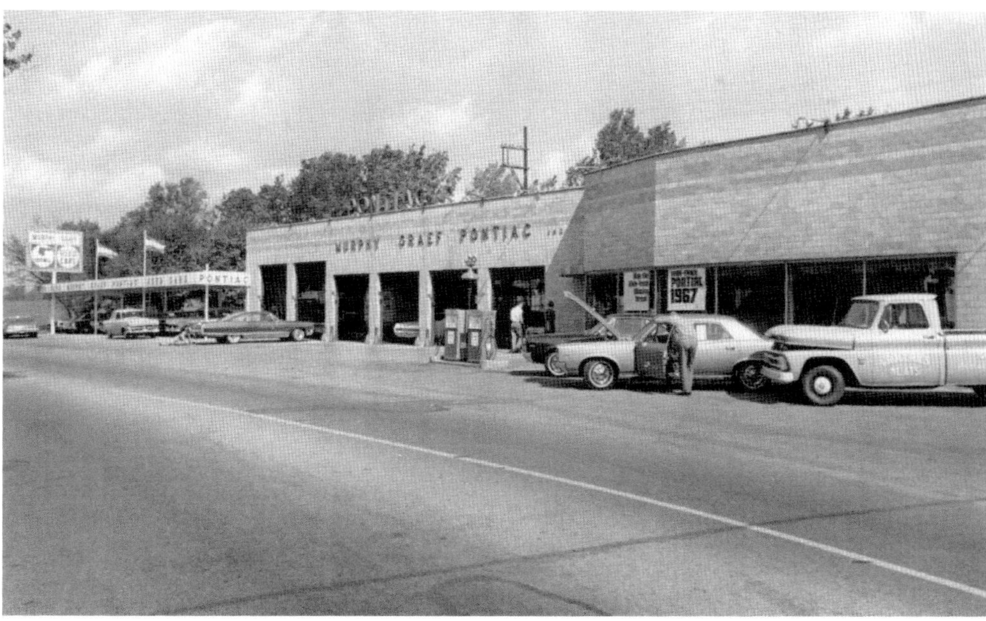

After retiring from hockey, Bill Murphy and his wife, Betty, stayed in Troy. Bill worked for Kruse Brothers Pontiac on State Route 25A north of the city. Along with Richard Graef, Murphy purchased the dealership in 1966, and it was renamed Murphy-Graef Pontiac. In 1969, Murphy bought the dealership outright and operated Bill Murphy Pontiac until 1986. (Courtesy of Bill Murphy.)

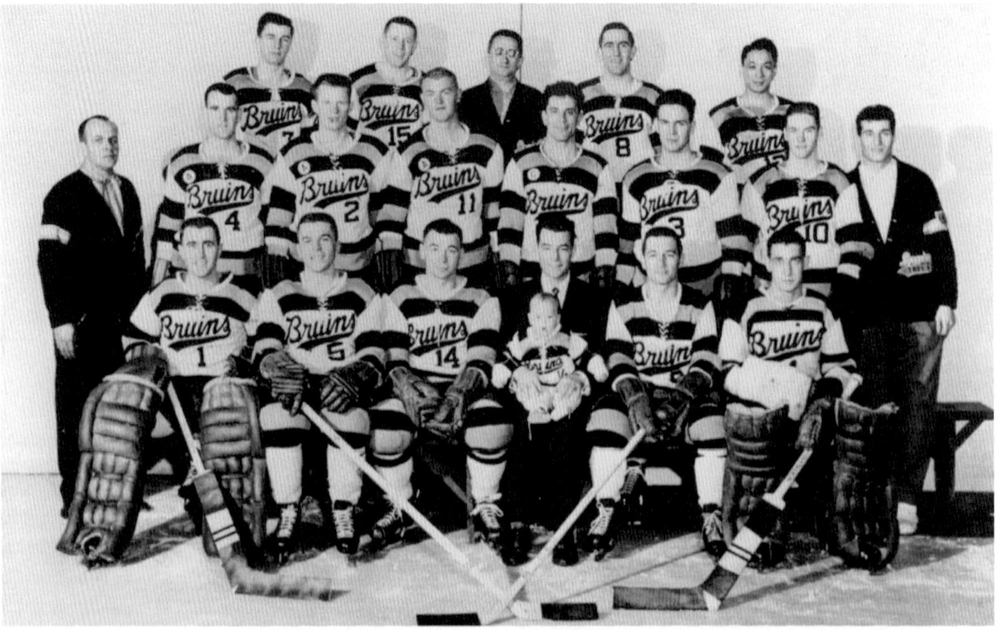

After losing the first game of the season, the 1955–1956 Bruins won 18 of their next 23 games and spent nearly two months atop the IHL. Though overtaken in the standings by the Cincinnati Mohawks, the Bruins finished second and won a team record 39 games. The team also won its first 11 home games and lost only four games at Hobart that year. (Courtesy of Bob Speck.)

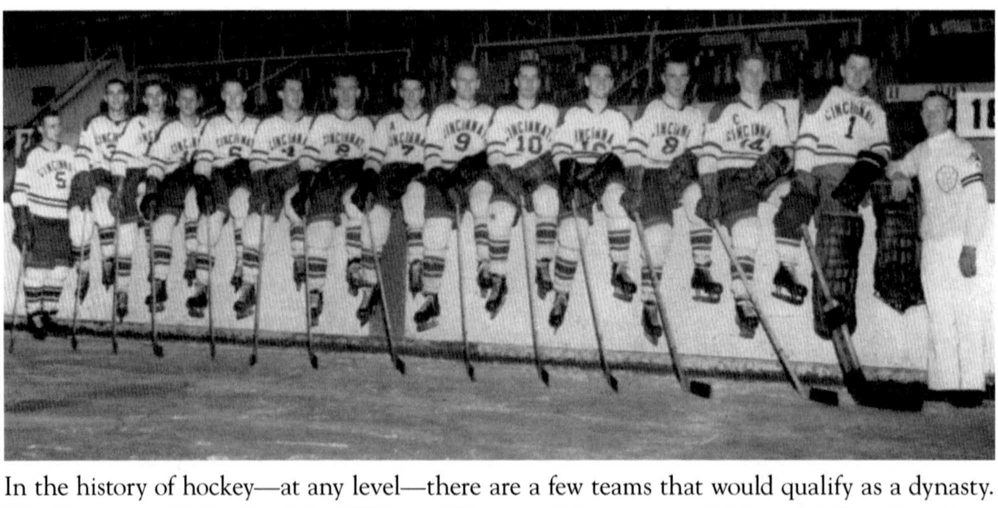

In the history of hockey—at any level—there are a few teams that would qualify as a dynasty. The Cincinnati Mohawks of the 1950s would be one of those teams. A Montreal Canadiens farm team, the Mohawks dominated the IHL, winning five consecutive Turner Cup championships between 1953 and 1957, including beating the Troy Bruins in 1955. The 1956–1957 Mohawks compiled a record of 50-9-1, for 101 points. This record for points stood until it was broken by the 1975–1976 Gems. (Courtesy of Kevin Anderson.)

Before bus travel, hockey teams would pile into the players' cars and drive themselves to road contests. Former Gems coach Warren Back said that with all the driving teams had to do during the season, often in treacherous winter conditions, it was amazing that no one ever got killed driving to a game. (Courtesy of Marty Szturm.)

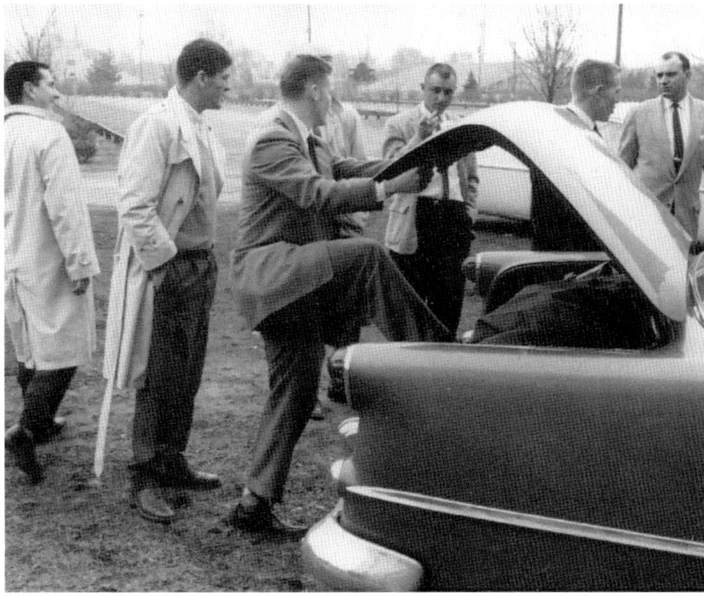

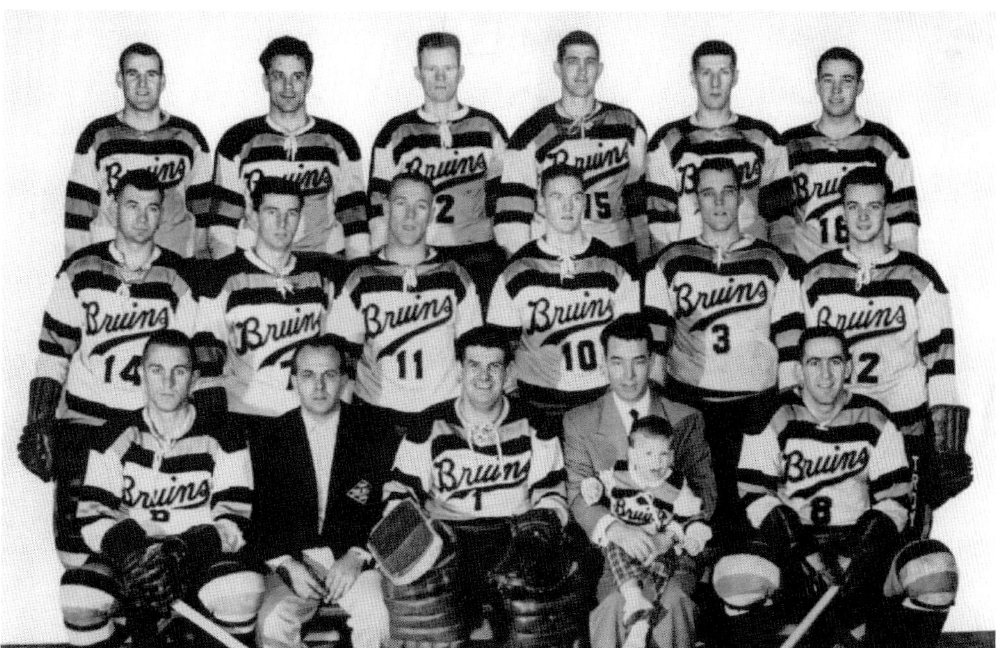

The 1956–1957 Bruins finished last in the IHL and failed to make the playoffs for the first time in team history. Larry "King" Kwong, the first player of Asian descent to play in the NHL, played with both the 1955–1956 and 1956–1957 Troy Bruins. (Courtesy of Bill Murphy.)

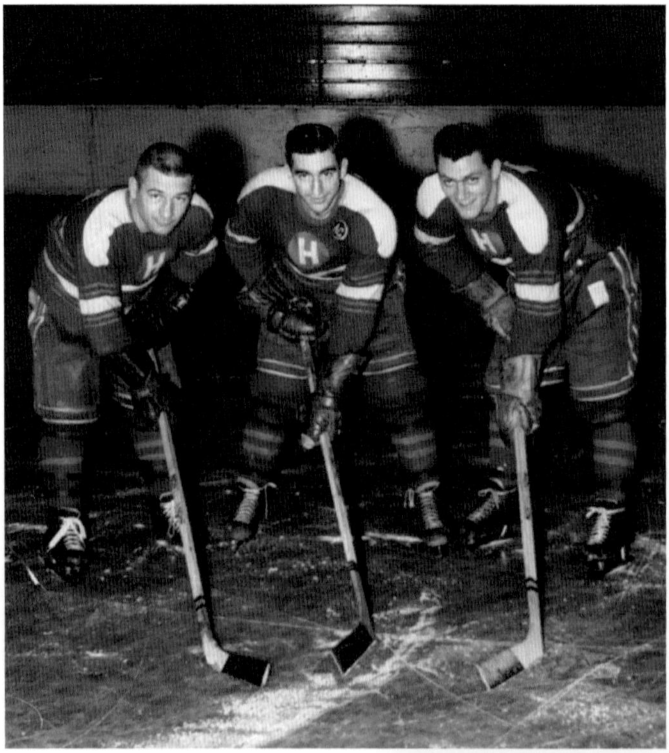

Steve Gaber (far left) finished his hockey career after playing with Huntington and Fort Wayne during the 1956–1957 season. He retired as the IHL's all-time leader in goals (222) and points (407), records that would stand for several years. (Courtesy of Bill Murphy.)

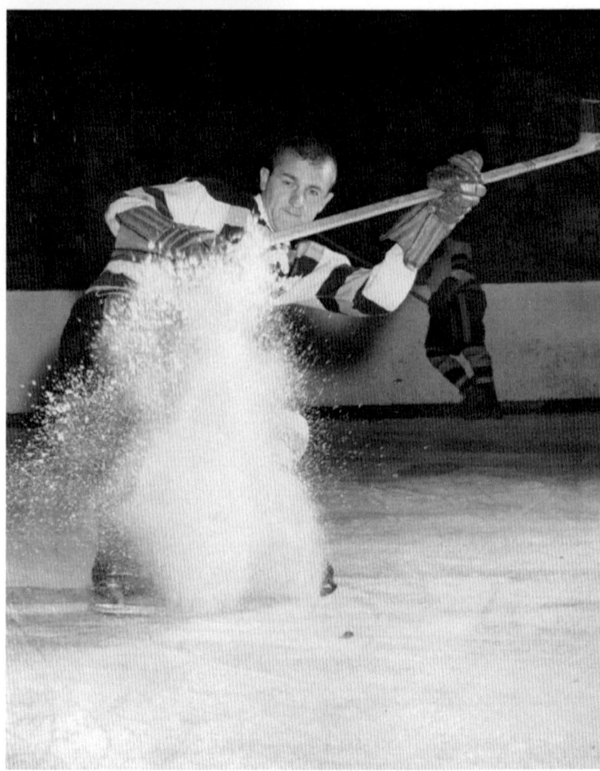

Max Szturm is the third-leading scorer in Troy Bruins history. In the 1954–1955 season, the center led the team in scoring with 57 points, including 23 goals. For his effort that season, Szturm won a set of golf clubs, which he put to good use, becoming a skilled golfer after his hockey days as well as the superintendent at Wildwood Country Club in Middletown, Ohio. (Courtesy of Marty Szturm.)

Brian "Killer" Kilrea played for the Bruins from 1955 to 1959 and is the team's second all-time leading scorer. He played with the Los Angeles Kings during their first season in the NHL. Kilrea made his mark not as a player, but as a coach. He spent 33 seasons as the coach of the Canadian junior Ottawa 67's, where he won 1,193 games. He was the winningest coach in junior hockey. In 2003, he was elected to the Hockey Hall of Fame under the Builder category. (Courtesy of Bill Murphy.)

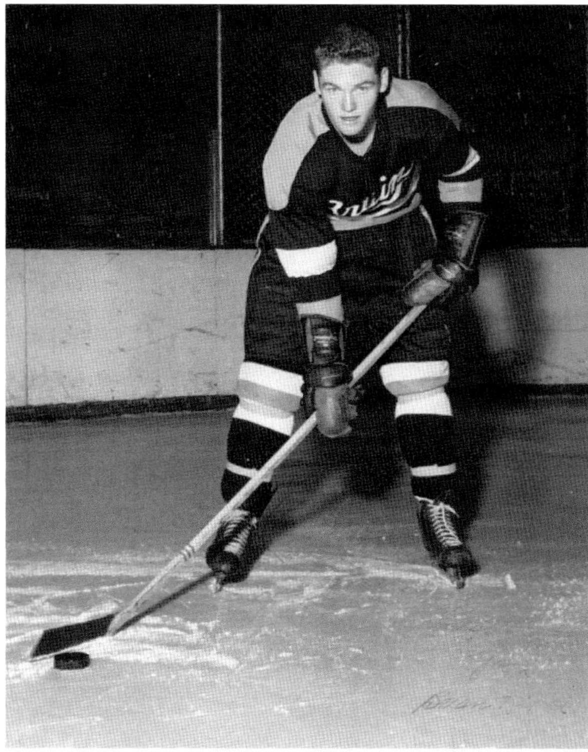

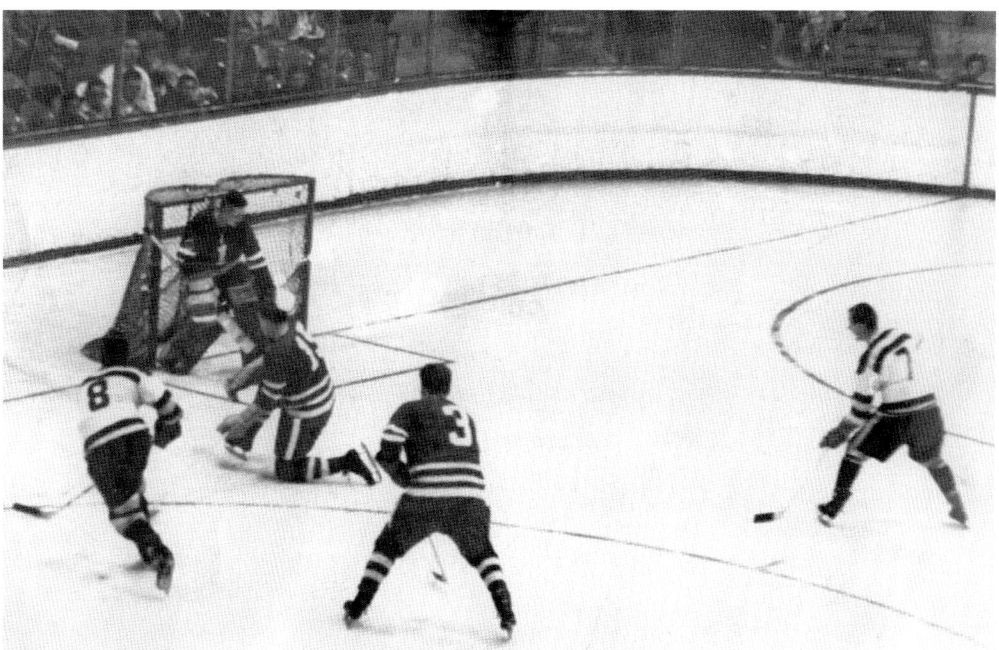

On November 8, 1958, the Fort Wayne Komets scored a 17-1 victory over the Bruins in Fort Wayne. The 17 goals stood as the record for most goals in a game until 1962. Fort Wayne scored 16 consecutive goals, which also set an IHL record. (Courtesy of Bill Murphy.)

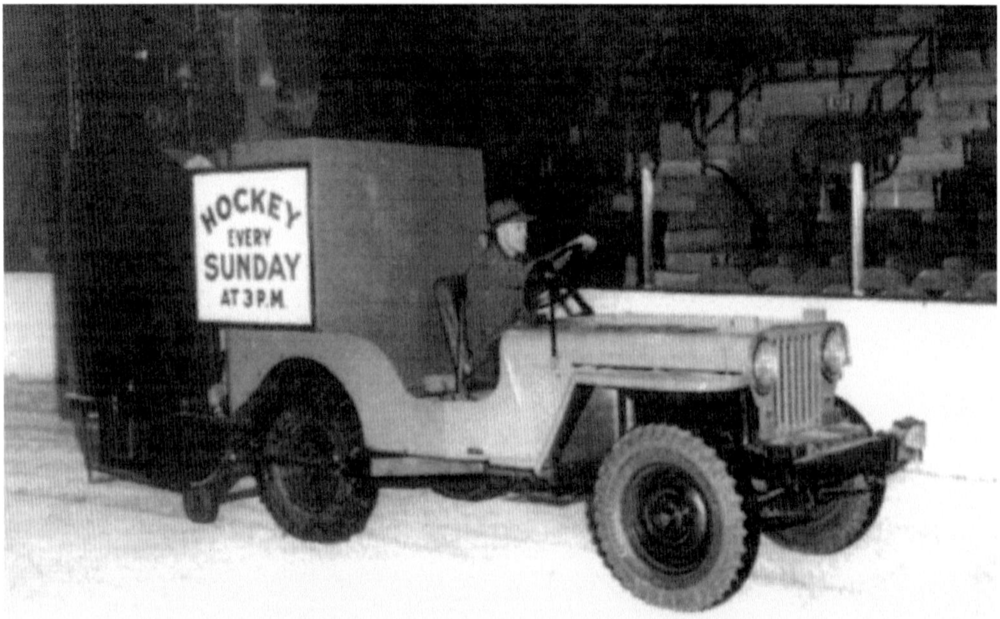

Just as popular as the Bruins was the ice-resurfacing machine that Hobart Arena employed for many years, as well as its driver. Before there was the Zamboni, Hobart Arena used a modified World War II jeep built by the Hobart brothers that shaved the ice and laid down hot water between periods. Aloye Yackels drove it and, eventually, the arena Zamboni, into the mid-1970s. (Courtesy of Hobart Arena.)

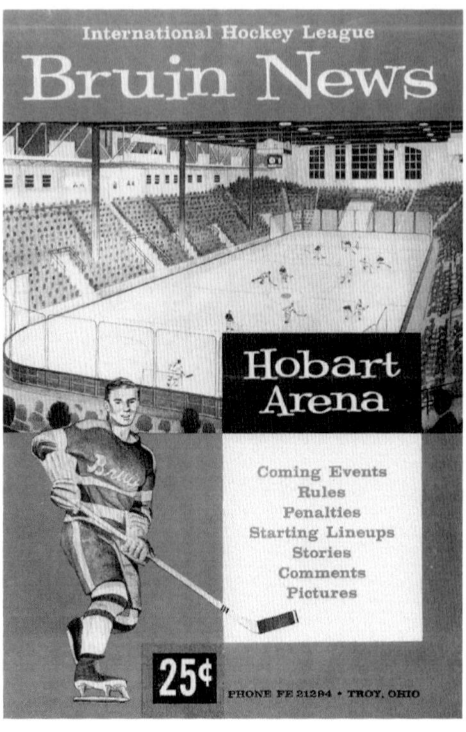

This is a program cover from the 1958–1959 season. Because of falling attendance and a poor showing on the ice the two previous seasons, it was uncertain if the Bruins would compete in the 1958–1959 season. However, hockey legend Eddie Shore, a friend and mentor to Ken Wilson, provided financial backing for the team to operate for an eighth season. (Courtesy of Hobart Arena.)

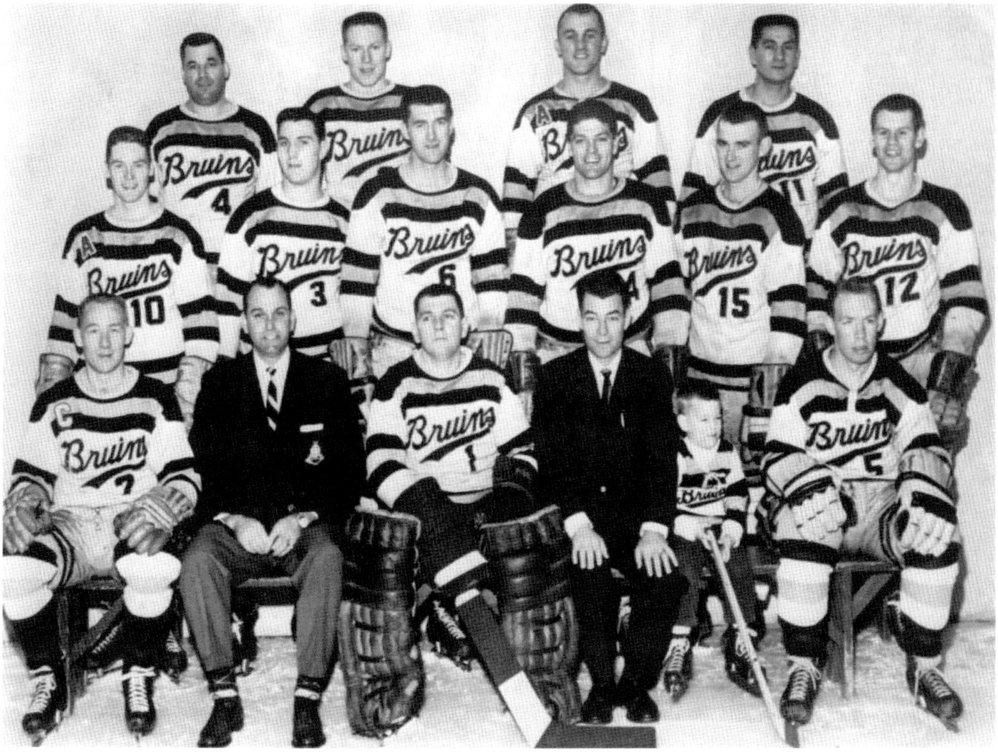

The 1958–1959 Bruins finished in third place in the IHL and made the playoffs for the first time in three years. However, the team continued to struggle at the box office, sometimes drawing less than 1,000 fans for a game. In early March 1959, Ken Wilson announced that the team would move to Greensboro, North Carolina, where they would compete in the EHL as the Greensboro Generals. (Courtesy of Bob Speck.)

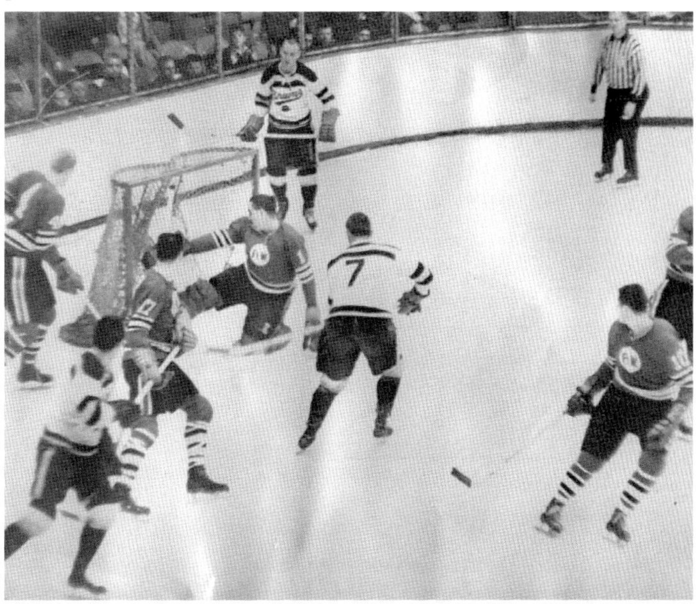

A crowd of about 2,000 fans attended the Bruins' last regular-season home game on March 29, 1959. The home team beat Fort Wayne 4-3 for Troy's 10th consecutive win over the Komets. Fort Wayne had won the first five season matchups. The Bruins finished third in the league and made the playoffs for the first time in three years. (Courtesy of Marty Szturm.)

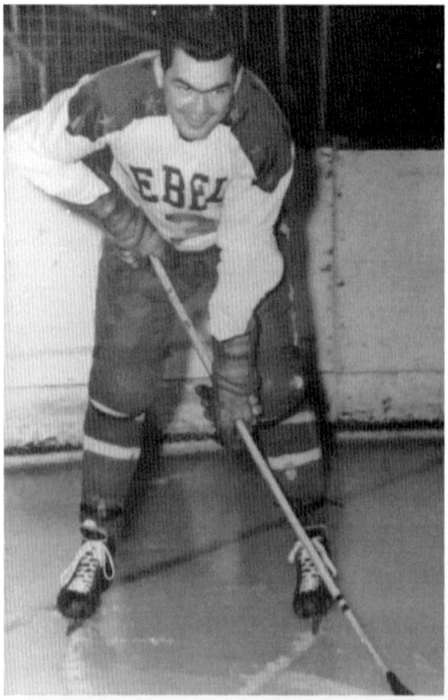

Troy met Louisville in the 1959 IHL playoffs. With Troy down three games to one, game five was played at Hobart on April 8. Tied 3-3 late in the game, Louisville defenseman Warren Back lifted a harmless shot that somehow found the net, giving Louisville the series win and ending hockey in Troy. Back would return to the area in 1964, when he became the first coach of the Dayton Gems. (Courtesy of Warren Back.)

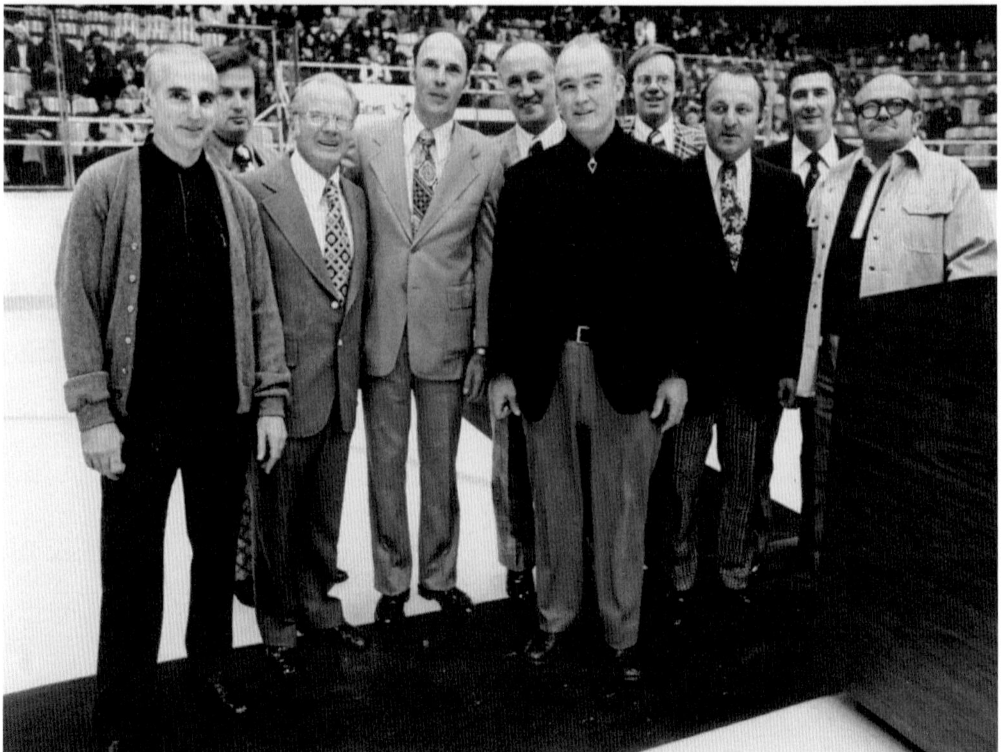

It was "Troy Night" at Hara Arena on November 22, 1974, when the Dayton Gems hosted the Saginaw Gears. Prior to the contest, the Gems honored the Bruins and recognized a number of former players who attended the game, which the Gems won 4-1. (Courtesy of Bill Murphy.)

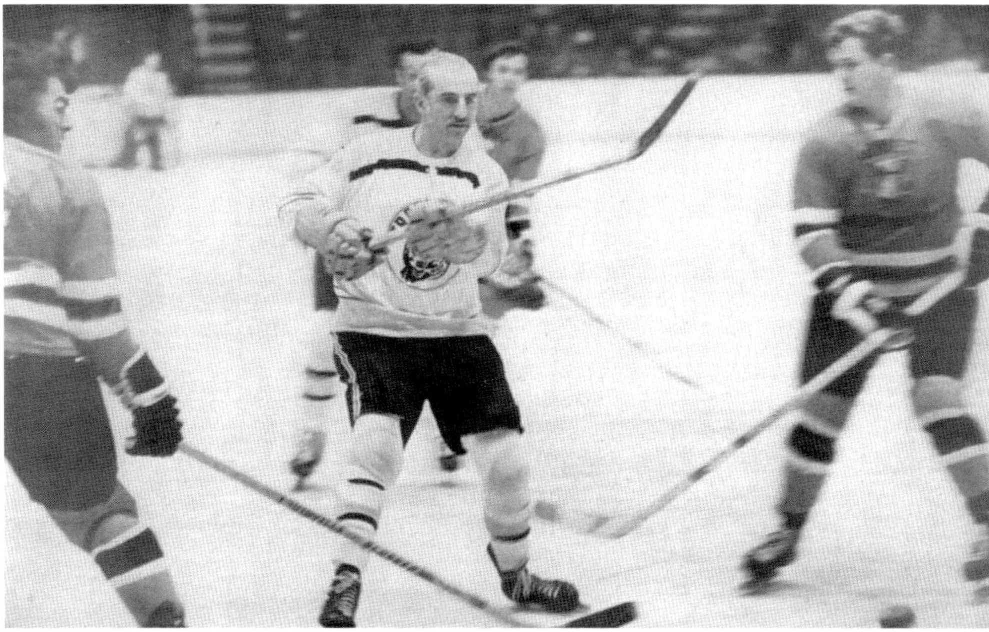

Over the years, Hobart Arena hosted many old-timers games, in which former Bruins players would team up with former Dayton Gems players—including Pat Rupp and Bob Bailey—and face off against teams of retired players from other cities. On March 17, 1974, the Troy Bruins took on the Fort Wayne Komets in an old-timers game at Hobart Arena. The Bruins came out on top, 7-5, before a crowd of about 2,000. On March 30, the Bruins beat the Lima Blues 7-2. Jim Campbell is pictured above in action against the Komets. Below, Bill Murphy looks on during the Bruins game versus Lima. (Both, courtesy of Bill Murphy.)

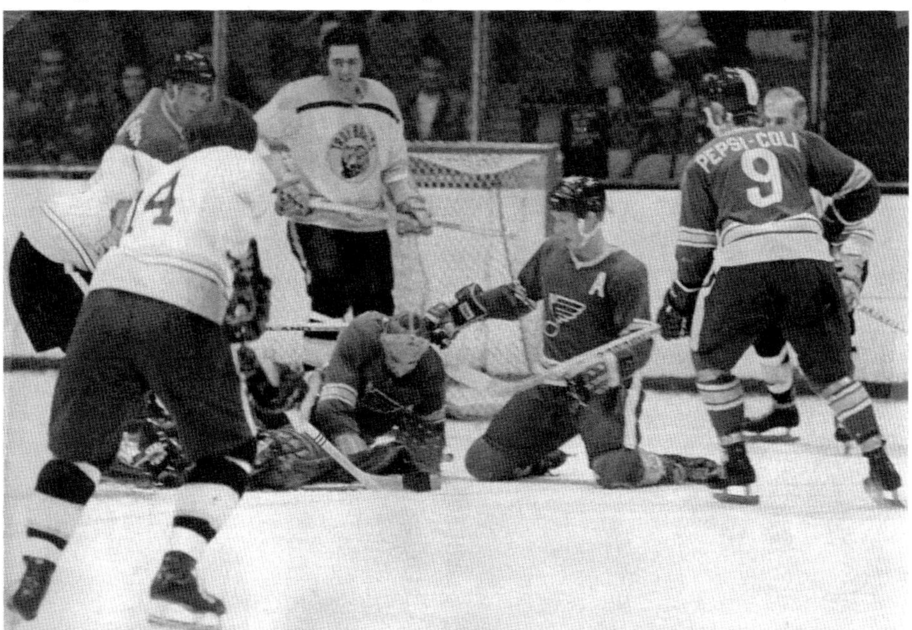

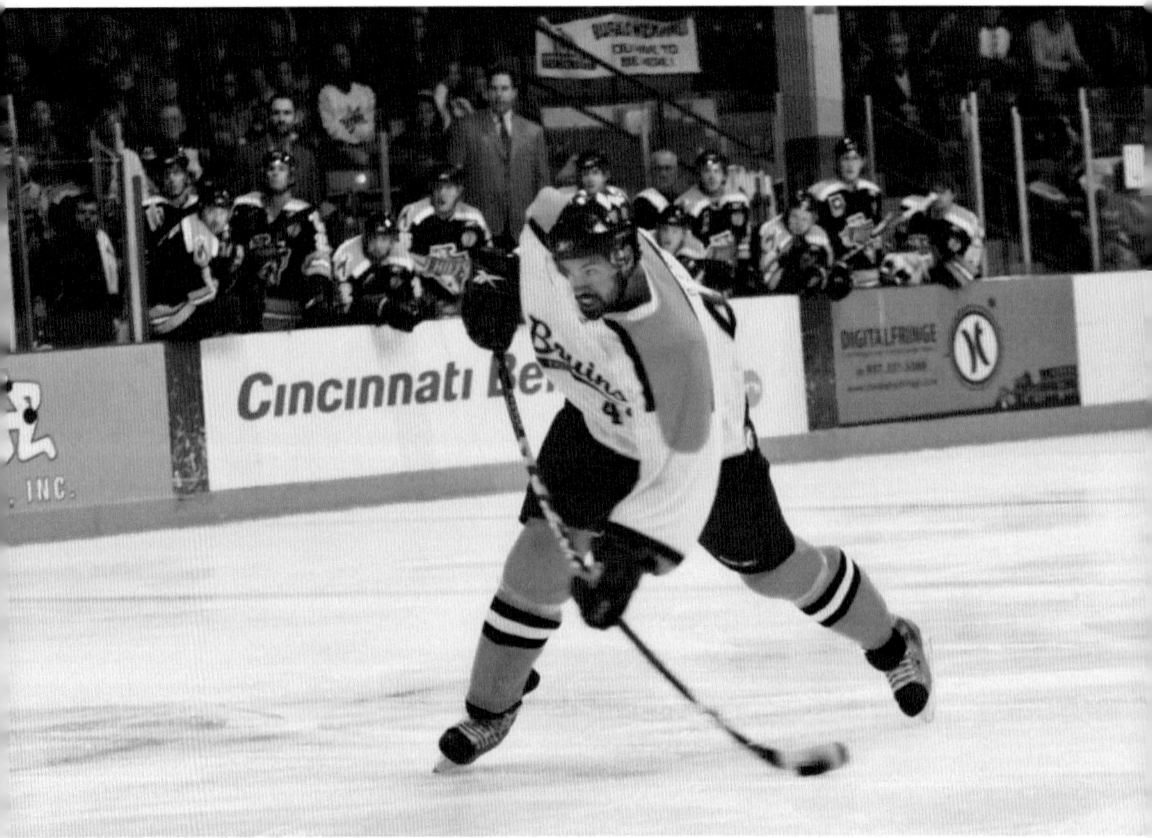

At 65 years old, Hobart Arena continues to be the home for area hockey leagues of all levels, as well as host to a variety of sporting and entertainment events. The facility went through major renovations in the late 1990s and will undergo additional improvements beginning in 2015. The arena hosted many Dayton Bombers games when the Nutter Center was unavailable, including the contest seen here, when the Bombers donned Bruins jerseys in a game versus the Johnstown Chiefs on November 15, 2008. The Chiefs won the game 3-1, in front of 3,011 hockey fans. (Courtesy of Max Surikov.)

2

Beautiful Hockey

The Dayton Gems

On June 24, 1964, the IHL held a press conference announcing its expansion to the city of Dayton. Lefty McFadden attended the event to pitch his advertising agency to the new owners. Little did he know that, later that day, he would be asked to lead the new team. Dad had been at the Dayton Speedway since 1961 and turned the failing track around financially. He now found himself with a new challenge. Despite a limited player pool, Dad, along with player-coach Warren Back, managed to put a team together. On November 1, 1964, the Dayton Gems took to the ice for their home opener, defeating the Port Huron Flags, 5-2.

It did not take long to create die-hard fans. Excitement was at a fever pitch during the 1966 playoffs, when the Gems' masterful stick-handler, Bob Bailey, was suspended for a spearing call. IHL commissioner Andy Mulligan upheld the call, but Gems fans disagreed. When Mulligan next came to town, the commissioner was hung in effigy at Hara Arena. The team won back-to-back Turner Cups in 1969 and 1970. In 1970, Dad was named Minor League Hockey Executive of the Year by the *Hockey News*. The recognition was a tribute not only to our dad, but also to the Gems and all they had accomplished in a short amount of time.

Our family had the privilege of witnessing it all firsthand; watching the Gems play each Sunday became part of our lifestyle. Looking back, names like Jack Walker, Stu Denmark, Art Bok, Russ Guerra, Ralph Skilken, and so many more fill us with fond memories. Our common interest in the Gems brought us together, and lifelong friendships were formed. Longtime staff members, including John Huffman, Sonny Tate, Warren and Mary Rose Back, Barbara Brigner, Walter Smith, Charlie Robinson, and their families were always present as we bonded over the fate of the Gems each week.

In 1974, our family headed to Washington, DC, where another expansion team, the NHL's Washington Capitals, required our dad's energy and expertise. It was not an easy decision, but Dad felt his 10 years with the Gems had prepared him for the challenge. He said goodbye to the city and the team he loved. He would be forever grateful and humbled to be known as the "Father of Dayton Hockey."

—Michelle (McFadden) Haas and Ava (McFadden) Rinkus

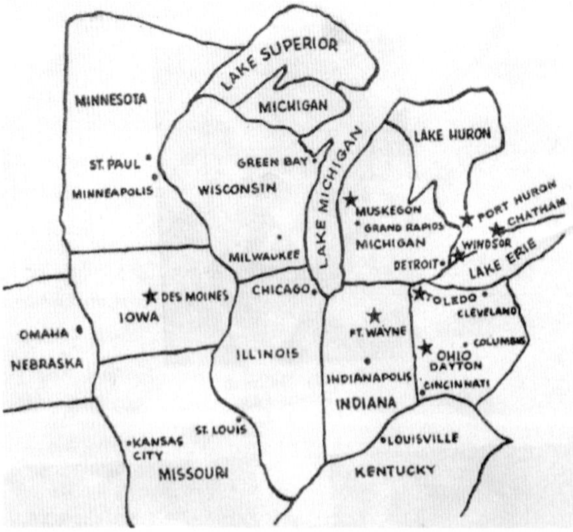

This map of the IHL is from the 1964–1965 league yearbook. The 1964–1965 season was the 20th for the league. By this time, the IHL had been in—and failed in—many major Midwest cities, including Indianapolis, Louisville, both Twin Cities, and Milwaukee. It had also been in smaller towns, like Muncie, Indiana; Marion, Ohio; and Johnstown, Pennsylvania. The league was beginning to run out of options to locate in new cities with a sizable arena to accommodate a team and where some league stability could be found. (Author's collection.)

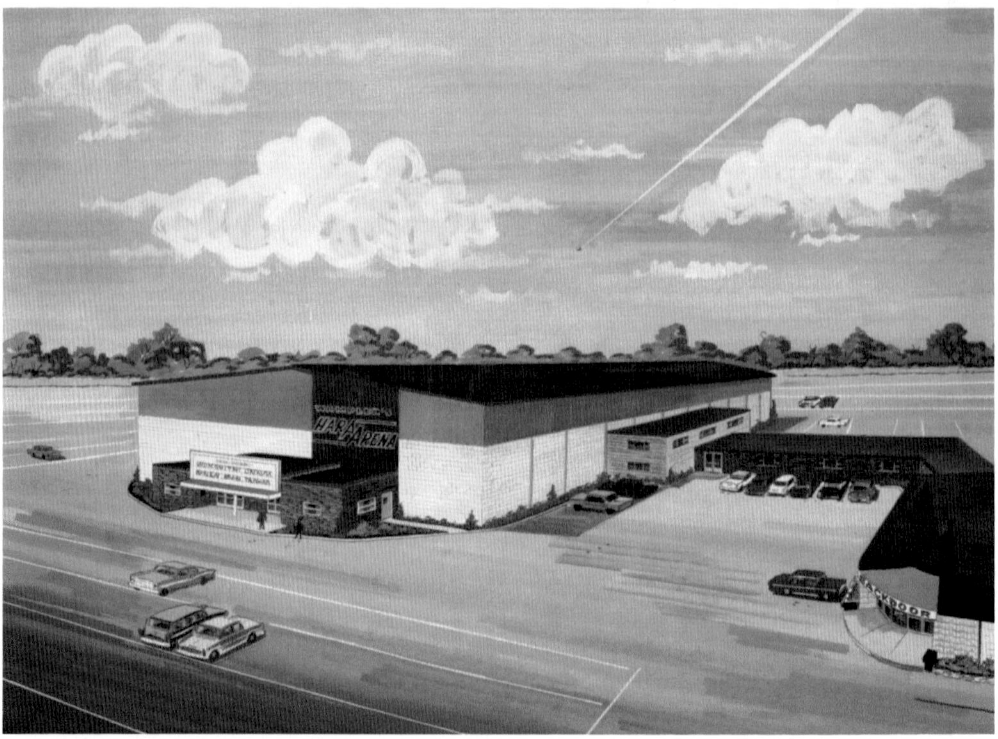

In the early 1960s, brothers Harold and Ralph Wampler began planning the construction of an exhibition arena that could host larger events—conventions, the circus, and trade shows—that no other Dayton facility at the time could accommodate. The arena would be built on the family property on the northwest side of Dayton, where the Wampler Ball Arena already stood. (Courtesy of Wright State Special Collections.)

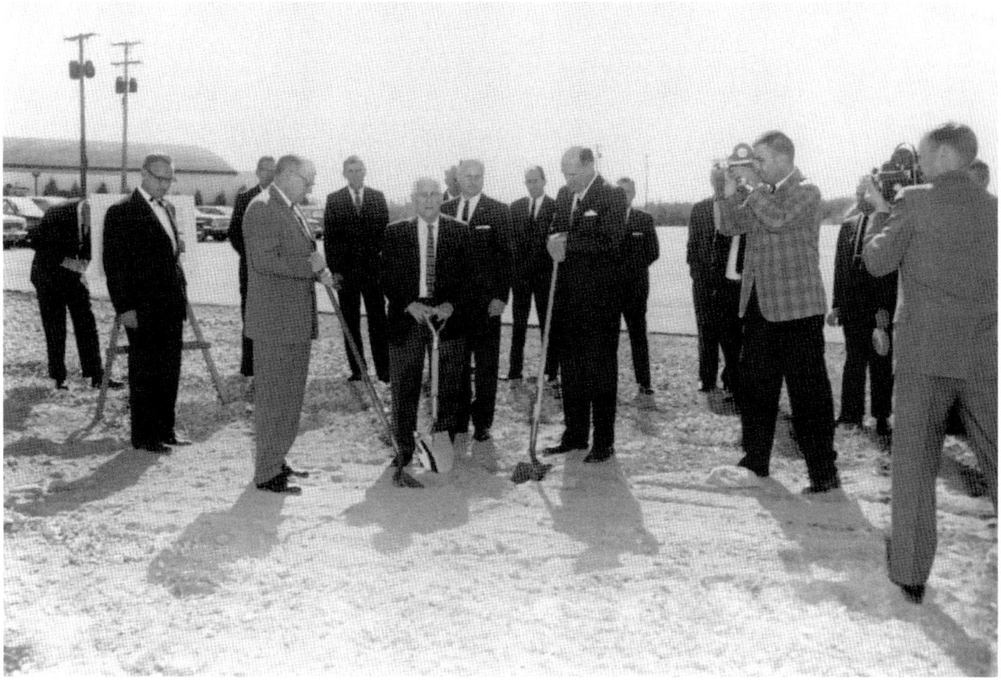

Ground was broken in October 1963 for the construction of Hara Arena, the name of which derived from the first two letters of the first names of Harold and Ralph Wampler. The arena would have 5,600 permanent seats. Initially, the plans did not include an ice rink, but this changed when the Wamplers were approached about hosting a hockey franchise. Within a few years, Hara Arena would become one of the most well-known buildings in hockey. (Courtesy of Wright State Special Collections.)

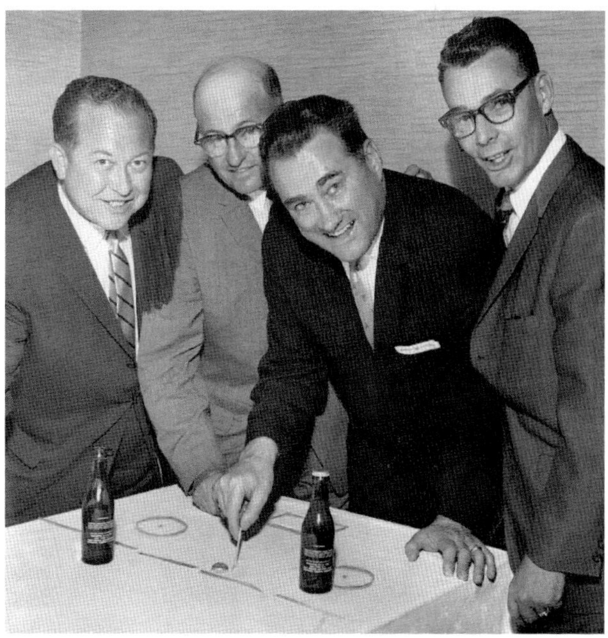

IHL commissioner Andy Mulligan (second from right) was in Dayton on June 24, 1964, for the announcement that a group of investors from Louisville would be locating a new franchise in Dayton to play at the newly built Hara Arena. When the investors failed to come up with the needed money, Mulligan and the other owners asked Lefty McFadden (far left) to take on the task of putting the new hockey team together. Ken Wilson is at far right and Harold Wampler is second from left. (Courtesy of Wright State Special Collections.)

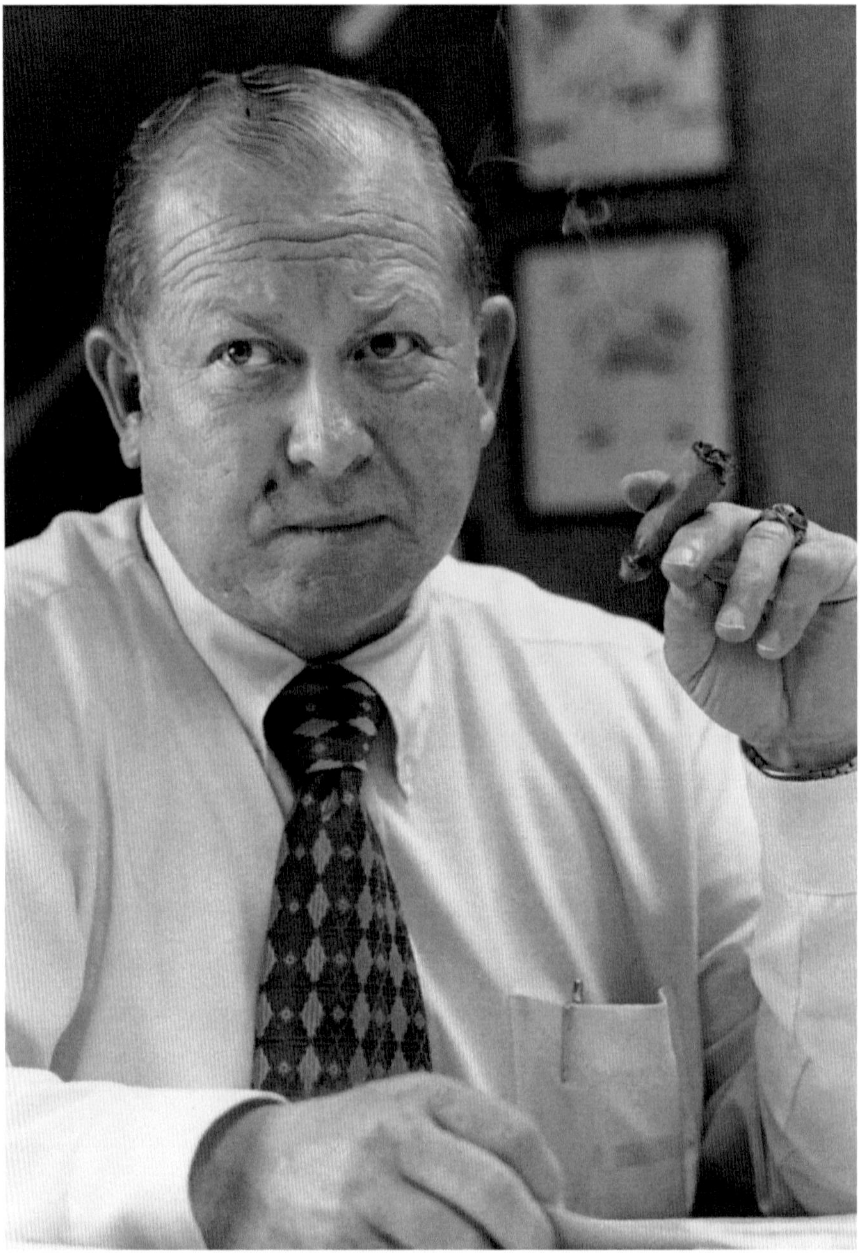

The cigar-smoking McFadden was the perfect choice to head the new hockey team. He was well known, well liked, and, most importantly, well connected in the Dayton area. He had an expansive sports background, having been a sportswriter, sporting-goods salesman, local sports radio host, and advertising agency owner. He became general manager of the failing Dayton and New Bremen Speedways in 1961 and turned them into successful moneymaking ventures within a few years. He knew very little about hockey when he took the new team on, but he said later, "I knew I liked the rough stuff." For the next decade, Lefty McFadden was the face of Dayton hockey and became known as the "Father of Dayton Hockey." (Courtesy of Wright State Special Collections.)

The league asked McFadden to raise $18,000 by a deadline of August 1. However, McFadden set a bigger goal of obtaining $40,000. His idea was to sell 40 shares of stock at $1,000 per share. In late July, McFadden had raised the money when he was notified that an $8,000 check had bounced. However, he met the $40,000 goal by the deadline date. The name of the new team would be the "Gems," as suggested by Jim Gabringer (the author's brother). (Courtesy of Wright State Special Collections.)

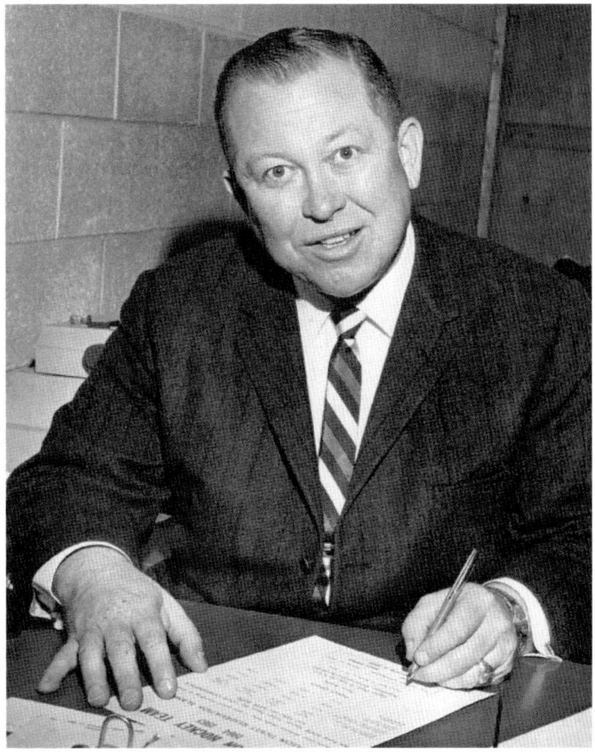

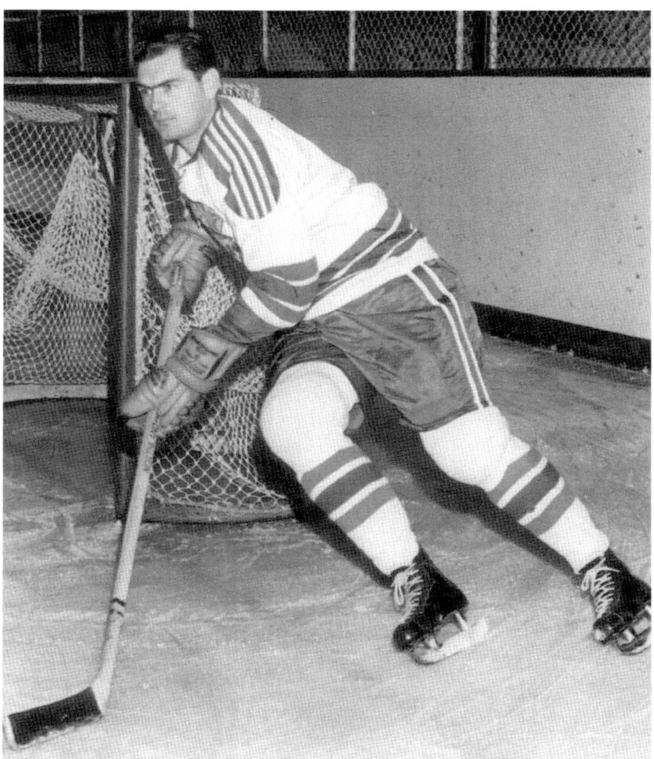

After spending seven years in the IHL with Louisville and Muskegon, Warren Back had decided to retire from hockey after the 1963–1964 season. When it was announced that Dayton would obtain an IHL franchise for the 1964–1965 season, commissioner Andy Mulligan recommended Back for the job as coach of the new team. After meeting Back for the first time, Lefty McFadden said he knew he had the right man for the job. (Courtesy of Wright State Special Collections.)

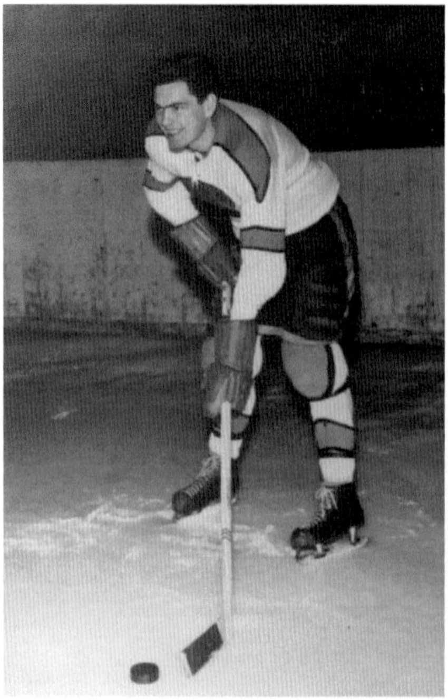

Warren Back grew up in Medicine Hat, Saskatchewan, and was a Boston Bruins farmhand. He had decided to quit hockey at age 27 to go into the management program at Sears when he took the offer to be the first Gems coach. For the first two years, he was a player-coach, lending his experience to the new team. (Courtesy of Warren Back.)

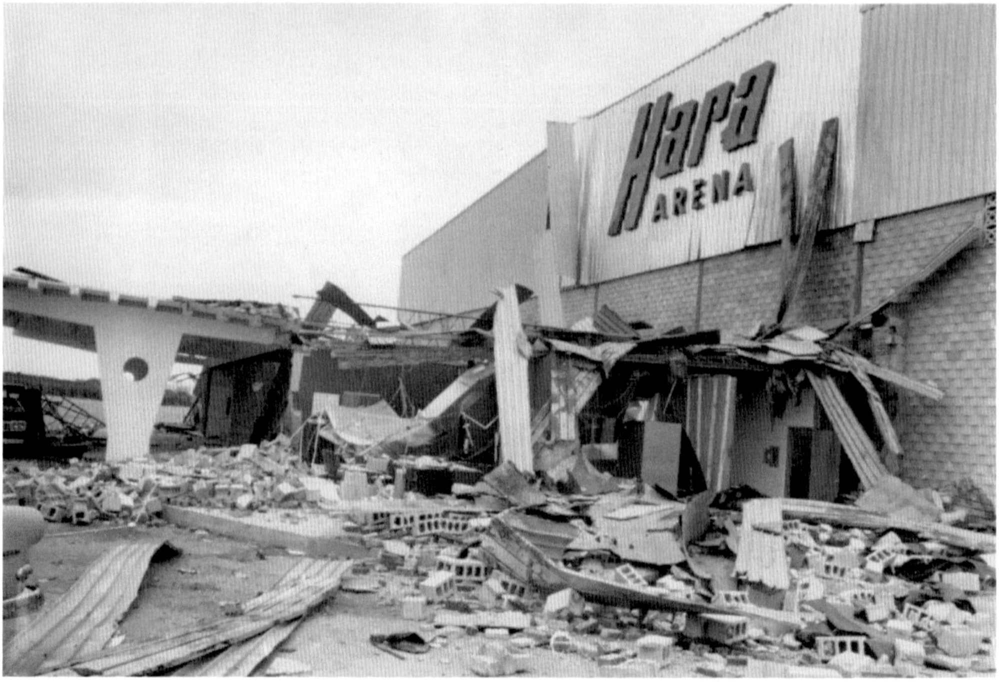

Lefty McFadden was at lunch when he learned that the front section of Hara Arena was severely damaged by an explosion during construction on October 4, 1964, just weeks before the start of the Gems' first season. Fortunately, no one was killed in the accident, and the main arena was not damaged. The Wamplers had the arena ready for the start of the season by month's end. (Courtesy of Wright State Special Collections.)

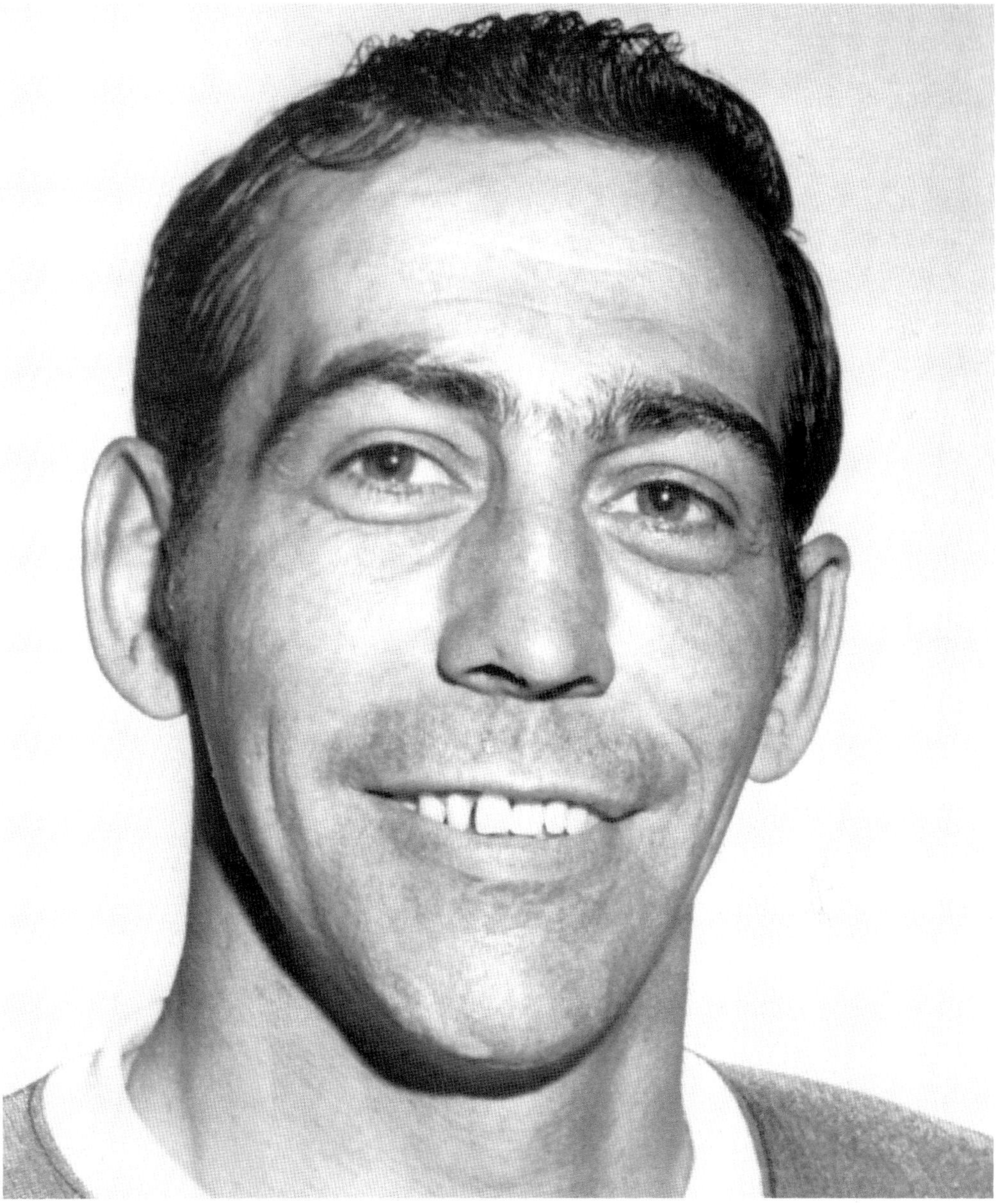

Three days before the start of the 1964–1965 season, the Gems acquired Guy Trottier from the Port Huron Flags for Tommy Clark, who wanted to play for a team closer to his mother's home in Sarnia, Ontario. The trade was a steal for the Gems, as, over the next three seasons, Clark would score a total of 43 goals, while the diminutive Trottier would net 185, including a Dayton record of 71 during the 1966–1967 season. While Sid Garant would score the most goals in Gems history, Trottier is thought of as the team's greatest goal-scorer because of the amazing numbers he registered in a short amount of time as a Gem. (Author's collection.)

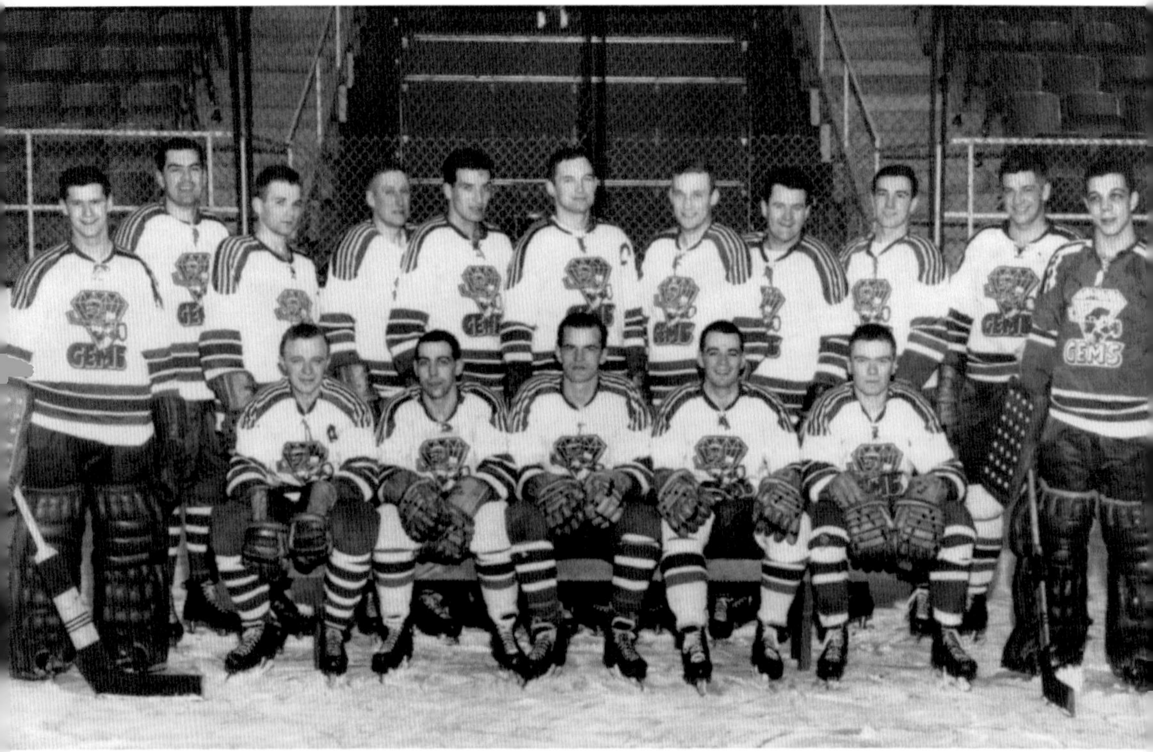

Dayton coach Warren Back said of the 1964–1965 Gems: "We had three teams that year. One coming, one going, and one playing." The startup squad struggled early in the season, at one time owning a 5-26 record and threatening to be the worst team in IHL history. But, with the addition of players like Bob Bailey, Pat Rupp, and Pat Donnelly, the team finished fifth with a record of 23-45-2. Guy Trottier led the team in goals (46) and total points (88). Though Dayton did not make the playoffs, it did not finish last in the six-team league. The first year, the Gems averaged 2,975 fans for their 35 home games at Hara Arena. (Author's collection.)

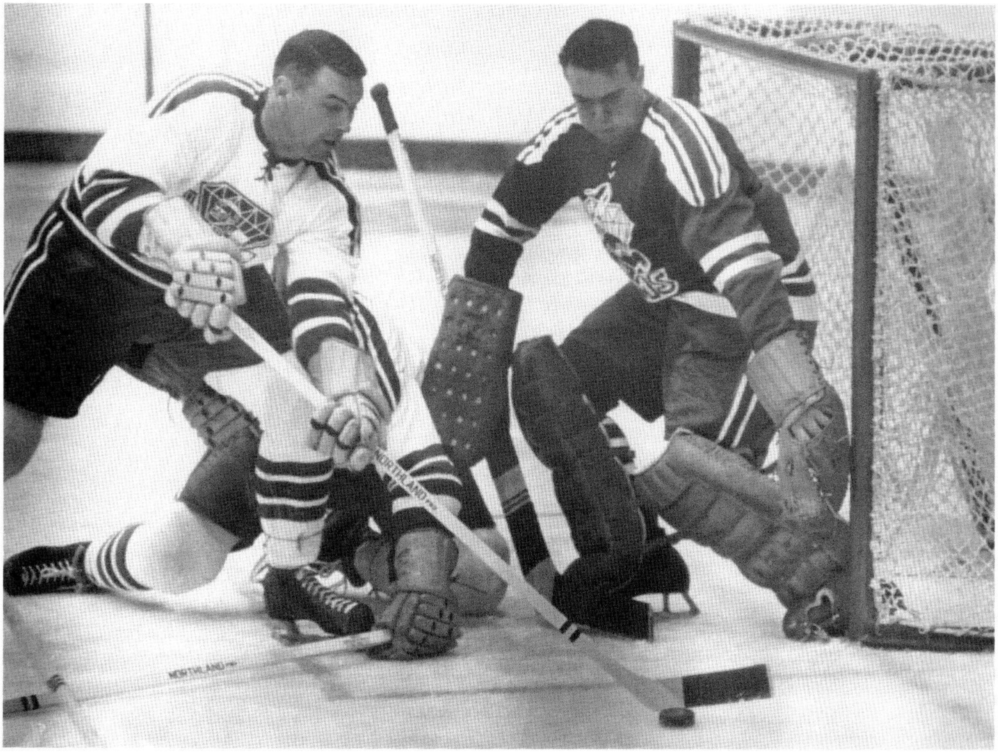

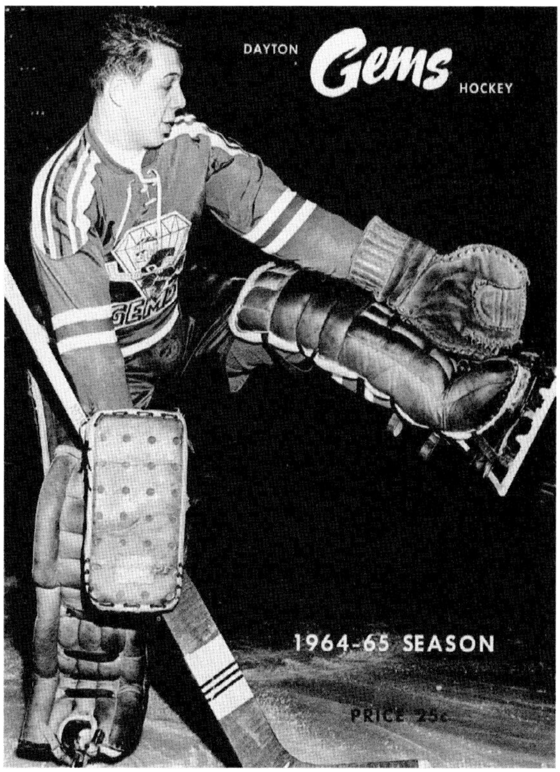

On October 27, 1964, a crowd of 1,420 turned out to see the Gems lose to Toledo 7-3 in the team's exhibition home opener. Lefty McFadden said, "there should have been that many people show up just to see why the lights were on at Hara Arena." On November 1, a respectable 2,871 fans watched the Gems beat the Port Huron Flags 5-2 in the first regular-season home game in Gems history. (Courtesy of Wright State Special Collections.)

The Gems program for the first season featured goalie Ludger Doucet on the cover. Doucet was the Gems' first-year netminder, until Pat Rupp arrived in January 1965. (Author's collection.)

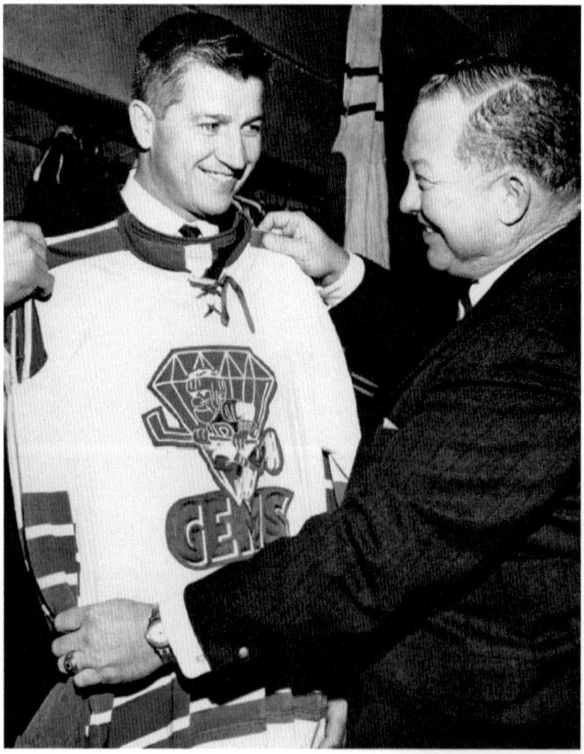

A few weeks into their first season, the Gems acquired veteran Bob Bailey from the Fort Wayne Komets. Bailey, who had spent time in the NHL with Toronto, Chicago, and Detroit, was on the IHL suspended list after shoving a referee during a game the year before. He was known as "Bashin" Bob Bailey for his tough and physical style of play. But he also was regarded as one of the most talented stick-handlers in all of hockey. Pat Rupp called him "a magician with a puck" who was capable of taking control of a game all on his own. (Courtesy of Wright State Special Collections.)

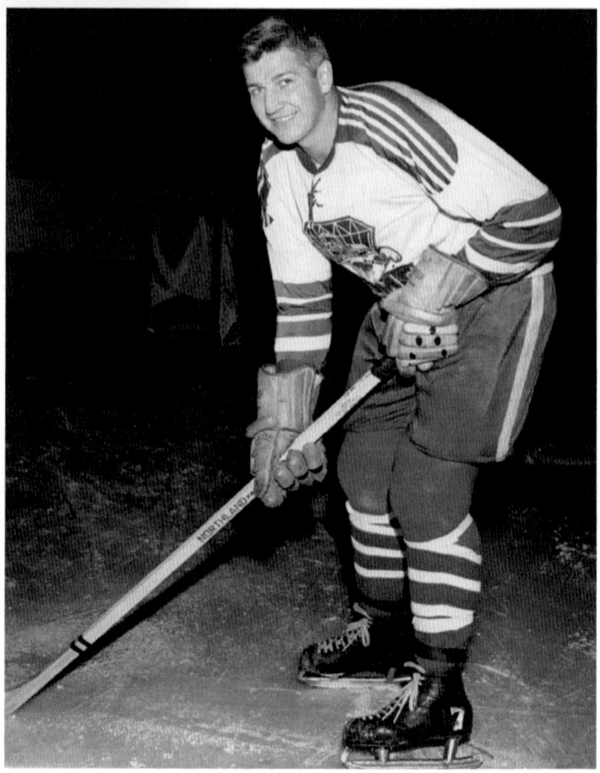

Bob Bailey's first game with the Gems was on November 25, 1964; he was credited with two assists in a 6-4 Gems win. He finished the 1964–1965 season with 87 points in just 54 games. The next year, he recorded 45 goals and 87 assists, a Dayton hockey record. He remained with the Gems until 1967, scoring a total of 319 points, including 215 assists, in just 204 games. (Courtesy of Wright State Special Collections.)

Rumor was, on nights when the Gems were not playing well, Lefty McFadden would signal from the press box for Ted LeBioda to start a scrap to get the home crowd excited. Whether or not this was true, LeBioda was the Gems' first "enforcer." Off the ice, LeBioda was a personable guy and a skilled hunter who would show up to camp each year with smoked meats from the game he had bagged during the off-season. (Courtesy of Kevin Anderson.)

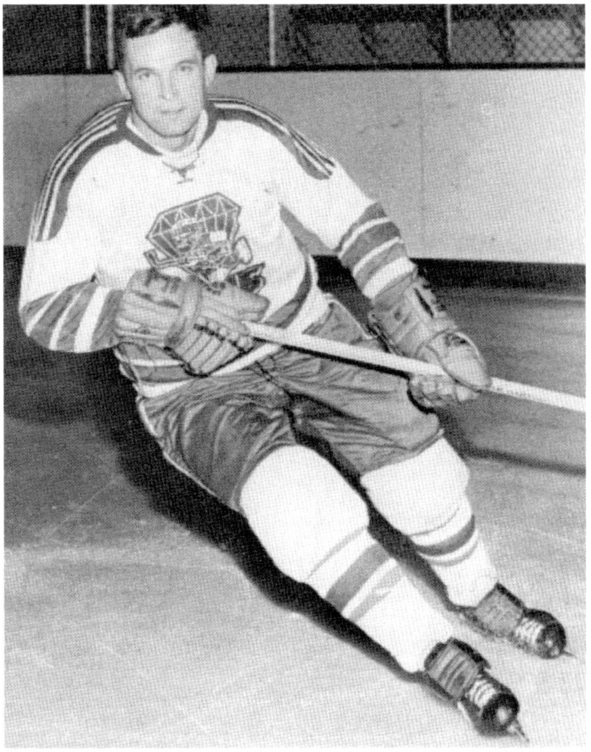

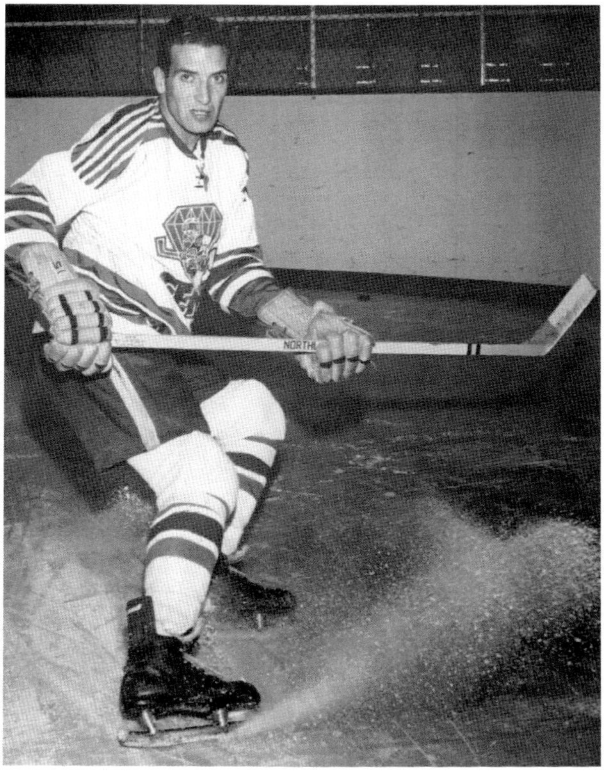

Sid Garant earned the name "Mr. Original" because, by 1969, he was the only player left from the start of the Gems' first year. Though overshadowed by Guy Trottier and Don Westbrooke in scoring, Garant was a fan favorite. He holds most of Dayton's career scoring records, including goals (204), assists (291), and points (495). (Courtesy of Wright State Special Collections.)

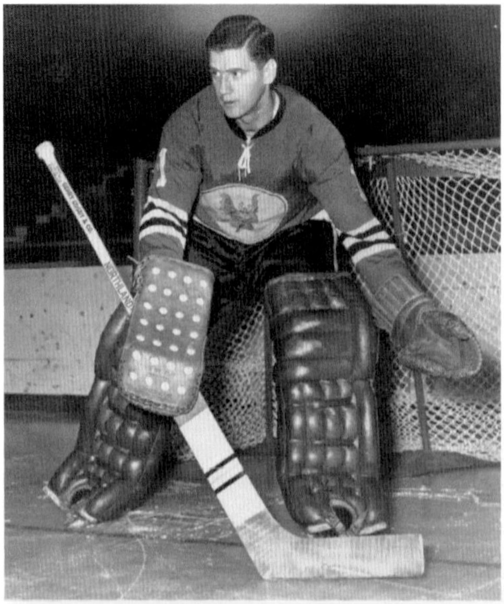

In early January 1965, the Gems obtained goaltender Pat Rupp from the Jersey Devils of the EHL. Rupp was from Detroit and played for the 1964 US Olympic hockey team. He also played one game for the Detroit Red Wings in February 1964. He debuted for the Gems on January 9, 1965, and was one reason the Gems finished above .500 for the second half of their first season. (Courtesy of Kathy Rupp.)

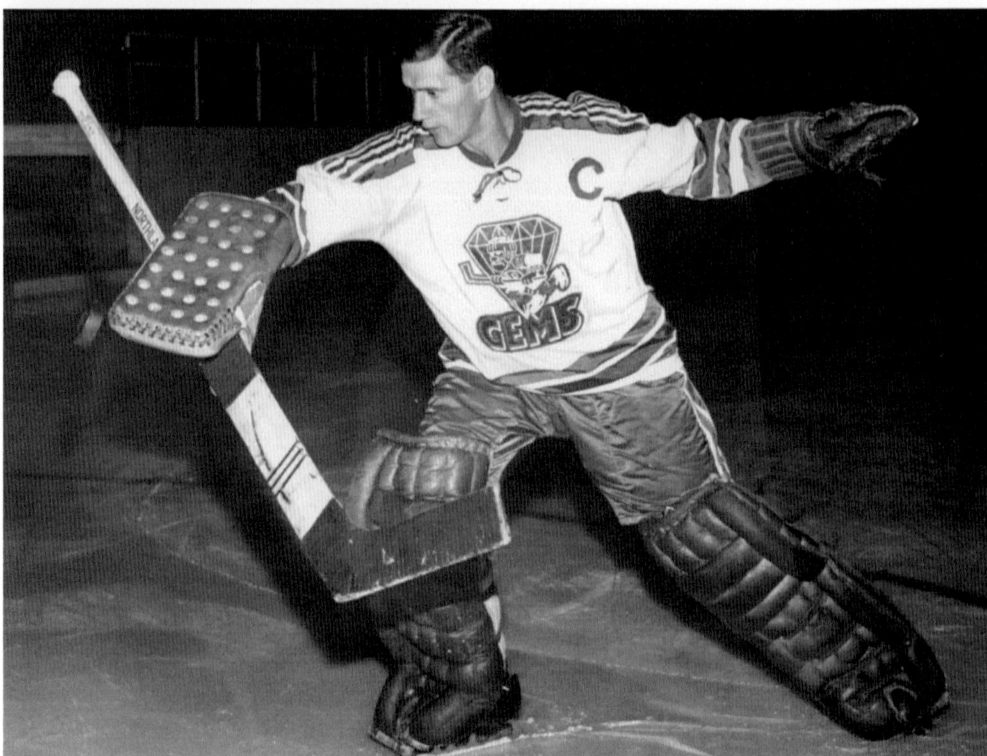

Two goalies were on one of Pat Rupp's youth hockey teams—he and Jimmy Hoffa Jr., son of the labor leader. "He [Hoffa] would arrive at the games in a limousine and had all new equipment and I had this ratty stuff from Goodwill," Rupp would say. Rupp played the majority of the games, and no one was found in the Detroit River wearing a pair of cement skates at the end of the season. (Courtesy of Kathy Rupp.)

In his first game as a Dayton Gem on December 26, 1964, Pat Donnelly (center) netted a hat trick in a 6-4 win over the Fort Wayne Komets. For his effort, Donnelly picked up a brand-new set of tires from a local tire dealer. Donnelly remained in Dayton until he was traded for Don Westbrooke in 1967. He is seen here with Bob Bailey (left) and Guy Trottier (right). (Courtesy of Kevin Anderson.)

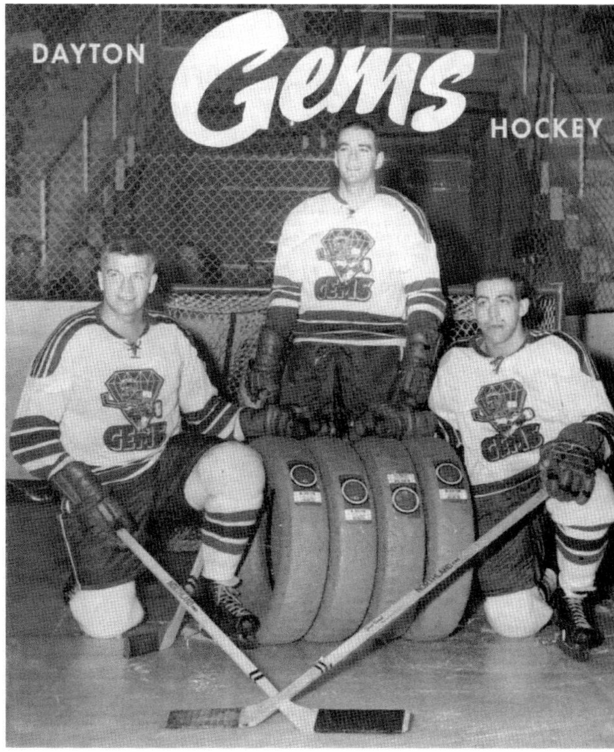

Dayton Hockey Team
HARA ARENA
1001 SHILOH SPRINGS ROAD
DAYTON, OHIO 45415
278-7991

NEWS RELEASE

FOR IMMEDIATE RELEASE

DAYTON, OHIO--Next Sunday night will be extra special for the kids in Dayton Gems Hockeyland.

The management of the Gems has announced that the first 500 youngsters, who sit in the $2, $2.50 or $3.00 seats at Sunday night's game will receive an official Dayton Gems hockey stick for free.

Dayton plays Toledo here Sunday night and the Blades will be under their new coach, Edgar (Chirp) Brenchley, former mentor at Port Huron. For the past 14 months Brenchley has been a scout for the Chicago Blackhawks and coach of the St. Catherines junior team in Canada.

Brenchley replaces Ken Wilson as coach. Wilson will continue as vice-president and General Manager of the Blades.

At Port Huron, Brenchley coached Sid Garant, Guy Trottier, Gerry Moore and Cliff Bristow, all current members of the Dayton Gems.

The Gems have beaten Toledo three straight games, two on Toledo ice, this season.

Game time for Sunday's game is 7 p.m., and tickets are on sale daily at the Hara Arena box office, 1001 Shiloh Springs Rd., from 10 a.m. to 10 p.m., and in downtown Dayton at the Dayton Inn, Jim Flynn's, Sears, Rikes and the AAA Club.

To maximize newspaper coverage of the Gems, Lefty McFadden would type up and hand deliver game stories to local newspapers following home contests in time for the next day's print run. Warren Back remembers delivering stories with McFadden long into the evening after Gems games, often on snowy and bitterly cold winter nights. This is a Gems press release from the 1965–1966 season. (Courtesy of the McFadden family.)

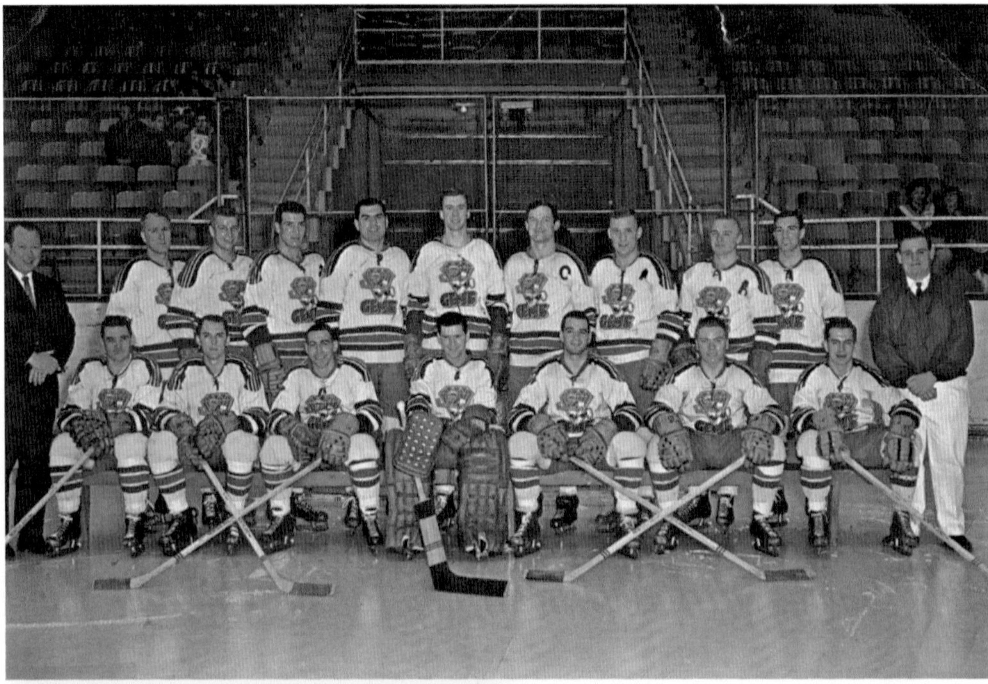

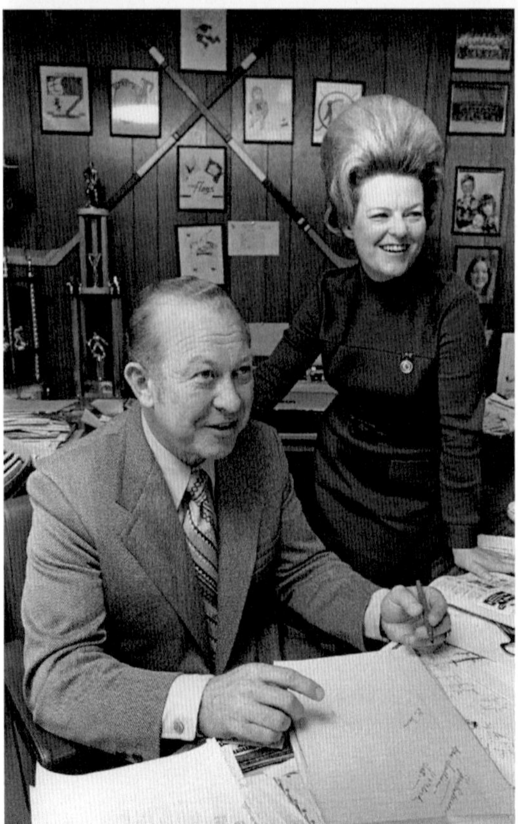

The 1965–1966 Gems team compiled a record of 33-35-2, ten more wins than in their first season. Guy Trottier and Bob Bailey each tallied an amazing 132 points. The team finished fourth and made the playoffs, defeating Fort Wayne in the opening round, but losing to Port Huron in the Turner Cup finals, four games to one. Regular-season home attendance grew to an average of 3,069. (Author's collection.)

Barb Brigner was hired by Lefty McFadden before the Gems' first season to be the team's office manager. She remained there for 13 years. Though she had a great relationship with McFadden, he once jokingly put her on league waivers—and she was claimed by three other teams. (Courtesy of Wright State Special Collections.)

After being suspended for an altercation the night before in Fort Wayne, Bob Bailey watched along with the first-ever Hara Arena sellout crowd of 5,283 as the Gems defeated the Komets 5-2 in game six of the 1966 playoff semifinals to advance to their first-ever Turner Cup final. That evening, the festive home crowd passed a hat to collect money to pay Bailey's fine. Lefty McFadden remembered that there was enough for the fine and then some. (Courtesy of Wright State Special Collections.)

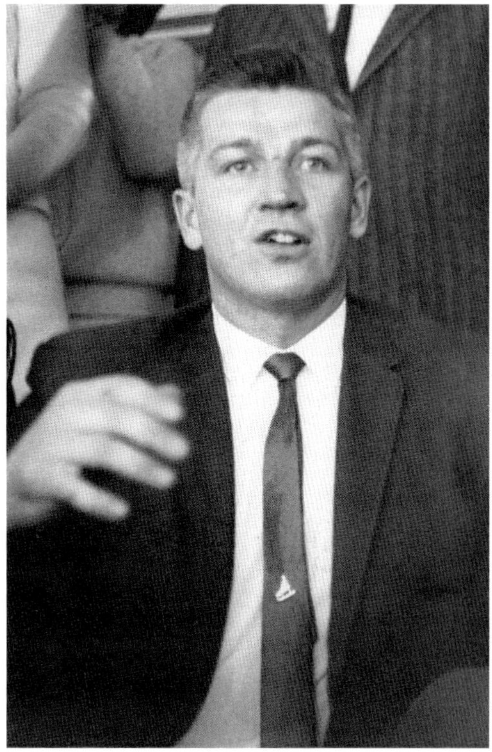

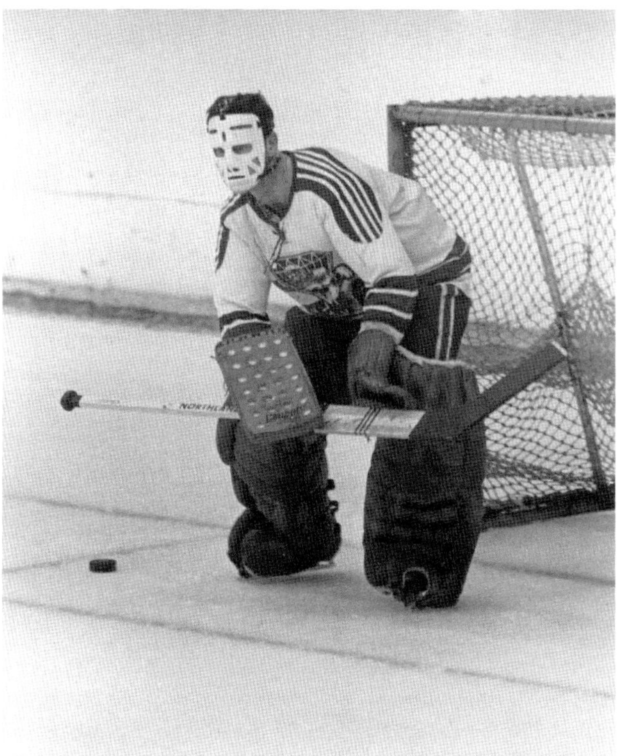

In the mid-1960s, Pat Rupp was one of a growing number of goalies who wore a face mask. "Hockey management felt that if you wore a mask you were either afraid or it impinged upon your vision," Rupp would say. "They were afraid a puck would wind up in the net because you wouldn't see it coming and it would cost you a championship. It had nothing to do with you wearing it because you had common sense." (Courtesy of Kathy Rupp.)

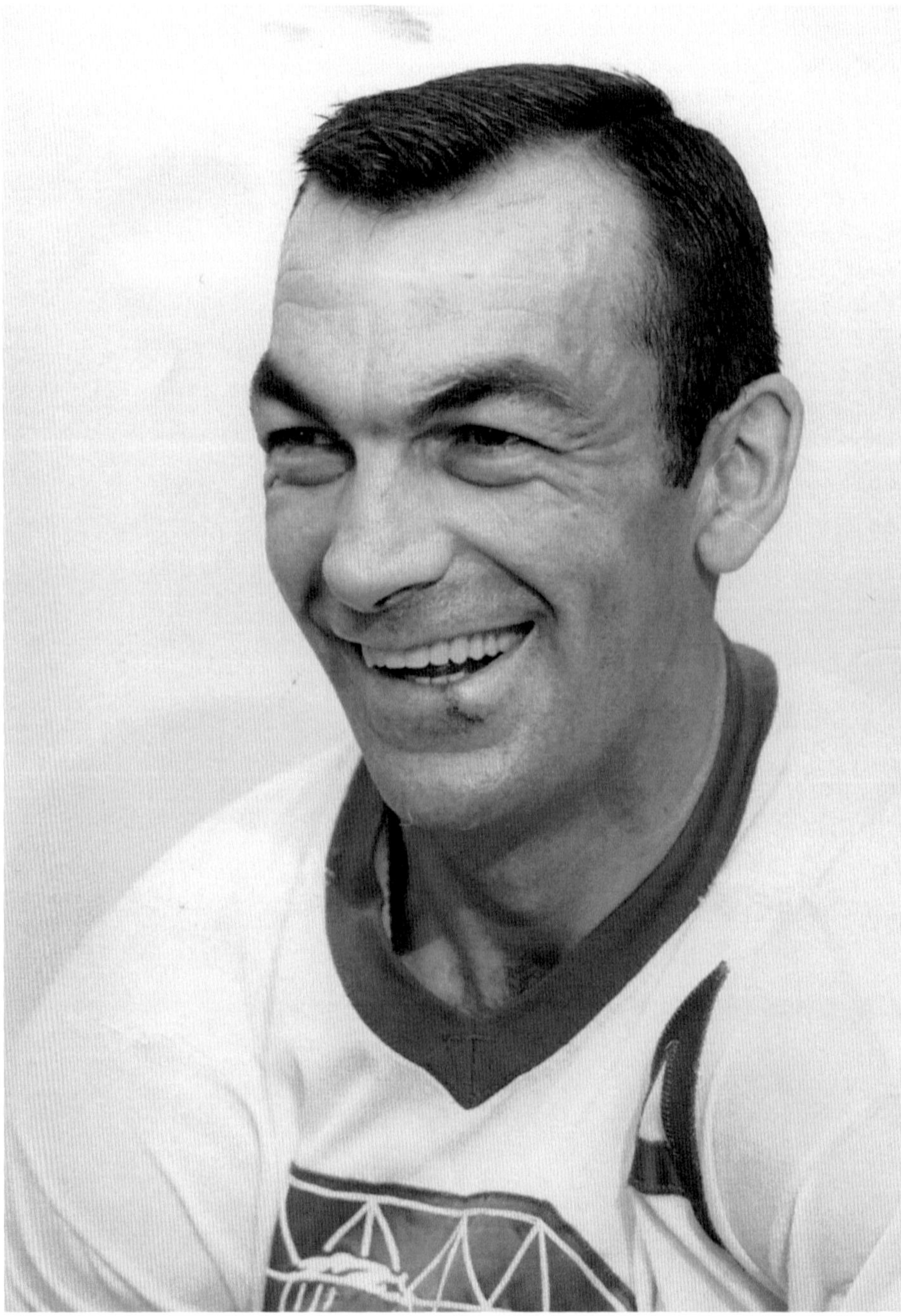

Moe Benoit was a longtime IHL veteran known for his leadership and defensive abilities. Benoit played on the 1960 Canadian Olympic hockey team that won a silver medal (the United States won the gold). He was coach of the Toledo Blades when the Gems acquired him before the 1966–1967 season. Benoit was key to the Gems winning two league championships and two Turner Cups from 1967 to 1970, and he became one of the most popular and recognizable Gems in history. (Author's collection.)

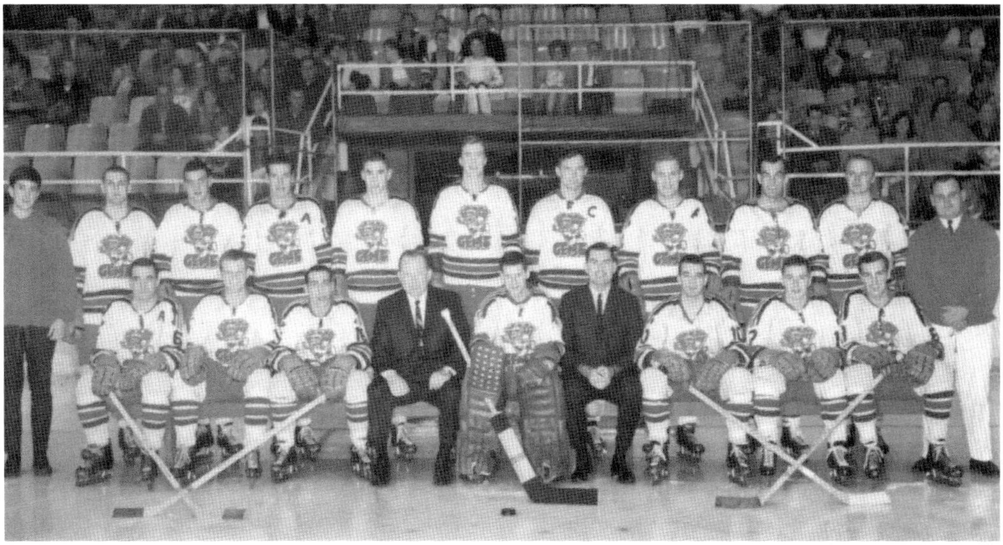

In only their third year, the Gems captured their first Huber Trophy as IHL regular-season champions. Warren Back became a bench coach, and the team added veteran defenseman Moe Benoit and rookies Gerry Mazur and Al Beaule. Guy Trottier netted a Dayton hockey record of 71 goals and 135 scoring points. Home attendance swelled to an average of 4,123. In the playoffs, the Toledo Blades swept the Gems in the first round, four games to none. (Author's collection.)

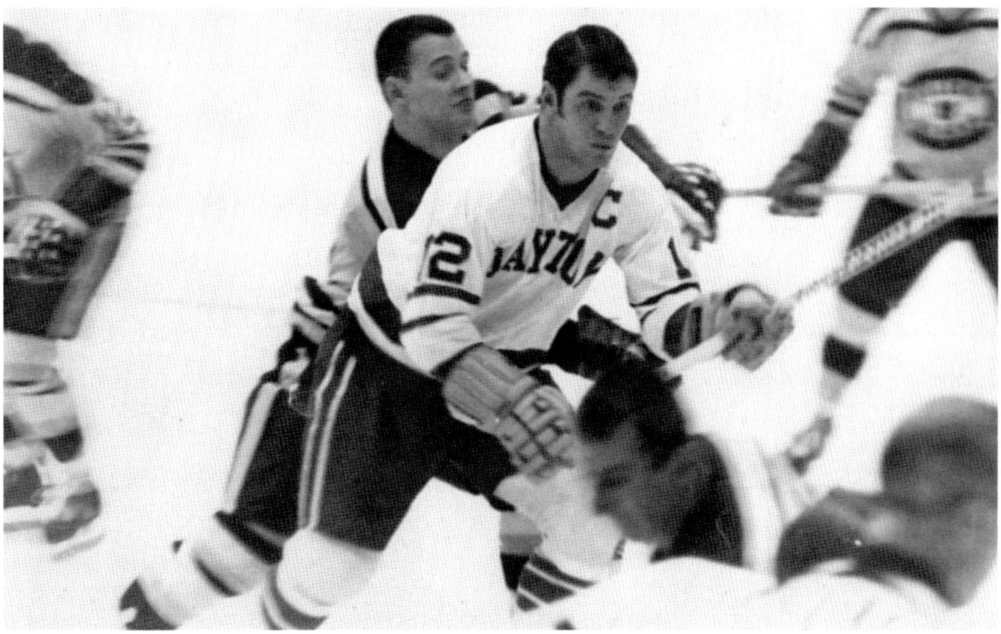

Duncan Rousseau was one of Lefty McFadden's favorite players. Rousseau's tough, hard-nosed style of play endeared him to Gems fans as well. The left winger played with the Gems from 1967 to 1970 and was the captain of the 1969 and 1970 Turner Cup champion teams. During the 1968–1969 season, he tallied 88 points playing on a line with Larry Wilson and Don Westbrooke. Rousseau also amassed 172 minutes in penalties. (Courtesy of Kathy Rupp.)

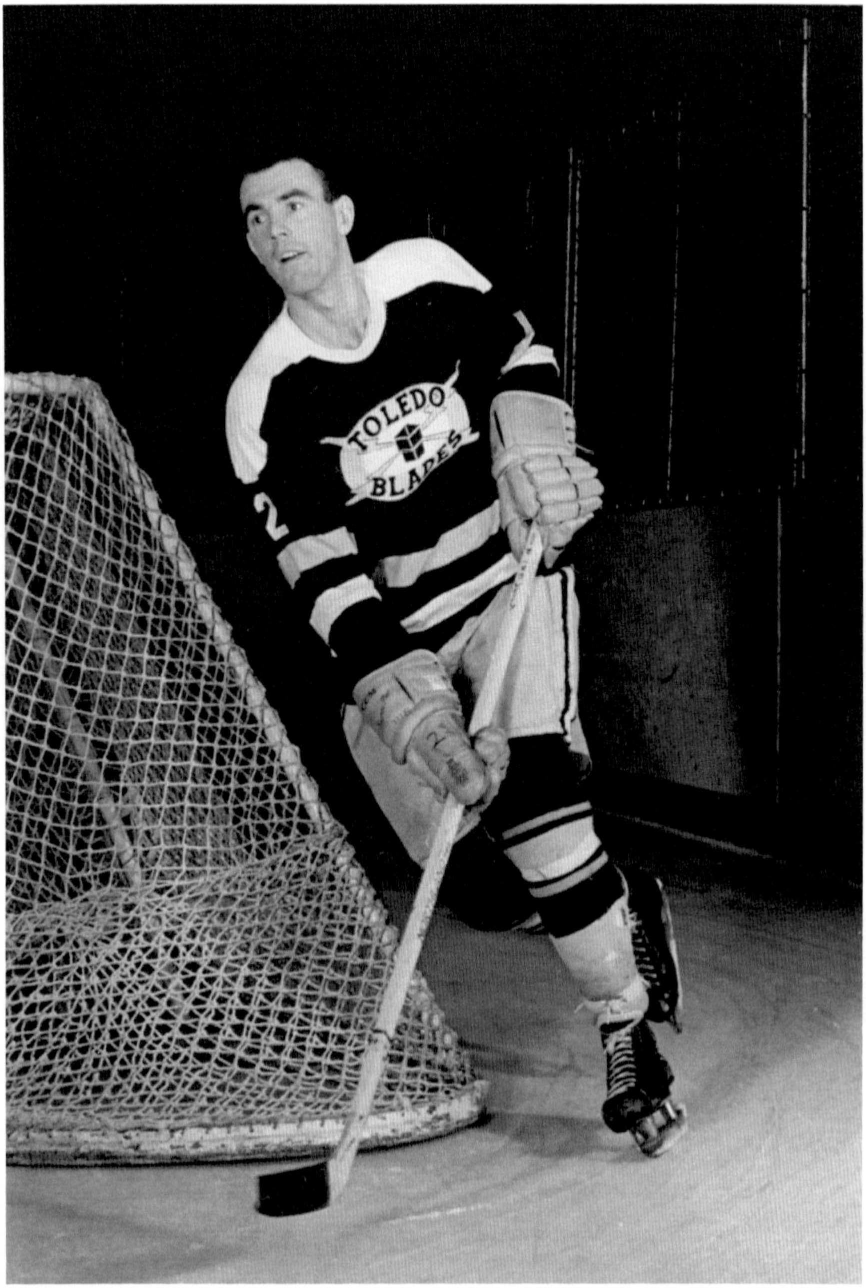

Don Westbrooke was named the 1963–1964 IHL Rookie of the Year while playing for the Toledo Blades. That year, he scored 70 points on 28 goals and 42 assists. Over the next several seasons, he failed to live up to the high-scoring potential the Blades felt he possessed. Following the 1966–1967 season, the Gems acquired Westbrooke from Toledo for Pat Donnelly. When hearing the news that he had been traded to Dayton, Westbrooke said, "I thought I'd died and went to heaven." A Toledo newspaper later called the trade the worst in the history of Toledo hockey. (Courtesy of Wright State Special Collections.)

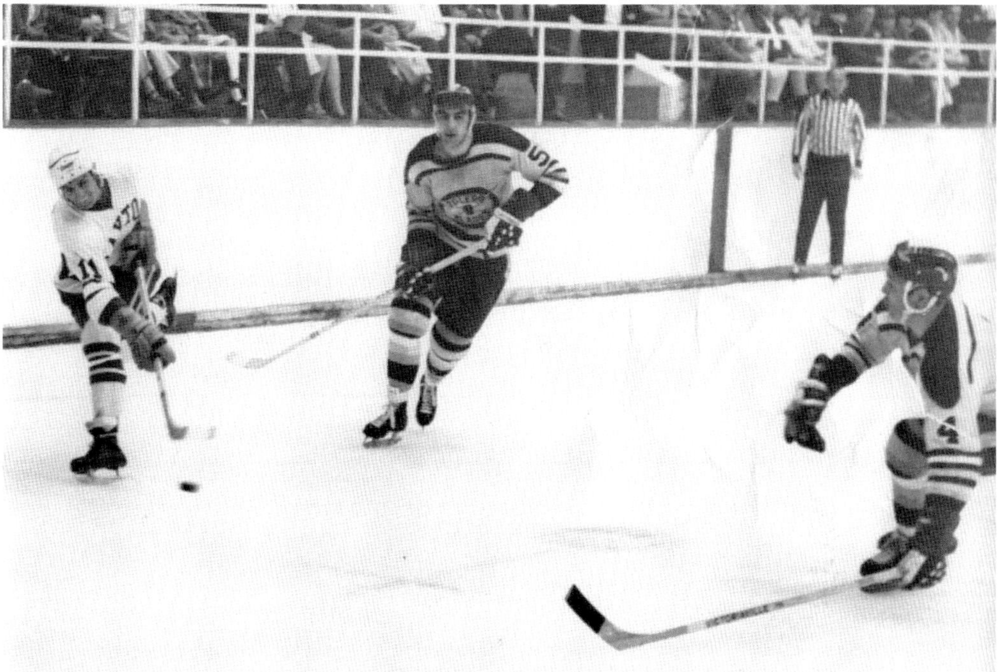

Westbrooke flourished upon coming to Dayton and became, along with Guy Trottier, the most prolific goal-scorer in Gems history. From 1967 to 1970, he scored 50, 59, and 59 goals. He won the Leo Lamoreaux Trophy as the league's leading scorer for the 1968–1969 season, when he scored 118 points, and won it again the next season, tallying 121 points. He was named IHL co-MVP for the 1967–1968 season and claimed the James Gatschene trophy for himself for the 1968–1969 season. (Courtesy of Wright State Special Collections.)

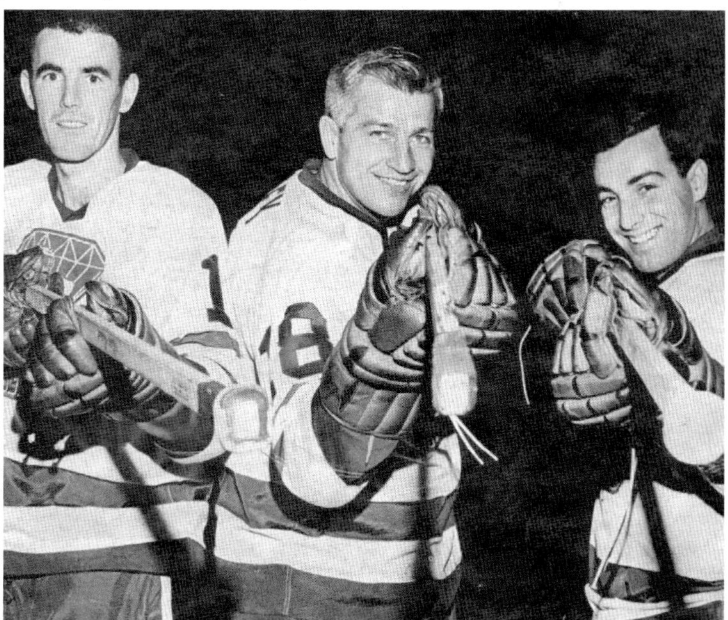

When Don Westbrooke (left) arrived from Toledo, he was put on a line with Bob Bailey (center) and Bob Regis (right), replacing Guy Trottier. The Westbrooke-Bailey-Regis line became one of the highest-scoring lines for the first part of the 1967–1968 IHL season. (Courtesy of Kevin Anderson.)

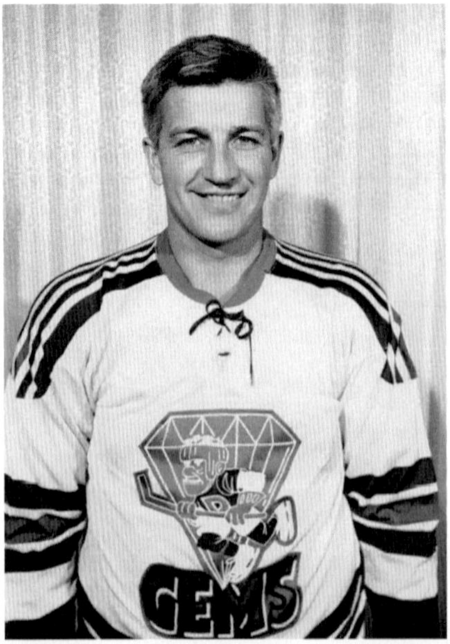

In December 1967, Bob Bailey was on pace to set a team record for points. Following an offside call during the third period of a game against the Komets in Fort Wayne on December 9, 1967, Bailey punched referee Billy Purcell. Bailey was ejected from the game and indefinitely suspended from the league. Subsequently, Bailey retired from hockey, ending the career of one of the most talented and colorful players in Gems history. (Courtesy of Wright State Special Collections.)

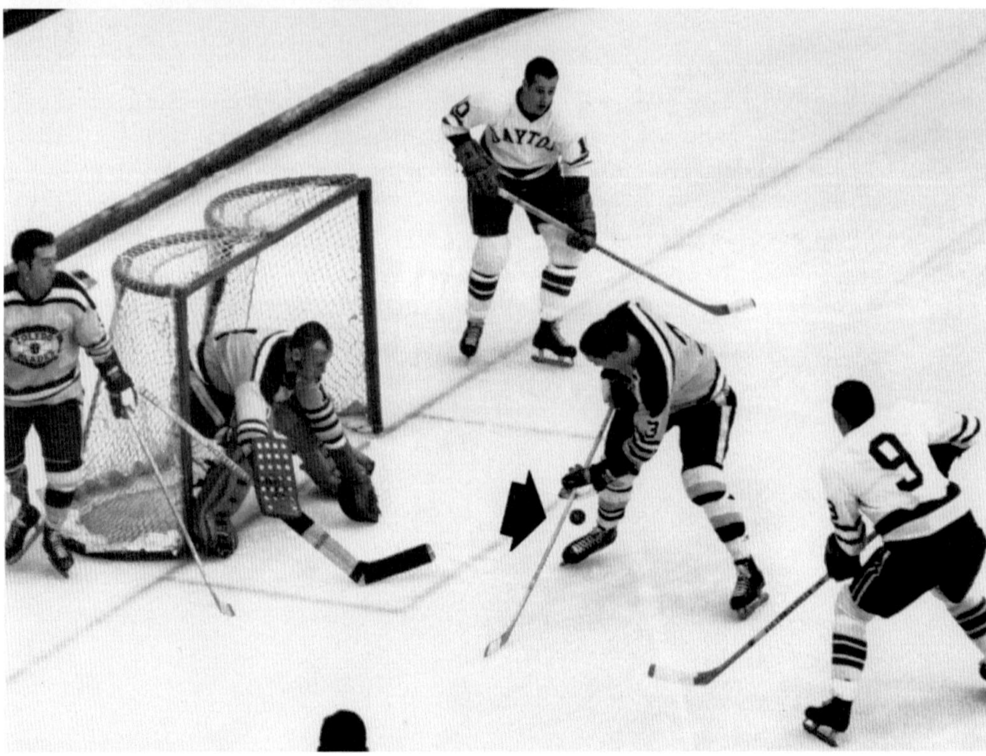

The Gems scored 31 goals in two nights—the most over two games—pounding the Toledo Blades 15-1 on New Year's Eve 1967 at Hara Arena, then following it on New Year's Day 1968 at home, demolishing Port Huron 16-3. Barry Merrell (top) led the scoring onslaught by netting seven goals over the two nights—four against the Blades and three versus the Flags. (Courtesy of Wright State Special Collections.)

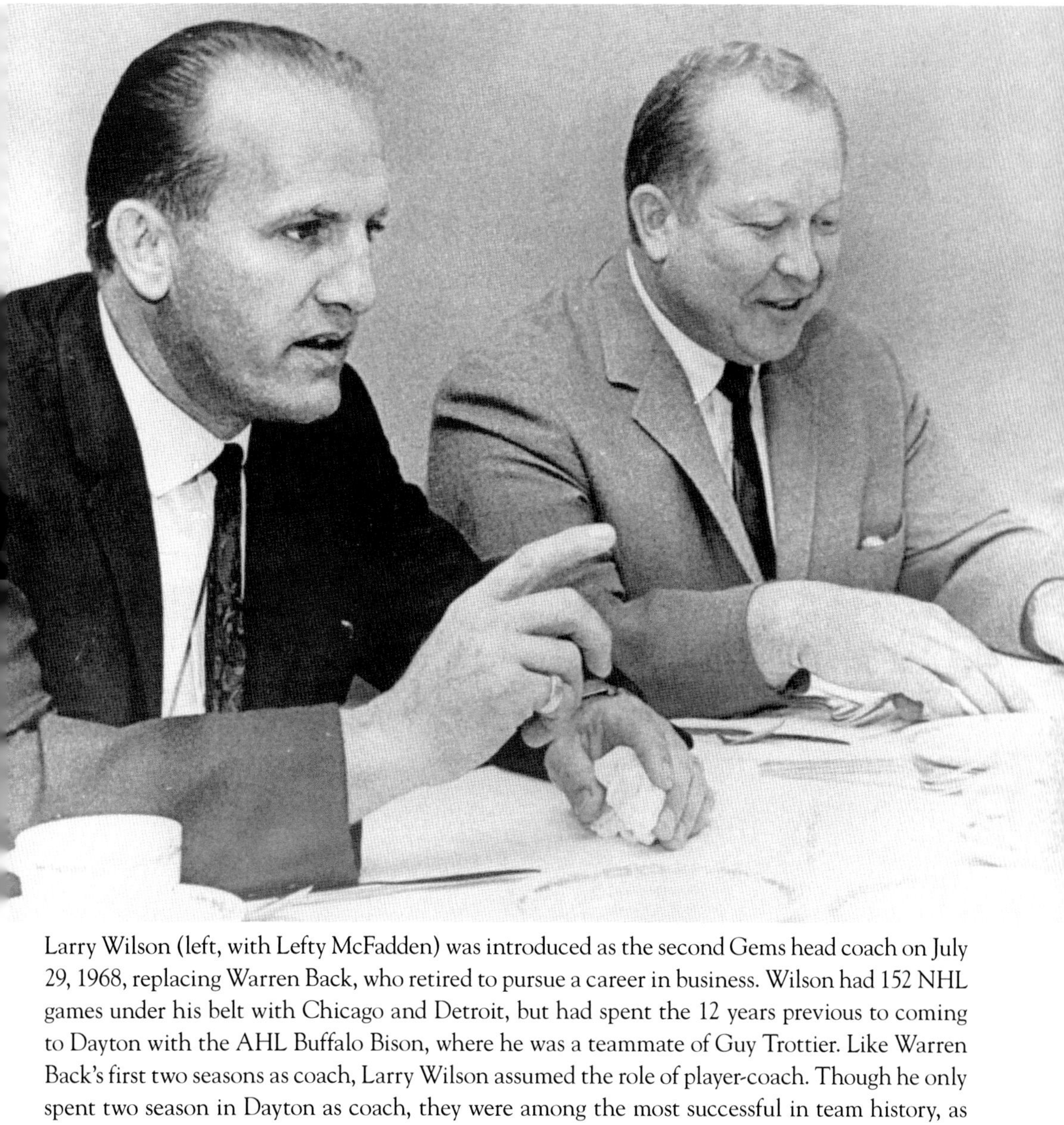

Larry Wilson (left, with Lefty McFadden) was introduced as the second Gems head coach on July 29, 1968, replacing Warren Back, who retired to pursue a career in business. Wilson had 152 NHL games under his belt with Chicago and Detroit, but had spent the 12 years previous to coming to Dayton with the AHL Buffalo Bison, where he was a teammate of Guy Trottier. Like Warren Back's first two seasons as coach, Larry Wilson assumed the role of player-coach. Though he only spent two season in Dayton as coach, they were among the most successful in team history, as he led the Gems to an IHL regular-season championship (1968–1969) and back-to-back Turner Cup championships (1968–1969 and 1969–1970). (Author's collection.)

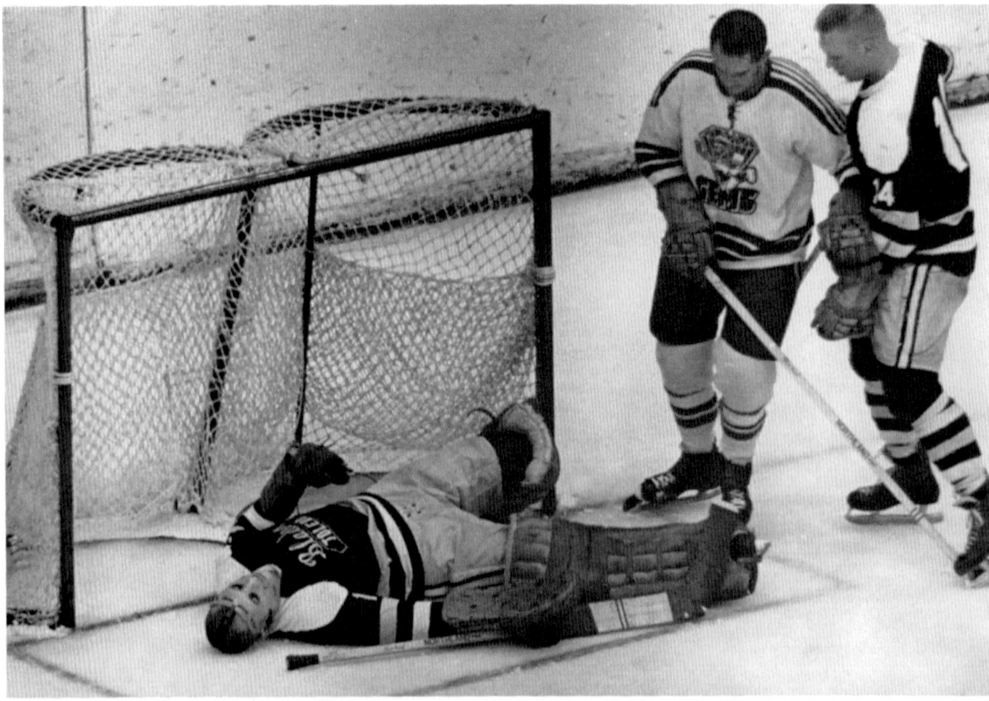

Following the Mercurys, the Blades were Toledo's second IHL team and the Gems' first real rival. Among the most recognizable Blades was goalie Glenn Ramsey (pictured). Ramsey was a talented netminder who, like many players of the 1950s and 1960s, had the misfortune of playing when the NHL only had six teams. Guy Trottier, who played in the National Hockey League, believed Ramsey would have easily played in an expanded NHL. (Courtesy of Wright State Special Collections.)

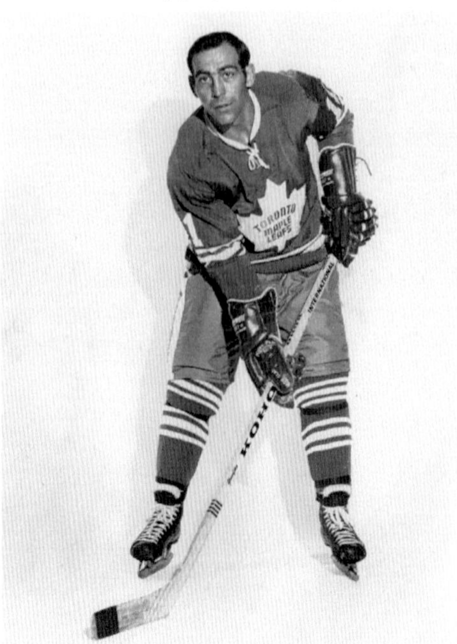

Guy Trottier became the first Gem to rise to the National Hockey League when he suited up for the New York Rangers on January 5, 1969. Beginning in 1970, he spent two years with the Toronto Maple Leafs, where he scored 28 goals in 113 games, including a game-winner at the Olympia versus Detroit on November 12, 1970. In all, he played in 126 NHL games, including nine playoff contests with Toronto. (Courtesy of Barb Brigner.)

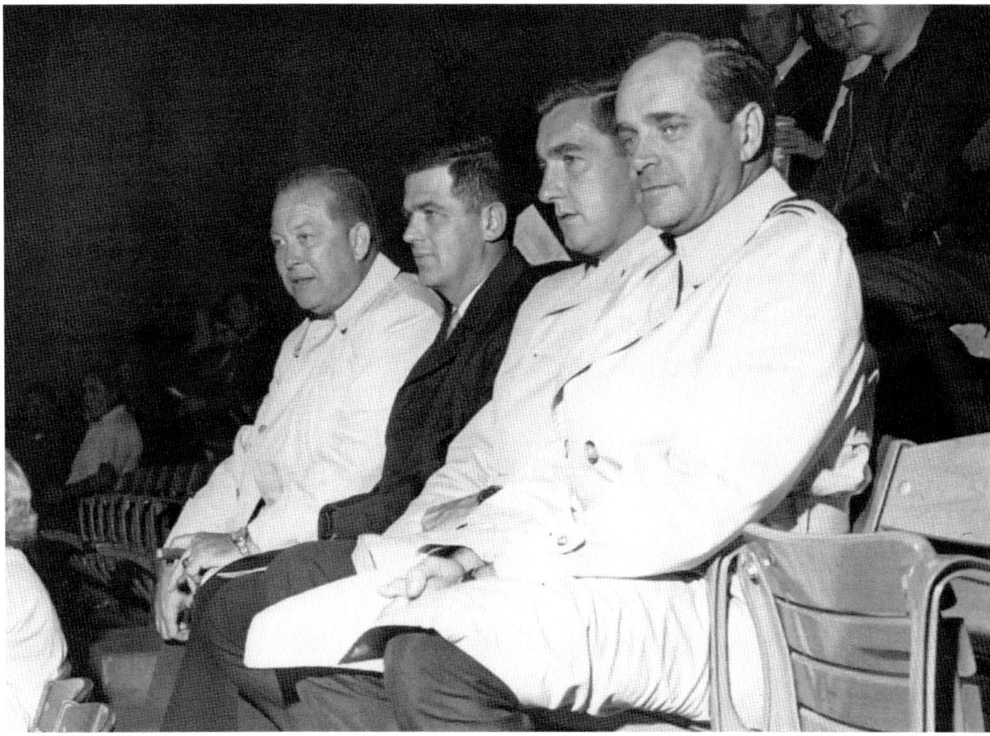

During the late 1960s and early 1970s, the Boston Bruins farm system included the Dayton Gems of the IHL and the Oklahoma City Blazers of the Central Hockey League, which was a step higher than Dayton. In this undated photograph, officials from the three teams watch a training-camp session. Pictured are, from left to right, Lefty McFadden, Boston Bruins coach Harry Sinden, Oklahoma City coach Murray Davidson, and Oklahoma City general manager Bill Levins. (Courtesy of the McFadden family.)

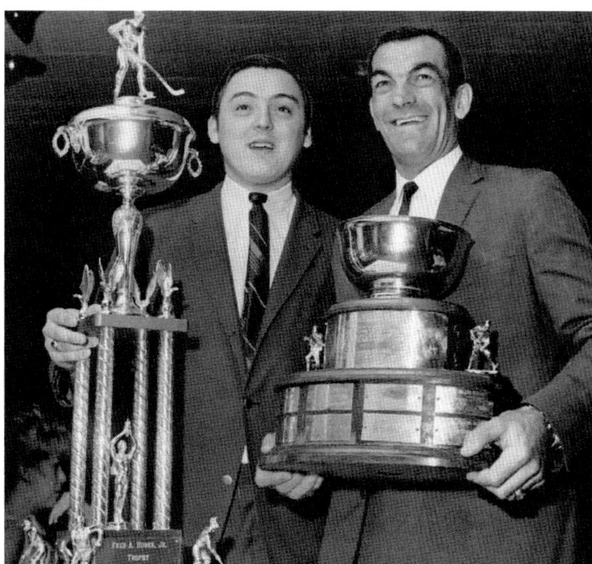

Moe Benoit (right) and goalie John Adams pose with the Turner Cup and Huber Trophy following the 1968–1969 playoffs. Joseph Turner was a Canadian goaltender who served in the US Army during World War II. He was killed in action in 1944. In 1945, the IHL named the league playoff championship trophy after Turner. The Cincinnati Mohawks won the most Turner Cups (five). The Gems were one of five teams to win the cup three times. (Courtesy of Wright State Special Collections.)

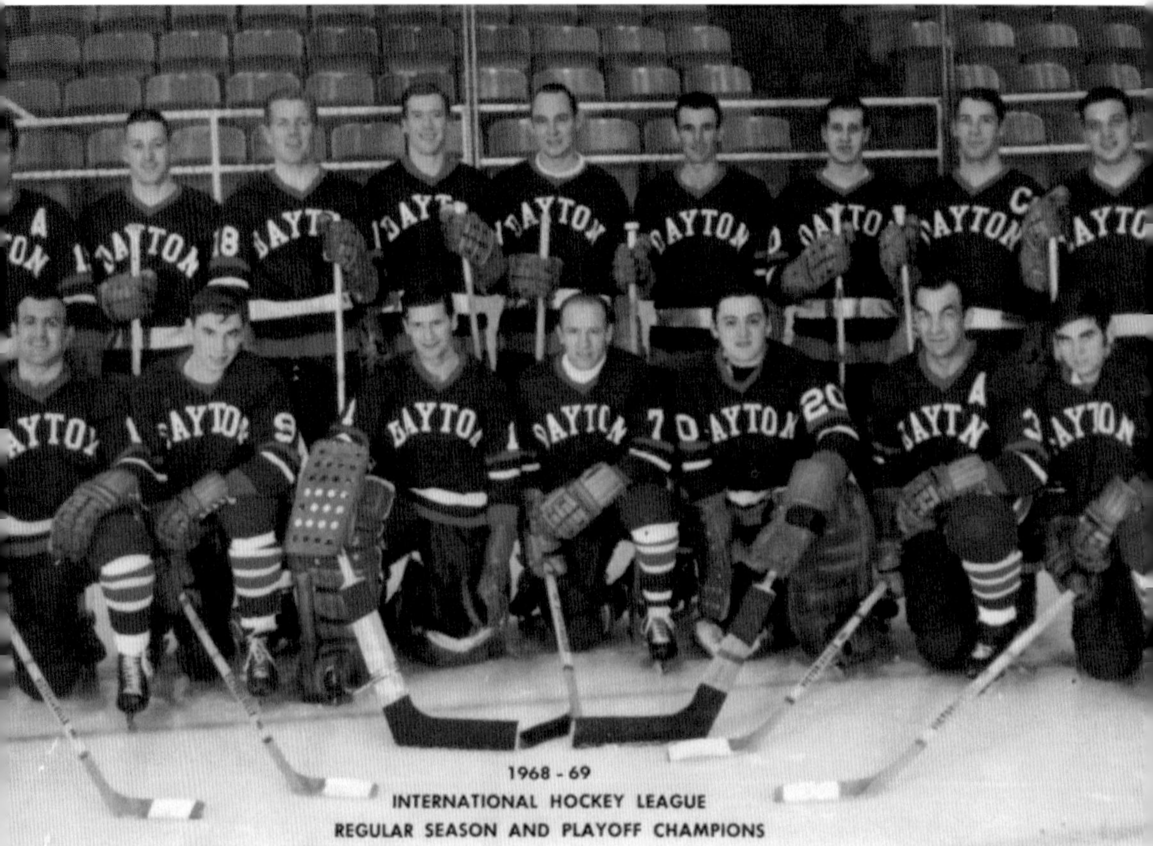

If there was a perfect Gems season, the 1968–1969 campaign was it. Under first-year coach Larry Wilson, the team won its second Huber Trophy as IHL regular-season champions. Pat Rupp and John Adams shared the Norris Trophy as the league's top goaltenders. Moe Benoit and Al Beaule won the best defenseman award, and Don Westbrooke was the league scoring champ and MVP. Attendance was at an all-time high. In the playoffs, the Gems compiled a 9-0 record, sweeping the Muskegon Mohawks in the finals to win their first Turner Cup. The Gems became the only IHL team to go unbeaten in the playoffs. (Author's collection.)

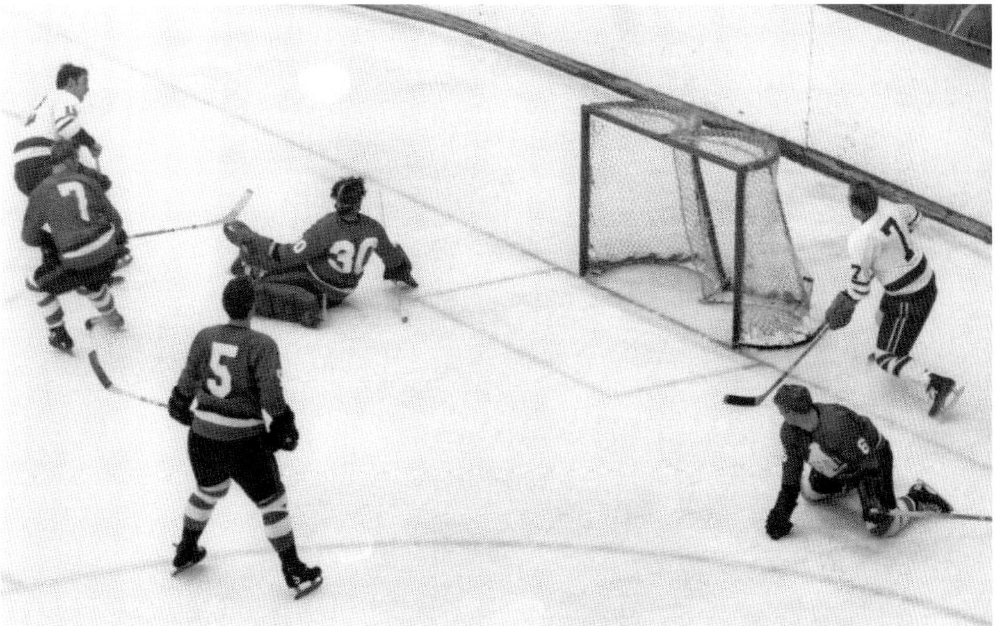

Duncan Rousseau (12) fires home a goal against Fort Wayne as Larry Wilson (7) looks on. As the Gems marched toward their first Turner Cup championship in 1969, crowds swelled at Hara Arena. Over the last two months of the season, the Gems averaged 5,211 fans a game and drew 11 crowds over 5,000 the last half of the season, including three sellouts. For the season, the team averaged 4,530 fans a game—the best in the team's history. (Courtesy of Kathy Rupp.)

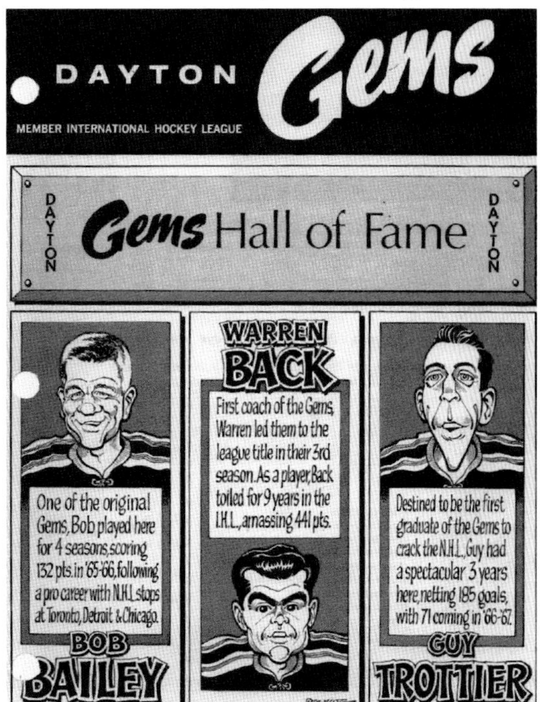

The Gems established the Dayton Hockey Hall of Fame to honor those who made significant contributions to Dayton hockey. On March 17, 1970, a Hara Arena crowd of 4,615 watched as Warren Back, Guy Trottier, Bob Bailey, and Hara Arena owners Harold and Ralph Wampler became the first members inducted, during the first intermission of that evening's game between the Gems and the Fort Wayne Komets. (Courtesy of Jerry Dowling.)

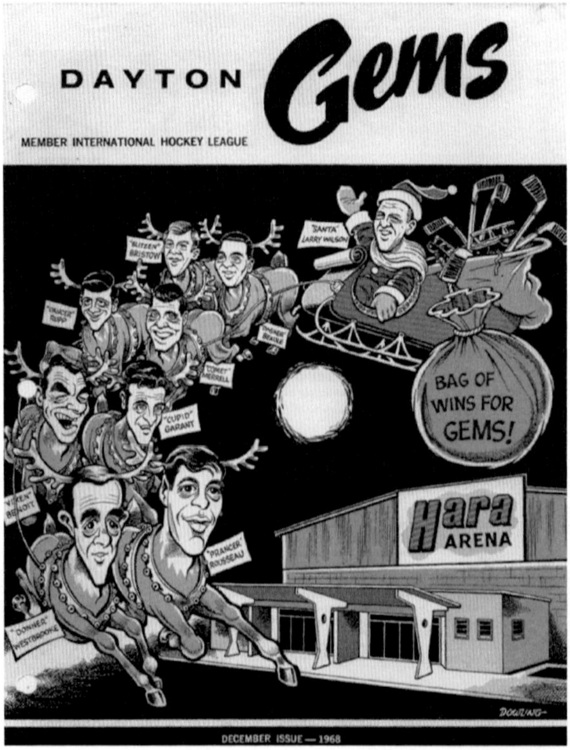

Cartoonist Jerry Dowling provided some of the most interesting program covers in all of sports when he drew covers for the Gems in the late 1960s. His work often depicted caricatures of Gems players in amazing detail. Dowling later became an award-winning cartoonist for the *Cincinnati Enquirer*. (Courtesy of Jerry Dowling.)

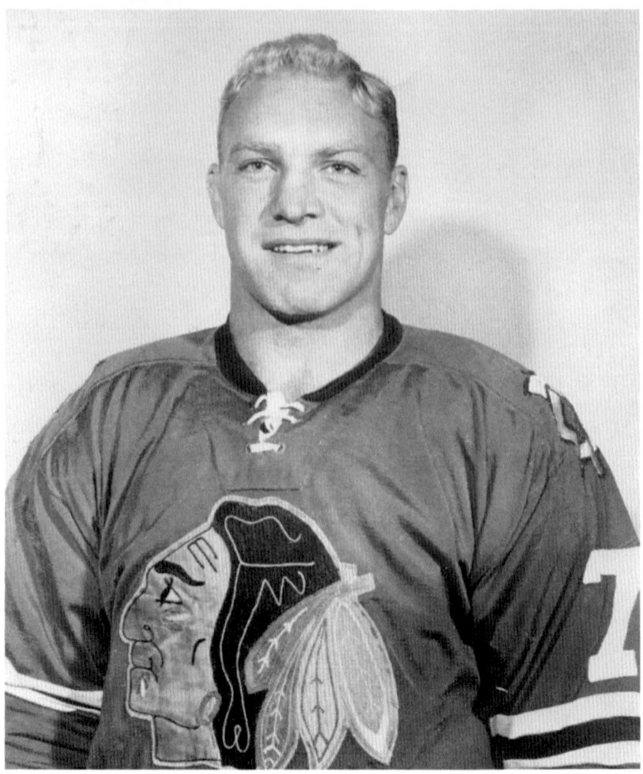

Bobby Hull sat out the beginning of the 1969–1970 NHL season, seeking a new contract from the Chicago Blackhawks. Being a public-relations genius, Lefty McFadden offered Hull the opportunity to come to Dayton and play with the Gems during his holdout. Hull never came to Dayton, but McFadden's scheme gave Dayton and the Gems some nationwide attention. (Courtesy of Bill Murphy.)

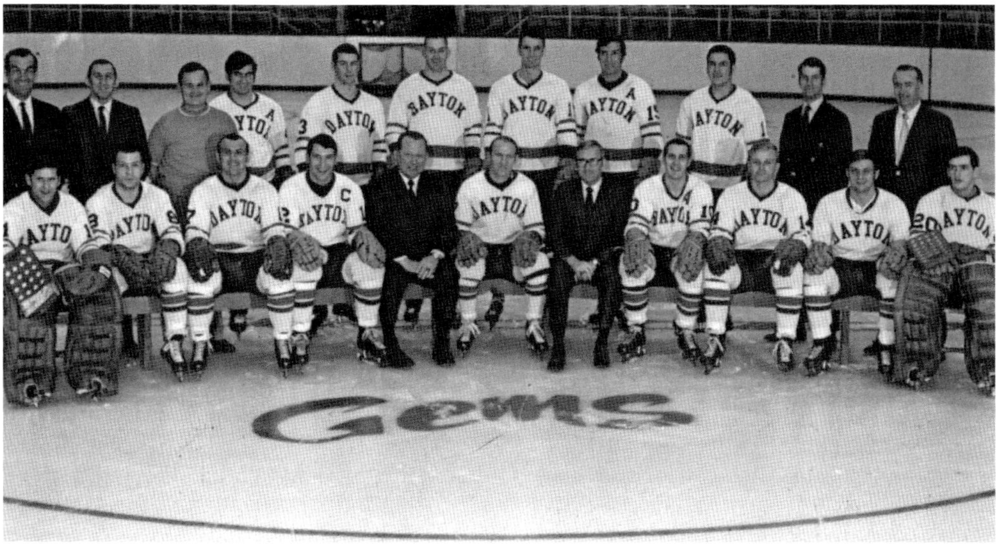

The 1969–1970 Dayton Gems beat the Port Huron Flags in seven games to win the Turner Cup for the second year in a row, becoming one of just six teams in the 56-year history of the IHL to win back-to-back Turner Cups. Larry Wilson left after the season and eventually coached the Detroit Red Wings during the 1976–1977 season. He passed away unexpectedly in 1979 at the age of 48. (Author's collection.)

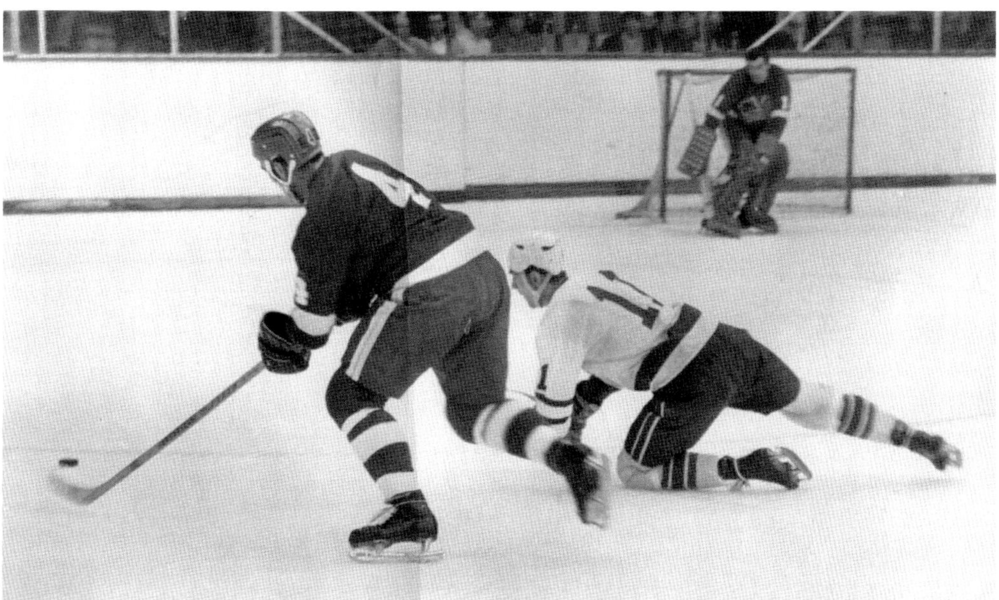

Game seven of the 1970 Turner Cup finals was played at Hara Arena in front of 4,519 fans. Don Westbrooke (11) injured his shoulder in the first period and left the game, not to return. Duncan Rousseau scored two goals, and the Gems defeated the Flags 5-2 to win their only Turner Cup on home ice. (Courtesy of Kathy Rupp.)

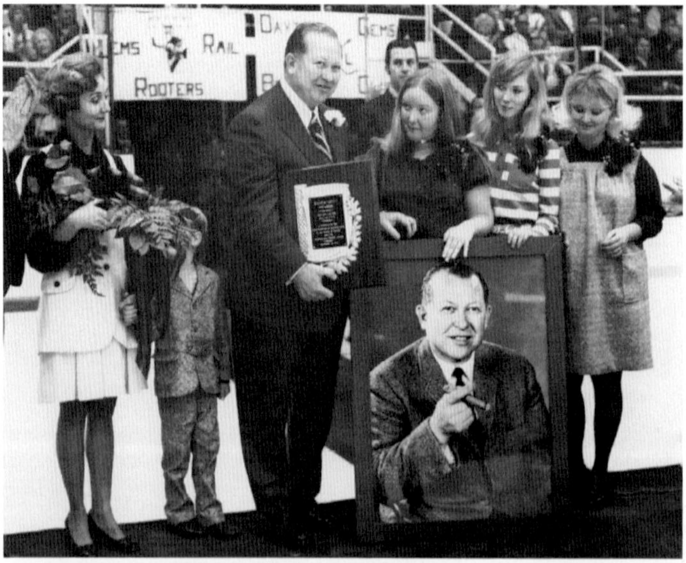

In 1970, the *Hockey News* named Lefty McFadden Minor League Hockey Executive of the Year. In five seasons, McFadden led the Gems from a startup hockey franchise in a brand-new market to one of the most successful and admired franchises in the IHL and in all of minor-league hockey. (Courtesy of the McFadden family.)

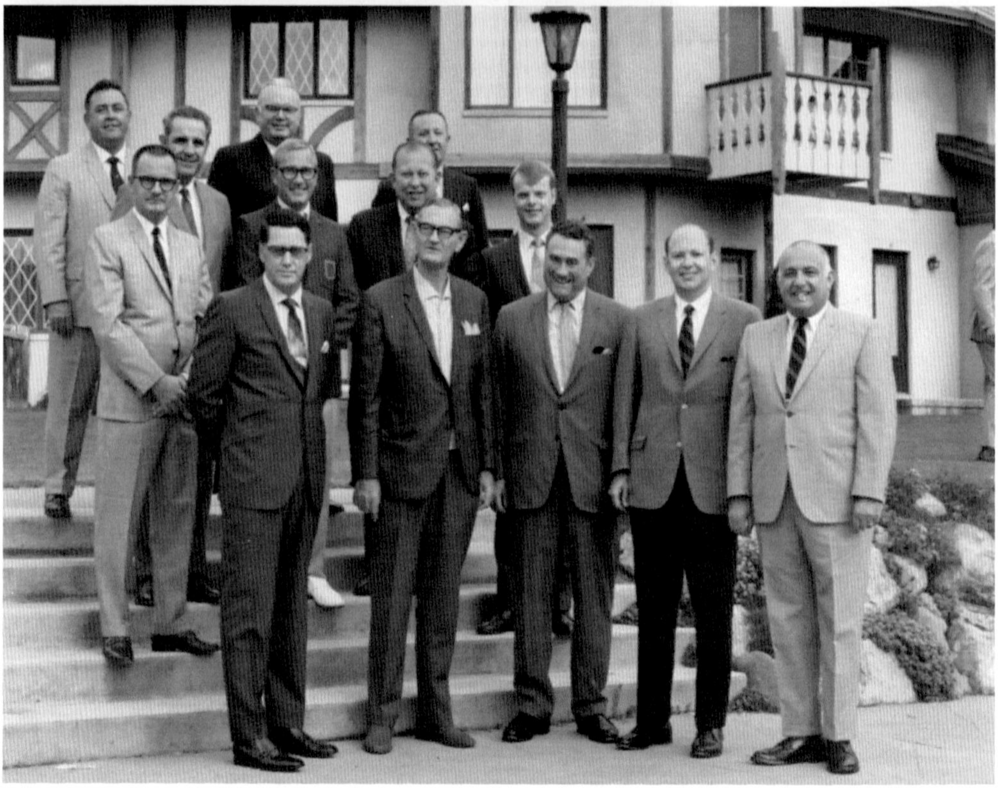

In this photograph from the late 1960s, IHL owners and executives pose at a league meeting in Harbor Springs, Michigan. While relationships could get tense when their teams competed on the ice, most of the IHL governors enjoyed friendly relationships off the ice. Lefty McFadden had a very good relationship with Ken Ullyot (first row, far left), the longtime owner and general manager of the Fort Wayne Komets. (Courtesy of the McFadden family.)

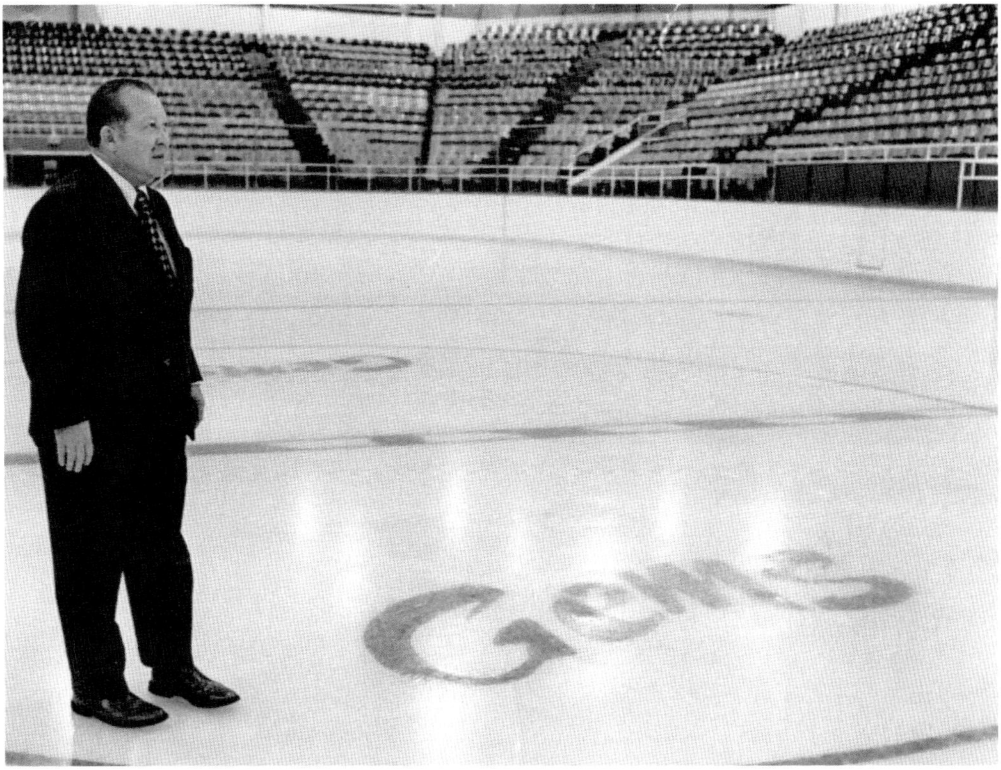

In the 1960s, Coca-Cola was a major sponsor of the Gems. Lefty McFadden had the idea to paint the Coke logo onto the Hara Arena ice. The IHL owners did not agree with his plan, turning it down as being too showy. Many years later, it became commonplace for teams to paint the logos of major advertisers on the ice, demonstrating how forward-thinking Lefty was. (Courtesy of Wright State Special Collections.)

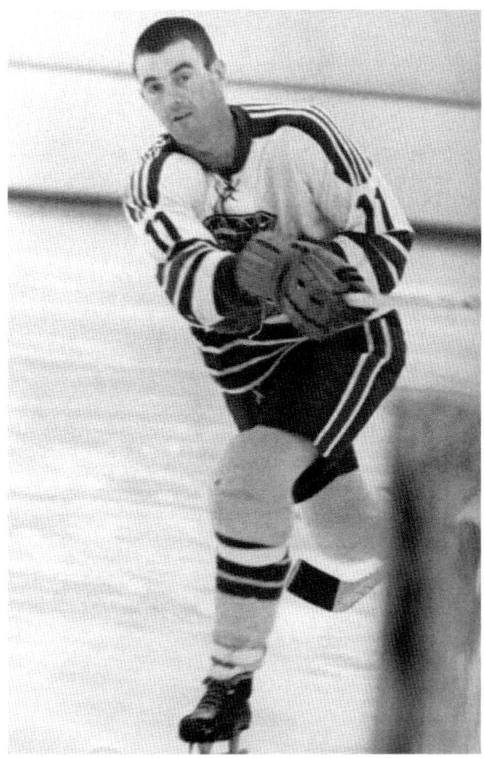

Don Westbrooke left Dayton after the 1969–1970 season. While he was with the Gems, the team went to the Turner Cup finals three times, winning twice and winning one regular-season league championship. He returned to the Gems briefly during the 1974–1975 season. In all, Westbrooke scored 368 points with the Gems, second all-time behind Sid Garant. He later said that his time in Dayton was the happiest time of his life. (Courtesy of Kathy Rupp.)

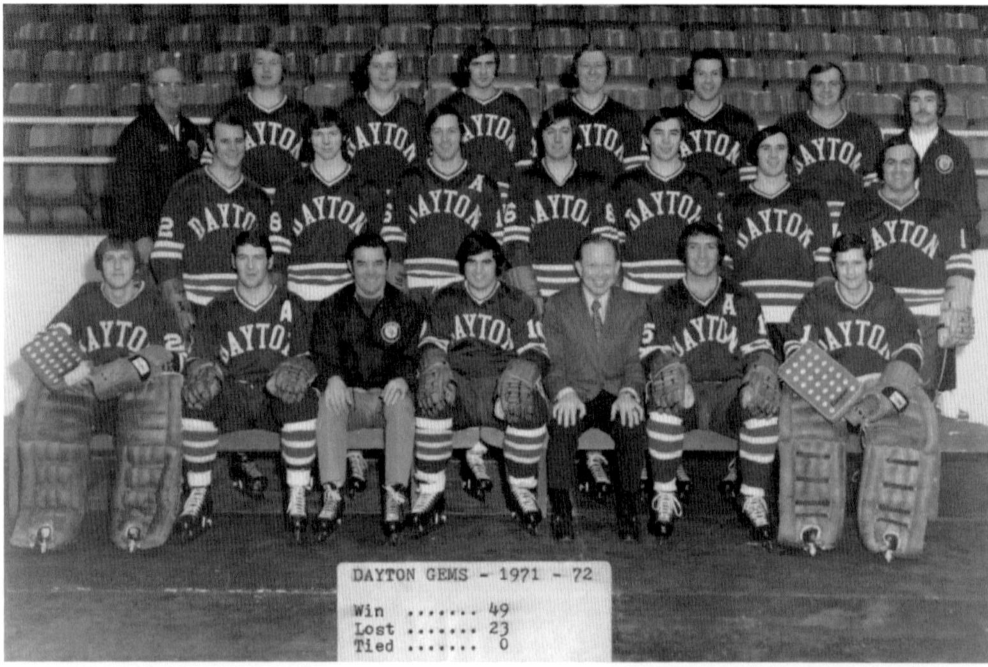

Under coach Gerry Moore, the 1971–1972 Dayton Gems won 49 regular-season games—more than any other Gems team and the most in Dayton hockey history. The squad fell one victory short of tying the IHL record of 50 wins. The team compiled an amazing 33-3 home record and won the IHL Southern Division by 22 points. Unfortunately, after a first-round bye, the Gems were eliminated by Muskegon in the playoffs, and Moore was let go as coach. (Author's collection.)

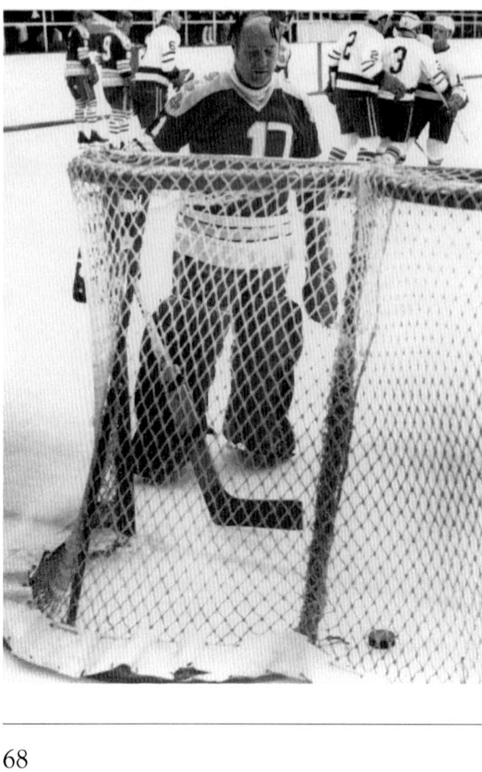

Des Moines Oak Leafs goalie Bob Perreault clears the puck from the net after a Gems goal. Perreault was an old-school goaltender who never put on a facemask, even as masks became standard goalie equipment. More amazing, until late in his career, Perreault never wore a chest protector. (Courtesy of Kathy Rupp.)

Pat Rupp makes a save in a game against Toledo on January 9, 1972. The 1971–1972 season was Rupp's best, as he registered a 3.38 goals-against average. He retired after the season—though he played in one game in 1980—and remained in Dayton, managing a successful financial planning business he started during his playing career. (Courtesy of Wright State Special Collections.)

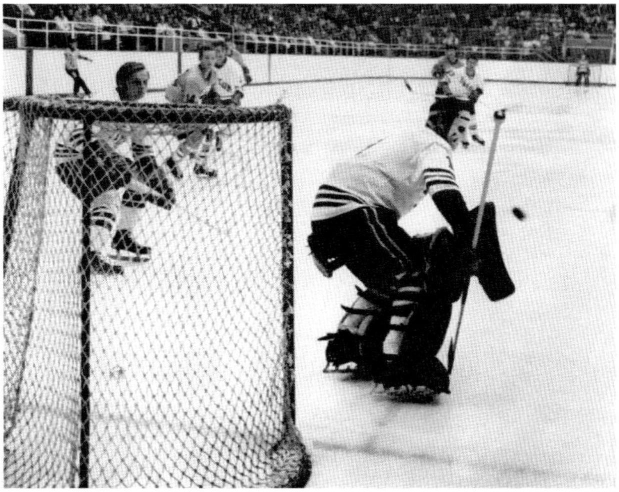

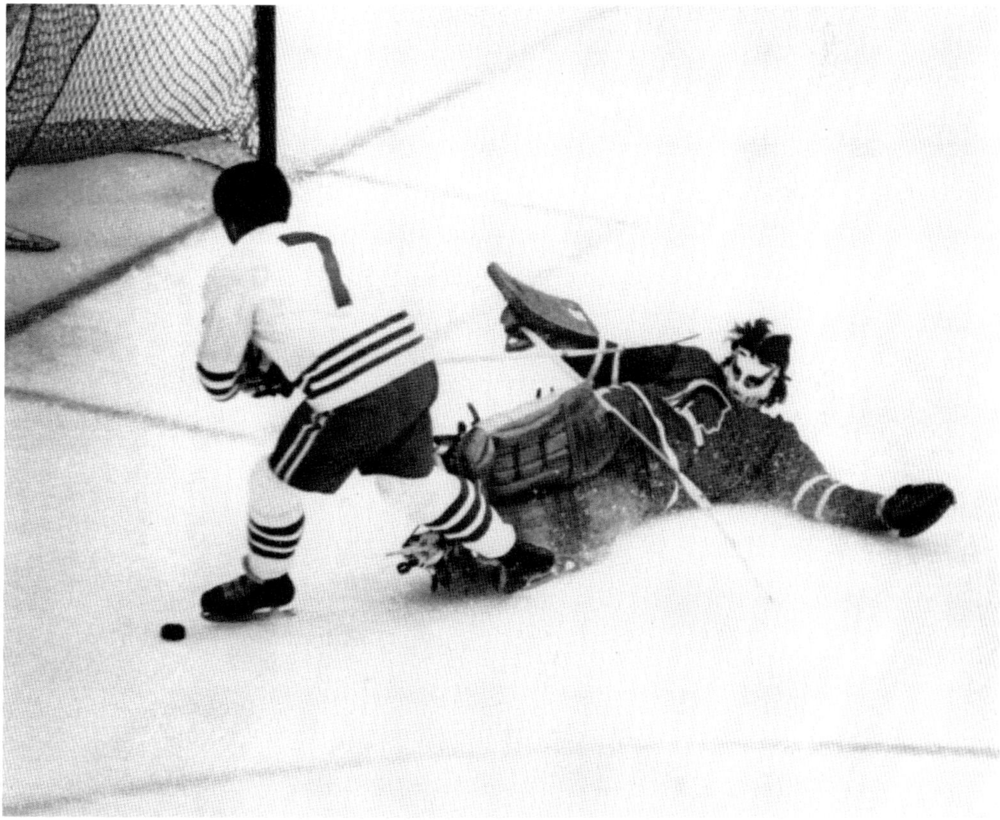

Muskegon put two teams on the ice during the Gems years: the Zephyrs and the Mohawks (dark uniform shown here). Quite possibly the most disliked of Gems foes, the Mohawks were always a big draw when visiting Hara Arena. The Mohawks were high-scoring teams that featured some of the IHL's all-time leading scorers, including Bryan McLay and Gary Ford. The Gems and Mohawks met twice for the Turner Cup, with each team winning once. (Courtesy of Wright State Special Collections.)

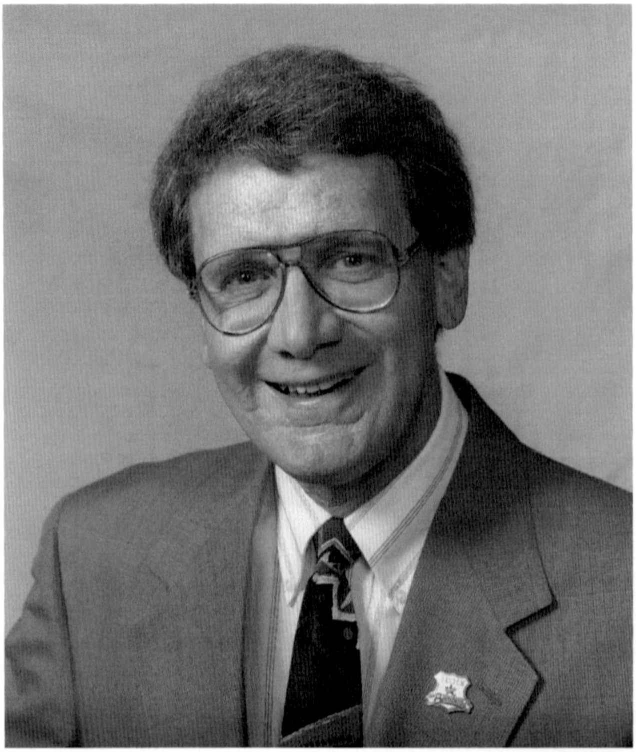

Lyle Stieg was the Gems play-by-play man on WHIO-AM from 1967 to 1977. He occasionally called games on television as well. Stieg opened his broadcasts with "From high above the ice at Hara Arena, home of the Dayton Gems." After the Gems, Stieg went on to call games for the NHL's Washington Capitals. He later called Dayton Bombers games. (Courtesy of Gregg Wurtzler.)

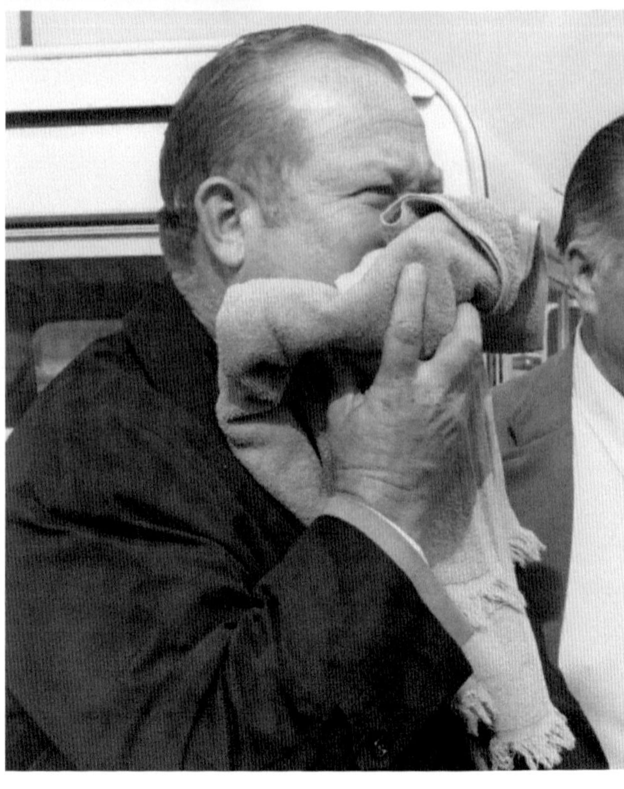

Players are not the only ones in danger of being injured by a flying puck. During the 1972–1973 season, Lefty McFadden was struck in the face during a team practice by a puck off the stick of Billy Staub. (Courtesy of the McFadden family.)

No Gem had scored five goals in a game—not even Guy Trottier or Don Westbrooke. That is, until "Cowboy" Jim Benzalock did it on February 6, 1972, in a 8-3 victory over Des Moines. Benzalock said he was still in disbelief when he did it again one week later, scoring five goals—the first three in a 45-second span of the first period—on February 13 in a 7-4 victory over Toledo. (Courtesy of Wright State Special Collections.)

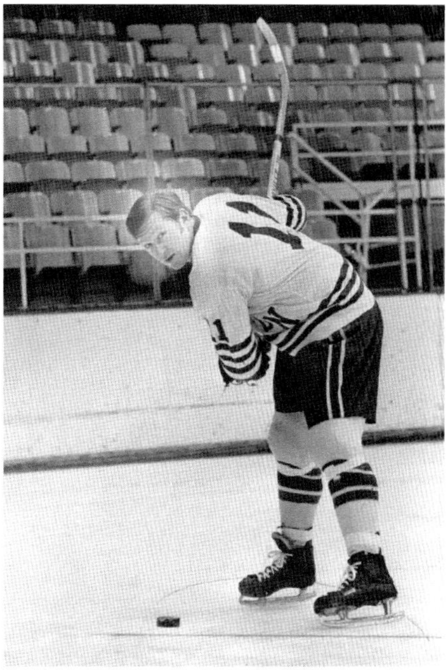

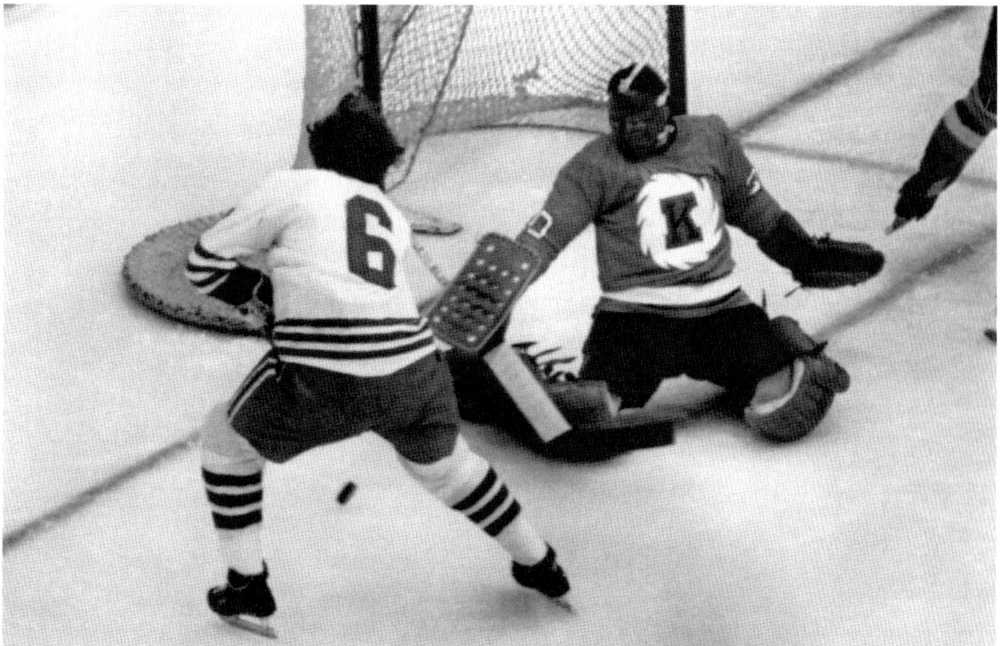

By the time the Gems entered the IHL in 1964, the Fort Wayne Komets had already been in the league for 12 years. From their beginning in 1952, the "K's" were immensely popular in Fort Wayne, often filling the giant (by the era's standards), 8,035-seat Allan County Memorial Coliseum. The Komets played in the IHL until 1999. When Gems games were not on the radio in Dayton, fans could listen to games on Fort Wayne's 50,000-watt WOWO radio station. (Courtesy of Wright State Special Collections.)

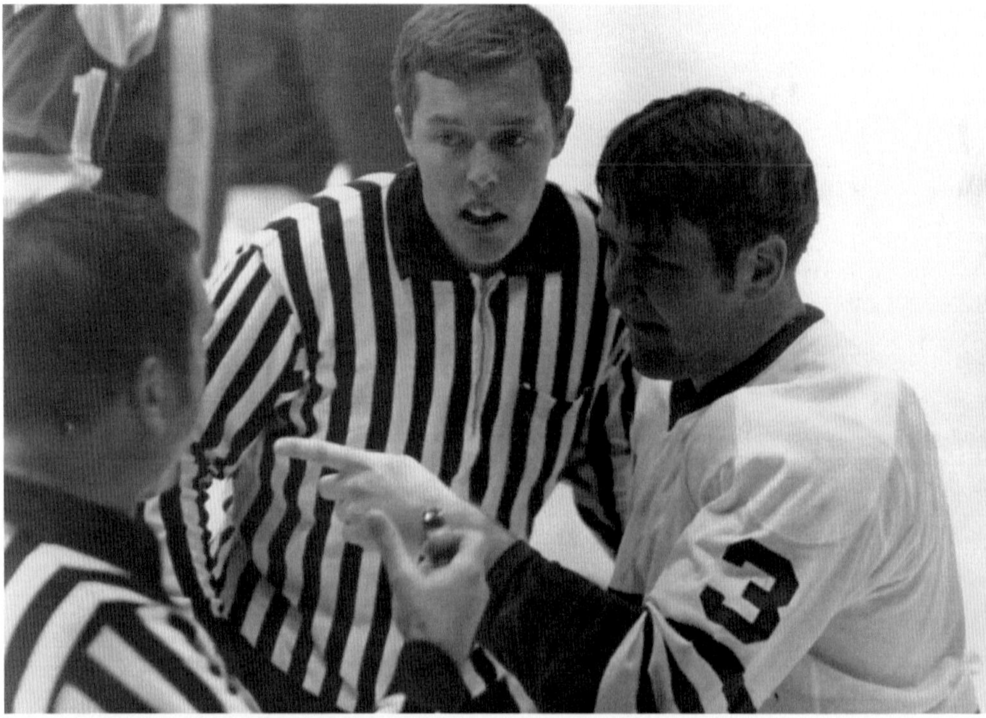

One of the toughest Gems in team history was Mike Sauter (pictured). Sauter was a part of the "Bulldog Line" with Gerry MacMillan and Dave Simpson that menaced the opposition in the early 1970s with tough defense and hard hits. While he could handle himself in a scrap, Sauter could also provide offense. During the 1971–1972 season, he scored 24 goals and added 50 assists. He also led the team in penalty minutes (242). (Courtesy of Kathy Rupp.)

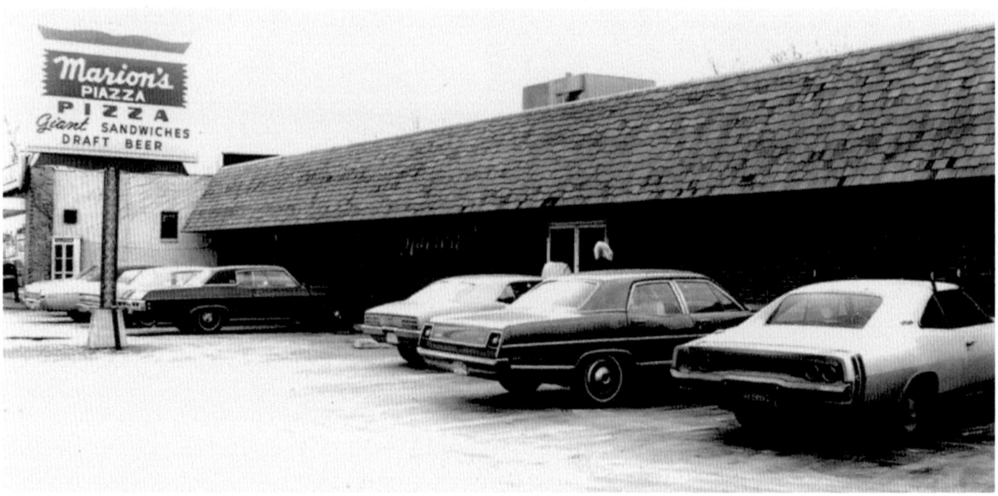

Lefty McFadden and Marion's Piazza founder Marion Glass were friends. For many years, after Sunday-afternoon games (and, later, Saturday-night games), fans had the opportunity to meet Gems players at the Marion's location on North Dixie Drive near the Traffic Circle. Marion's would often be packed after games with fans and players meeting and eating pizza. (Courtesy of Marion's Piazza.)

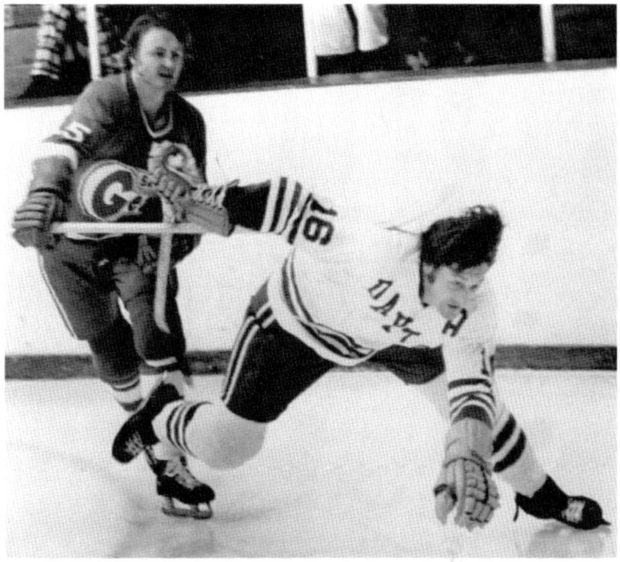

During a game in Flint on January 11, 1973, Dayton's Lorne Weighill (right) was checked from behind into the boards by the Generals' Doug Kerslake, sparking one of the worst brawls in Dayton hockey history. On January 27, Flint came to Hara Arena for the highly anticipated grudge match. In a relatively tame game that featured just one fight, a Gems Hara Arena record crowd of 5,665 watched the home team thump the Kerslake-less Generals 5-2. (Courtesy of Wright State Special Collections.)

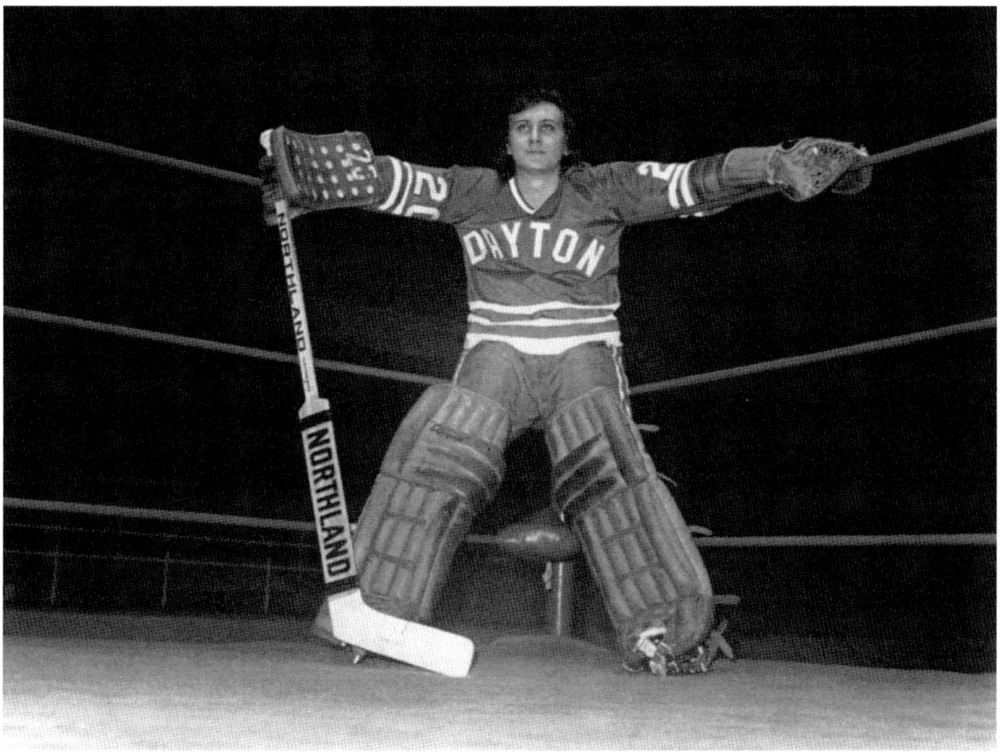

Jim "Peppermint" Pettie was probably the most colorful player to put on a Gems uniform. A goaltender, Pettie was assigned to Dayton by the Boston Bruins in 1973. Over the next three seasons, he established himself as one of the top goaltenders in the IHL. He also got a well-deserved reputation of not being afraid to engage in fisticuffs. For his career, he amassed 314 minutes in penalties—more than all other Gem goalies to that time combined. Pettie played in 21 games with the Boston Bruins. (Courtesy of Wright State Special Collections.)

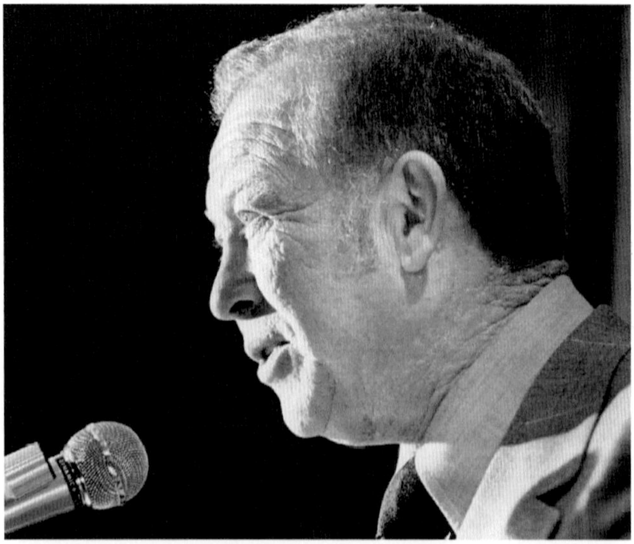

On December 9, 1973, Lefty McFadden announced that he would be leaving the Gems to become an assistant general manager with the expansion Washington Capitals. Though Lefty would be gone from the Gems, he continued to wield an influence on the team from Washington, as the Capitals assigned many of their prospects to Dayton. (Courtesy of Wright State Special Collections.)

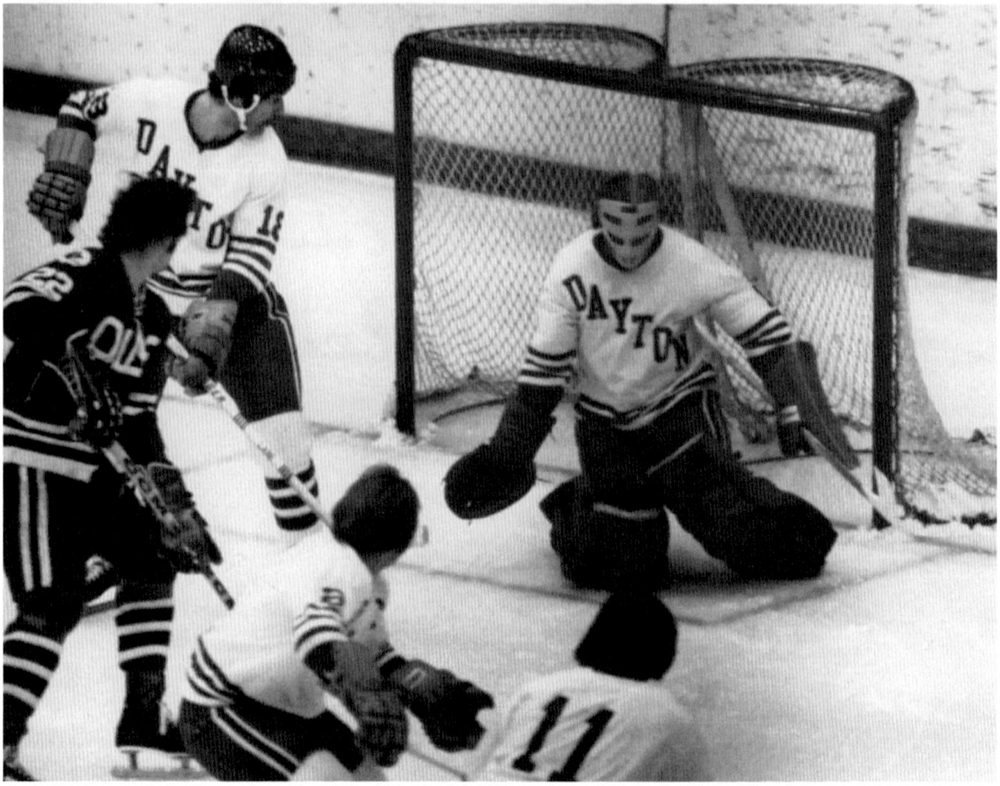

The Columbus Owls were the third IHL franchise to locate in Ohio's capital city, following the Checkers and the Golden Seals. The Owls were coached by IHL veteran Moe Bartoli, who put tough and physical teams on the ice. Along with the Toledo Goaldiggers, the Owls became the primary rivals of the Gems in the mid-1970s. (Courtesy of Wright State Special Collections.)

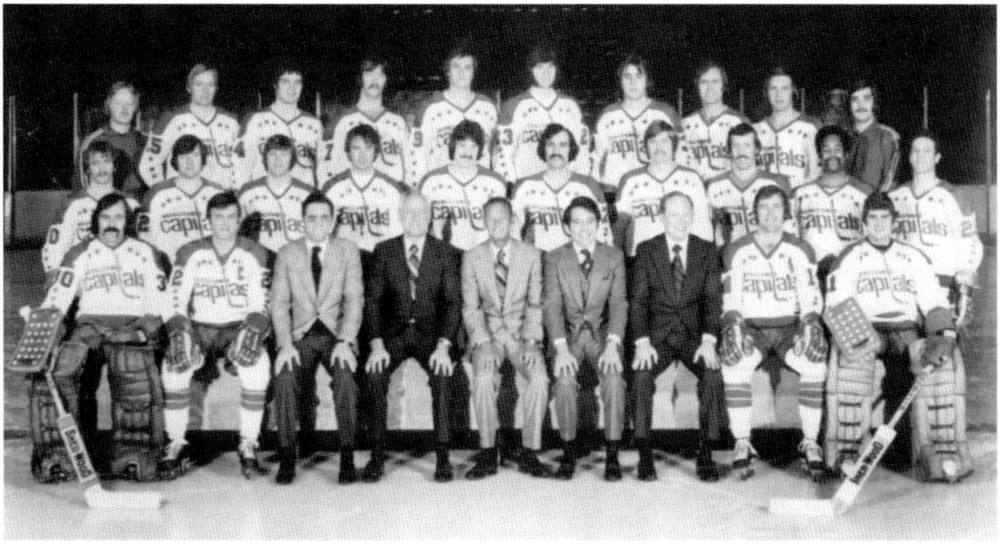

Lefty McFadden spent three seasons (1974–1977) as an assistant general manager of the Washington Capitals. During those years, many promising Capitals prospects were sent to Dayton to play with the Gems and were the core of great Gems teams—including Tony White, Brian Kinsella, and Jim Bedard. Paul Nicholson, who played with the Gems from 1975 to 1977, is pictured in the third row, third from left, in this photograph of the 1974–1975 Capitals. (Courtesy of the McFadden family.)

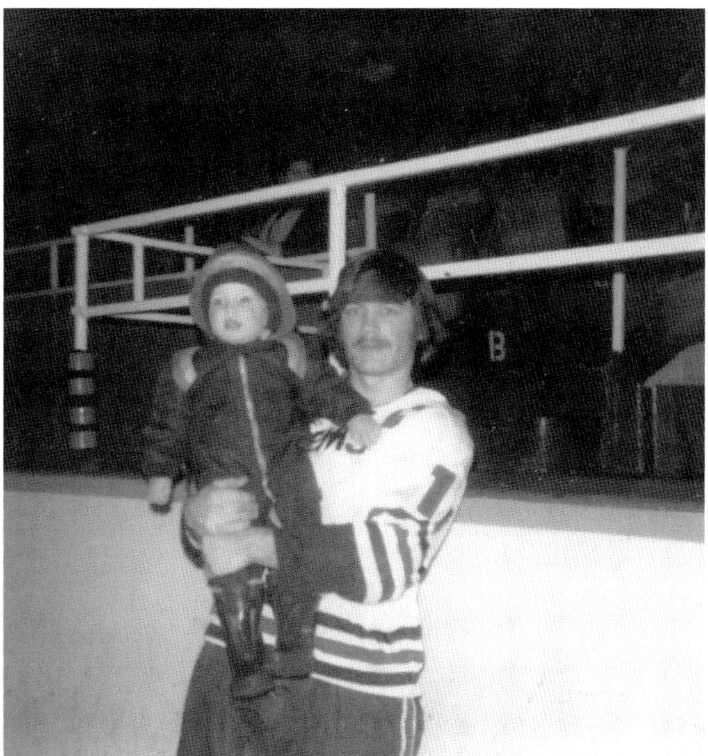

Steve Self enjoyed his time playing with the Gems so much that he named his son Dayton. The boy was born on October 4, 1975, just before Self's third year with the team. (Courtesy of Steve Self.)

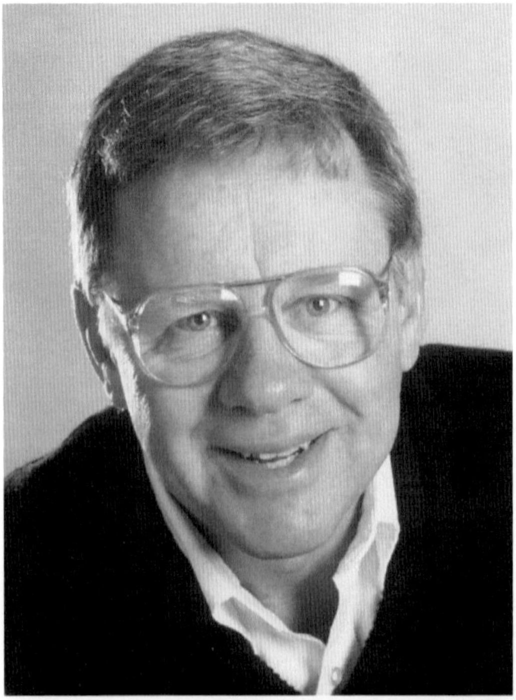

Bucky Albers grew up in Fort Loramie in Shelby County. As a boy, he traveled to Troy with his dad to watch the Bruins at Hobart Arena. He covered the Gems during their early years for the *Journal Herald*. "Everything I knew about hockey I learned from Eddie Shore's hockey talks before Bruins games." Albers served as Gems general manager for the 1974–1975 season. After the financial struggles of the year before, the team nearly broke even for the one year Albers guided the front office. (Courtesy of Bucky Albers.)

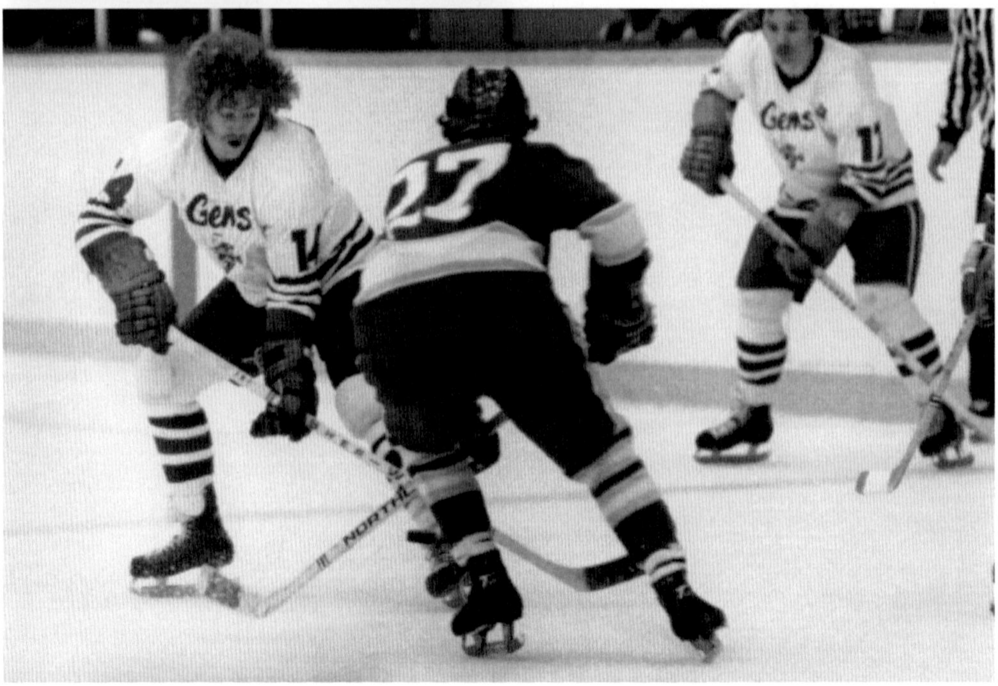

Tony White (14) was the first Dayton Gem to be promoted to the NHL's Washington Capitals. In an almost unheard-of move, White went from Dayton straight to the parent NHL team without making a stop in the American League or Central League. He played 164 NHL games and scored 37 goals. (Courtesy of Wright State Special Collections.)

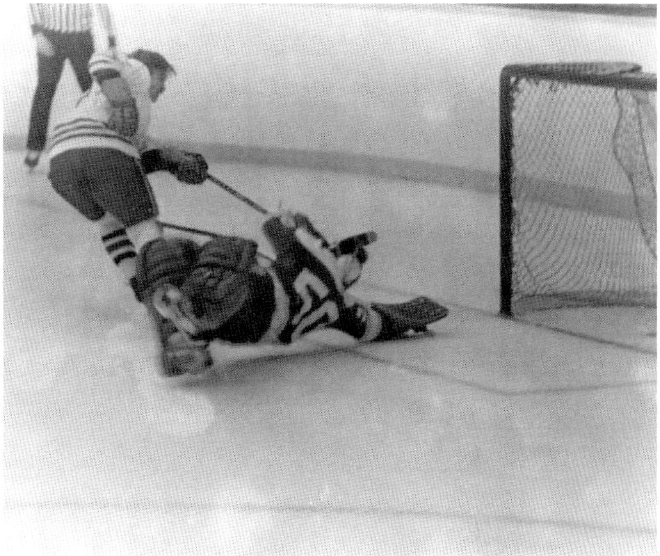

Steve Self scored 56 goals for the 1974–1975 Gems, joining Guy Trottier and Don Westbrooke as the only Gems to score 50 or more goals in a season. Self's 50th goal came on a penalty shot against Des Moines at Hara Arena on March 9, 1975. For his career, Self amassed 306 points for the Gems, fifth on the team's all-time list. (Courtesy of Steve Self.)

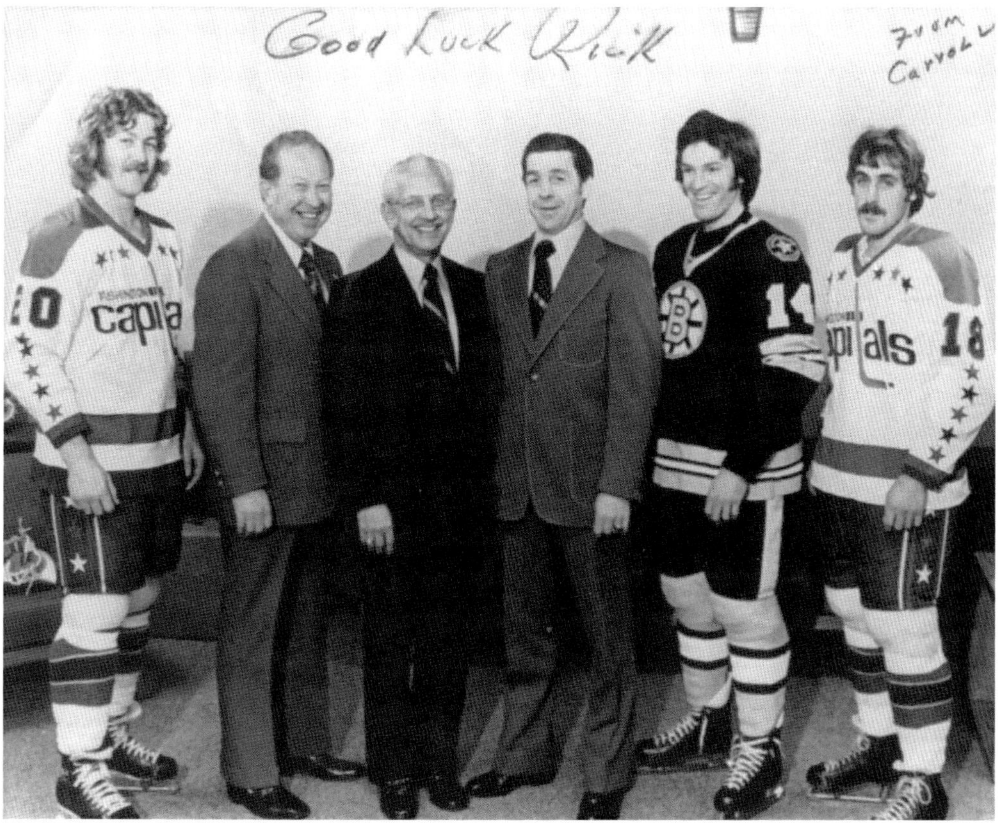

Former Dayton Gems players and officials gather before a Washington Capitals and Boston Bruins game on February 27, 1975 in Washington. From left to right are Tony White, Lefty McFadden, former Dayton Gems board member Carroll Studebaker, Tom McVie, Dave Forbes, and Rick Bragnalo. (Courtesy of Rick Bragnalo.)

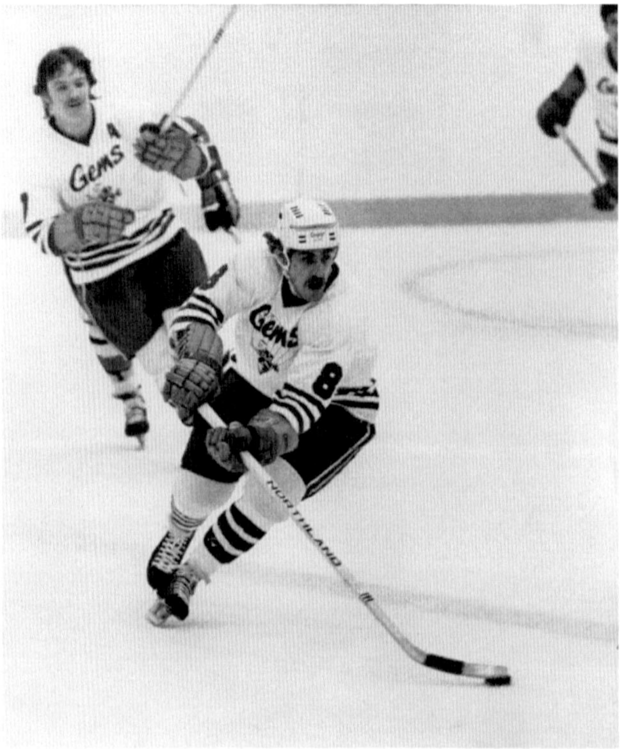

During the 1974–1975 season, Rick Bragnalo (foreground) and Steve Self (rear) became the first linemates to score 100 or more points in a season since Bob Bailey and Guy Trottier did so during the 1965–1966 season. That year, Self totaled 103 points and Bragnalo 113. (Courtesy of Wright State Special Collections.)

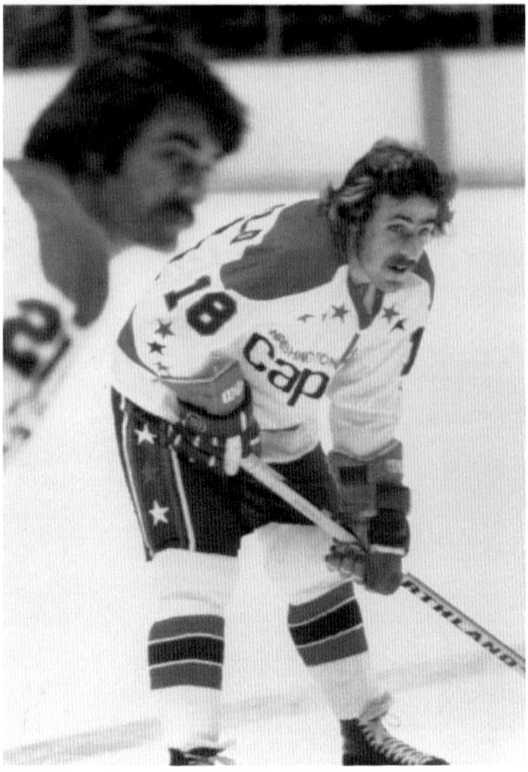

Rick Bragnalo was named the 1974–1975 IHL Rookie of the Year as he led the league in scoring with 113 points. He was the second Gem to win the award; Herb Howdle was the other. Bragnalo would play 145 games with the NHL's Washington Capitals. (Courtesy of Rick Bragnalo.)

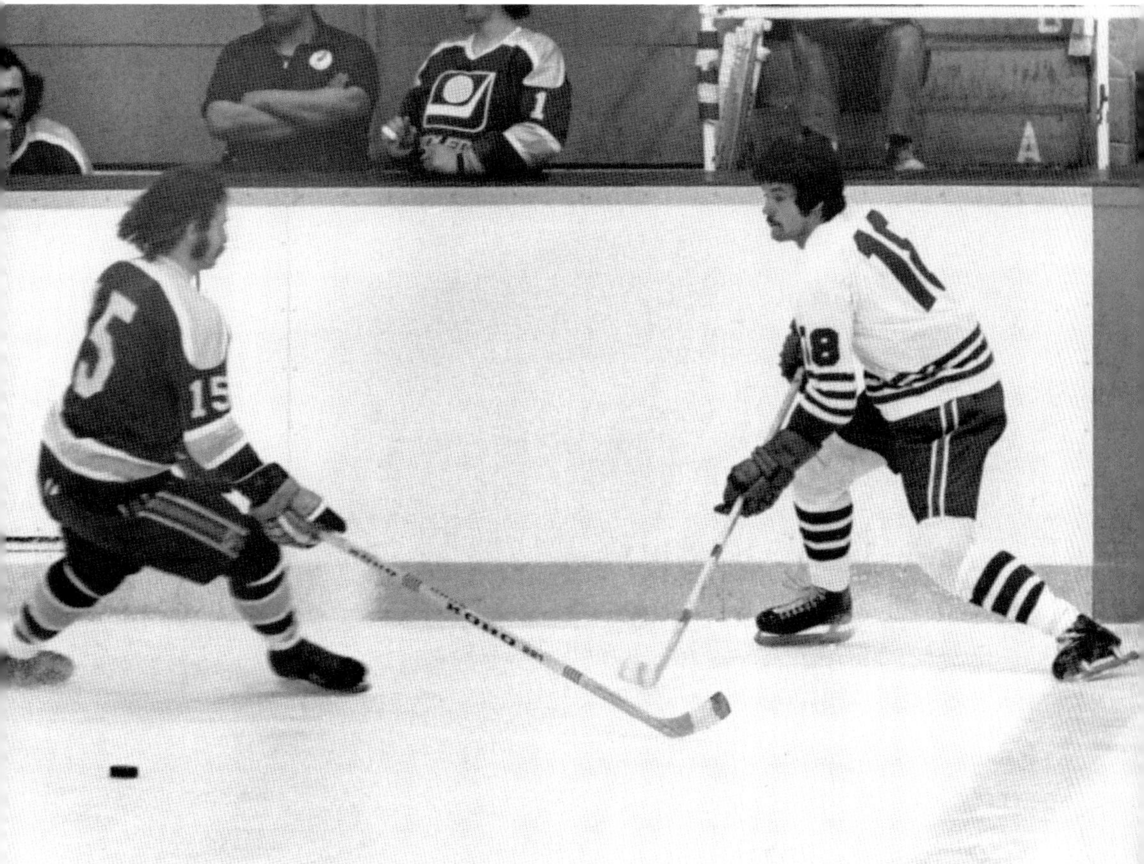

Gems defenseman Gord Lane (right) battles during the 1975 Turner Cup semifinals with the Toledo Goaldiggers. The Gems were heavily favored in the series, but the teams went to a decisive game seven, which had to be played at Hobart Arena, as Hara Arena was unavailable. Toledo fans traveled south and outnumbered Gems fans in Troy. Toledo stunned the Gems in the rubber game, 6-3, and went on to win the Turner Cup. (Courtesy of Wright State Special Collections.)

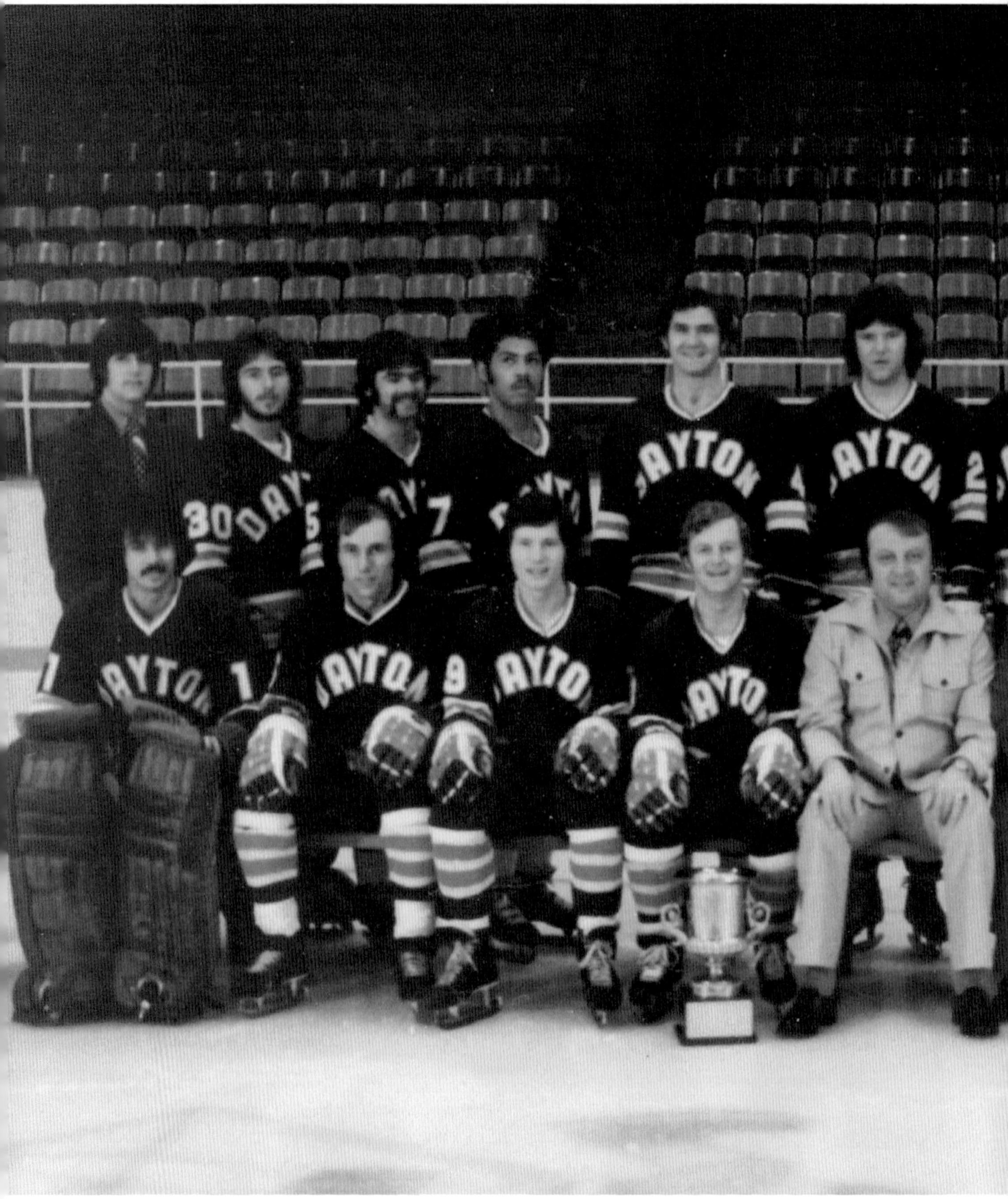

The 1975–1976 Dayton Gems set the IHL record for points in a season (104) and cruised through the playoffs to secure the team's third and final Turner Cup championship. The talent-rich team featured nine players who would see time in the NHL, including Jim Pettie, Stan Jonathan, and Gord Lane, who all enjoyed lengthy careers in the NHL. Lane had the most success of any Gem in the NHL, winning four Stanley Cups with the New York Islanders. The Gems won their last 14

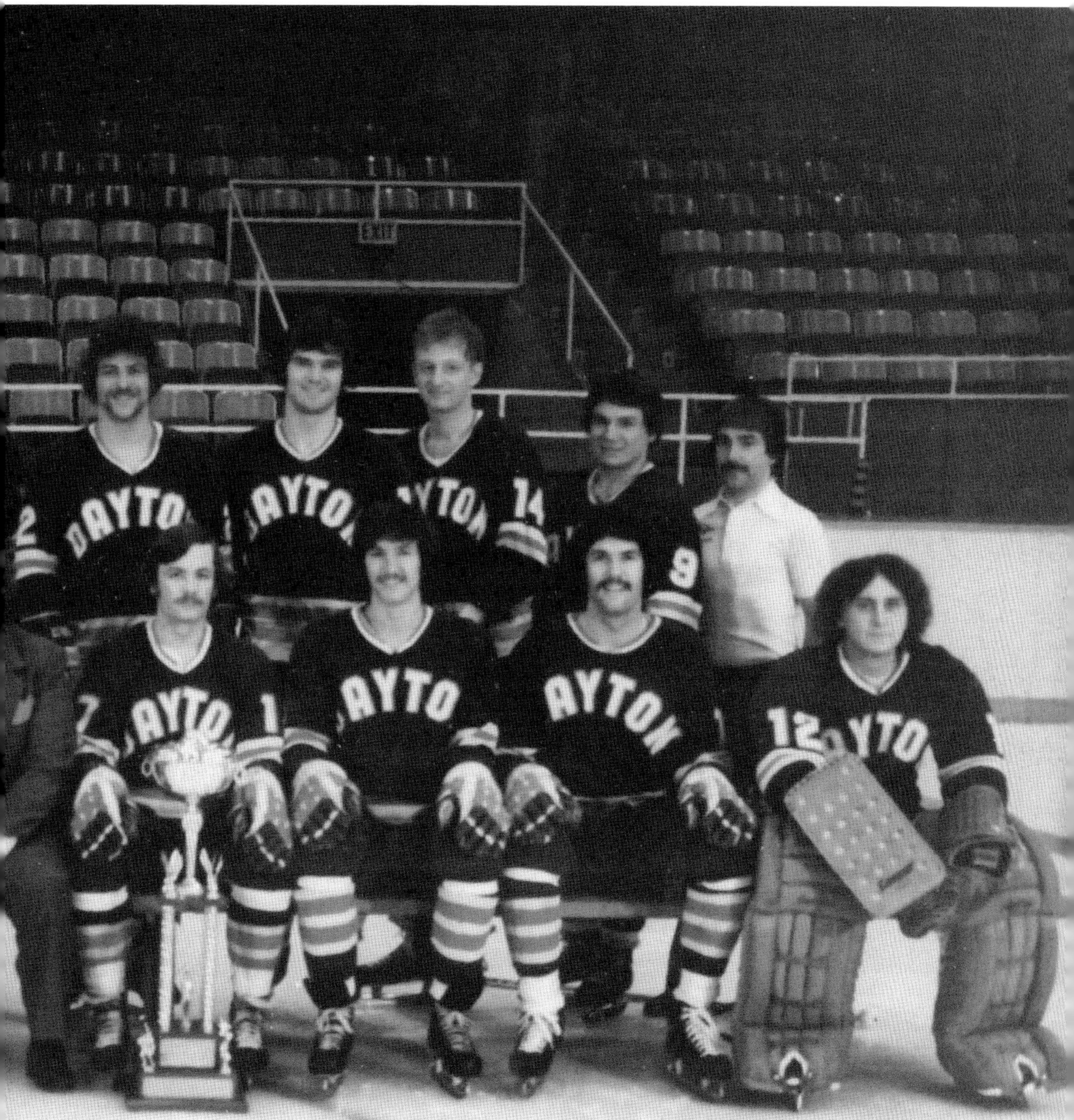

games to capture the IHL regular-season championship. In the playoffs, the Gems beat Kalamazoo and Fort Wayne, then swept the Port Huron Flags to win the Turner Cup. Amazingly, the team lost nearly $100,000 due to lackluster attendance and needed additional financial backing to operate the next season. (Author's collection.)

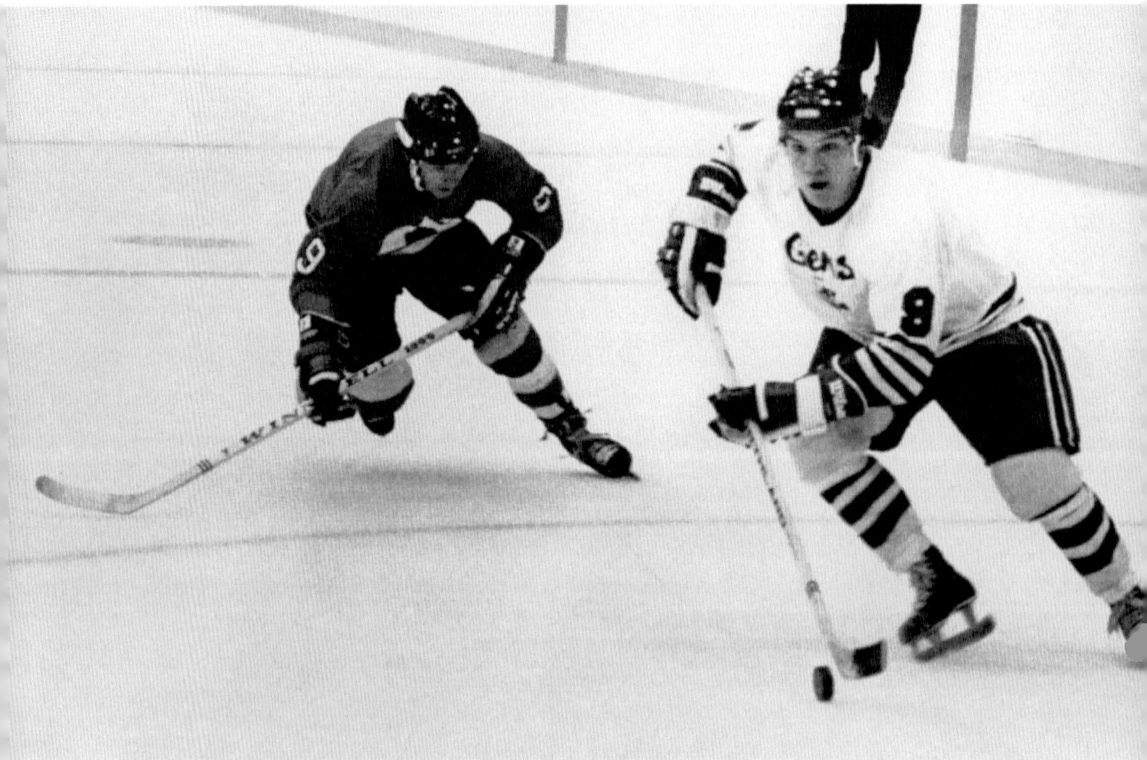

Stan Jonathan played one season in Dayton, with the 1975–1976 Turner Cup championship team. He played 411 games in the NHL, mostly with Boston. Teammate and IHL great Jim Bannatyne called Jonathan "pound for pound the toughest player I've ever seen." Bannatyne remembered a scrap between Jonathan and Ian McPhee of the rival Toledo Goaldiggers: "It was toe to toe and they were just giving each other shots. Then Jonathan switched hands on him and put him down. He threw a left and just drilled him right on the beak and down he [McPhee] went." (Courtesy of Wright State Special Collections.)

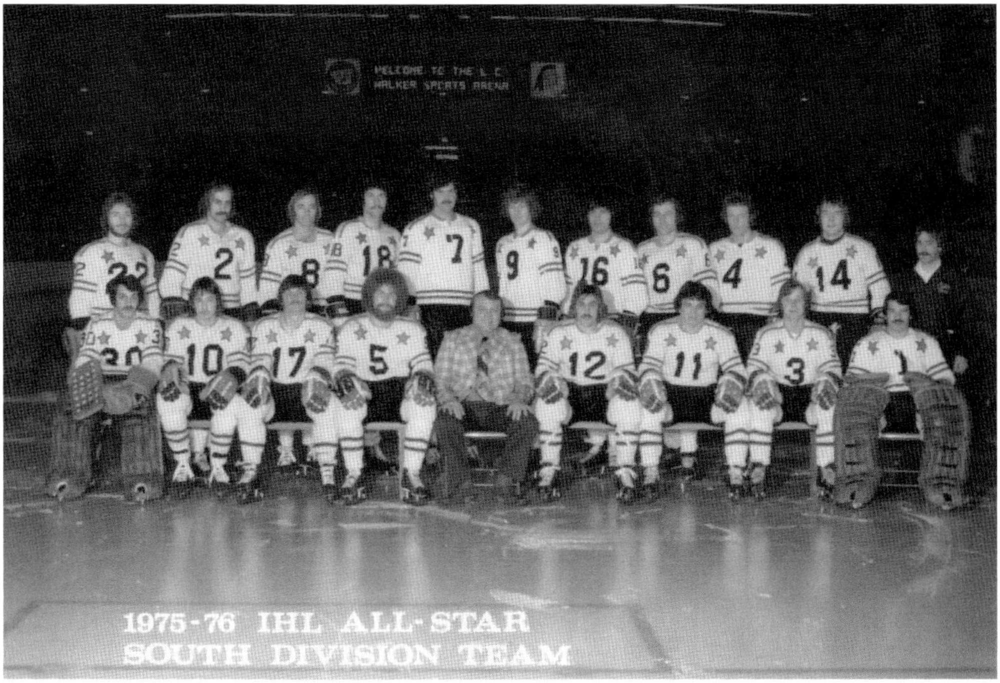

The 1975–1976 IHL South Division all-star team could have been manned by all Gems, given the success of the team that year. As it turned out, six Gems made the squad: Steve Self (17), Rick Bragnalo (12), Stan Jonathan (11), Jim Bannatyne (3), Gord Lane (18), and Larry Bolonchuk (6). Gems coach Ivan Predigar (first row, center) and trainer Keith Parker (second row, far right) were also selected for the team. (Courtesy of Rick Bragnalo.)

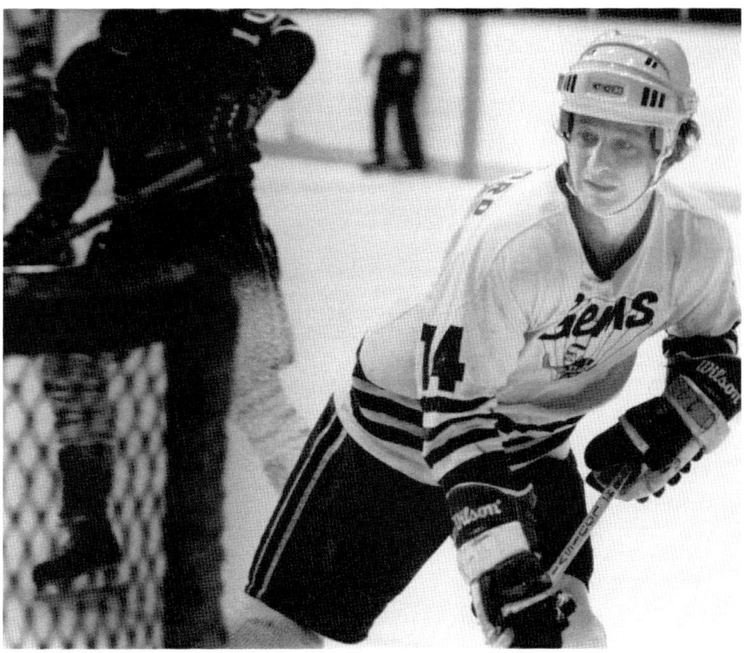

Tim Ampleford was one of the few players who returned from the Turner Cup champion team to play for the 1976–1977 Gems. The team finished below .500 for the first time in 11 years and lost to Fort Wayne in the first round of the playoffs. (Courtesy of Wright State Special Collections.)

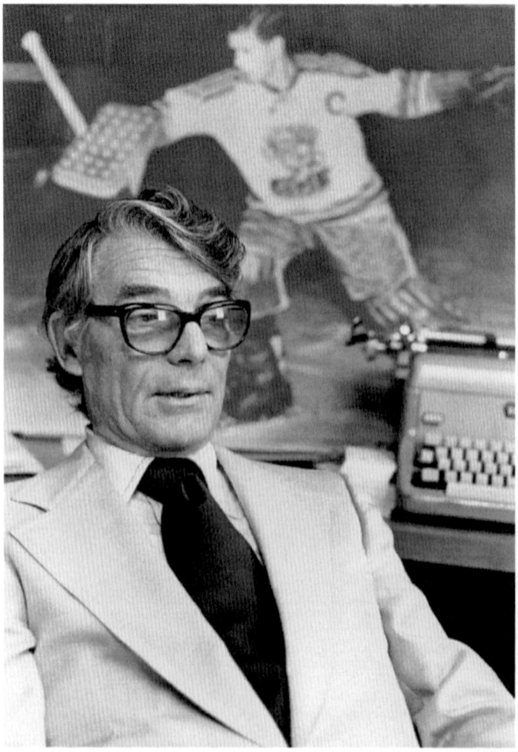

In 1976, seventeen years after leaving Troy with the Bruins, Ken Wilson returned to the arena to become general manager of the Gems. To make the team a financial success, he had to overcome a bad economy, a brutal winter, and a mediocre team. Unfortunately, at season's end, the franchise lost nearly $200,000 and suspended operations for the next two seasons. (Courtesy of Wright State Special Collections.)

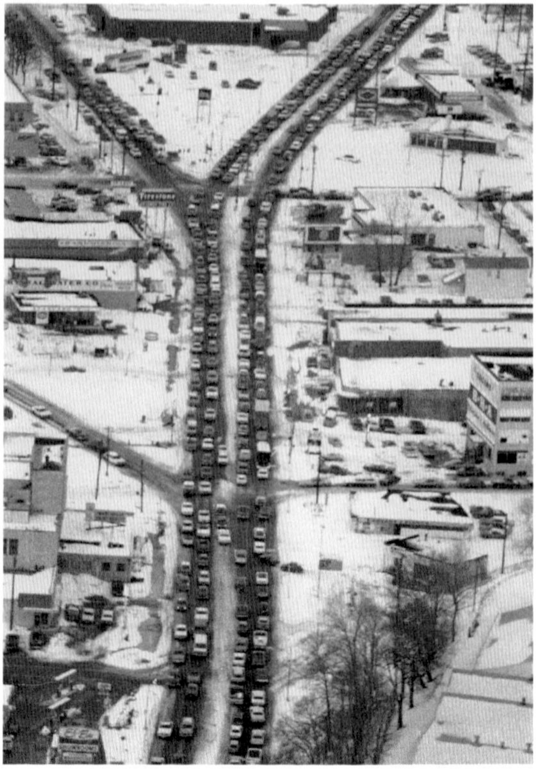

The winters of the late 1970s were among the worst in Dayton's history. The extreme cold and heavy snow of the winter of 1977 caused crowds to dwindle at Hara Arena. On January 26, 1977, in a game against Flint, the announced attendance was 935—the smallest crowd in Gems history. (Courtesy of Wright State Special Collections.)

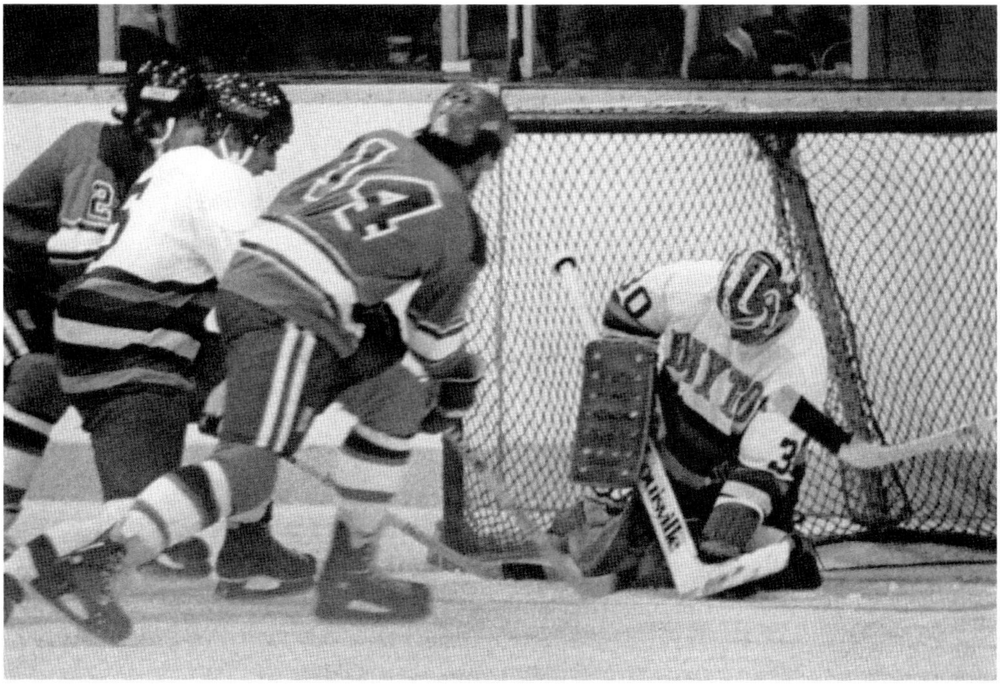

After being dormant for two seasons, the Gems played their first home game of the 1979–1980 "Second Coming" season on Sunday, October 21, 1979. They took on the Fort Wayne Komets in front of a disappointing Hara Arena crowd of 2,663. Ted Tucker, who played goal for the rival Toledo Goaldiggers in the mid-1970s, was between the pipes for the Gems that evening. Dayton beat the Komets 6-3. (Courtesy of Wright State Special Collections.)

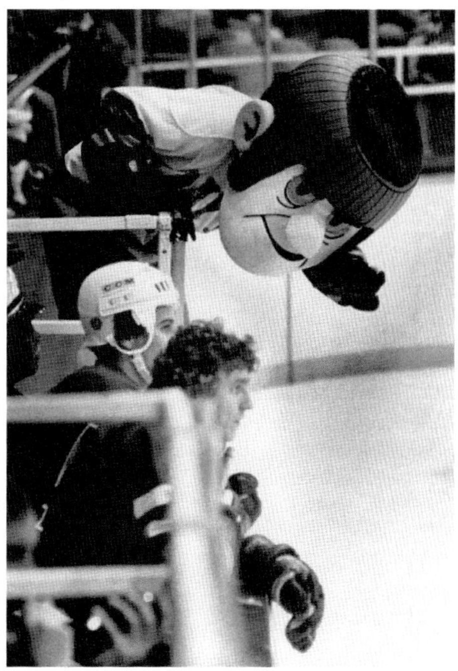

In the mid-1970s, Patty Puck was the Dayton Gems mascot. During the 1979–1980 season, Freddie Gemstone entertained the often-sparse Hara Arena crowds. Some nights, when the Gems were playing poorly at Hara, fans could depend on Freddie to supply some laughs by aggravating opposing players or referees. (Courtesy of Wright State Special Collections.)

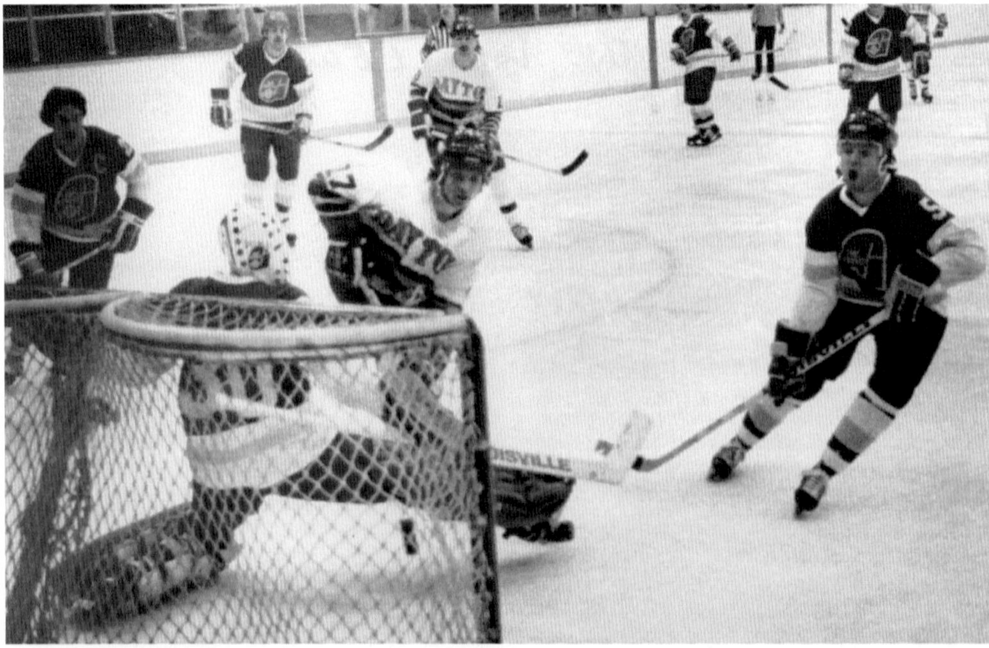

Benoit Gosselin scores one of his four goals against the Flint Generals at Hara Arena on February 10, 1980. The talented left winger played with the New York Rangers two years before coming to Dayton. He was one of the few bright spots for the 1979–1980 Gems, scoring 37 goals in just 42 games. (Courtesy of Wright State Special Collections.)

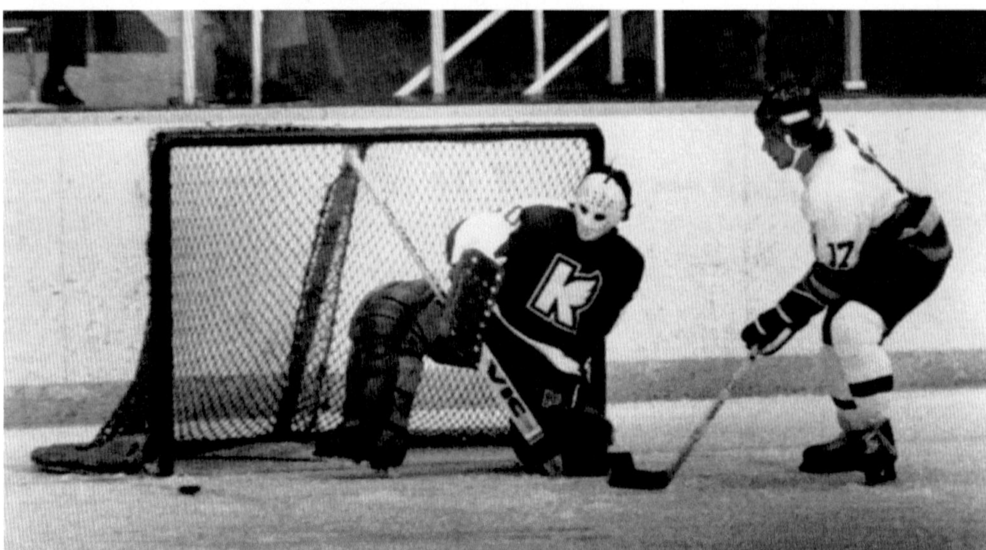

Dayton's Benoit Gosselin skates by Kalamazoo Wings goalie Larry Lozinski. The Gems took on the Wings in the final game of the 1979–1980 season at Hara Arena on April 6, 1980. The game ended in a 1-1 tie before a crowd of 2,185. The contest also turned out to be the final game in franchise history for the Gems. A few weeks later, the team suspended operations for good due to heavy financial losses. (Courtesy of Wright State Special Collections.)

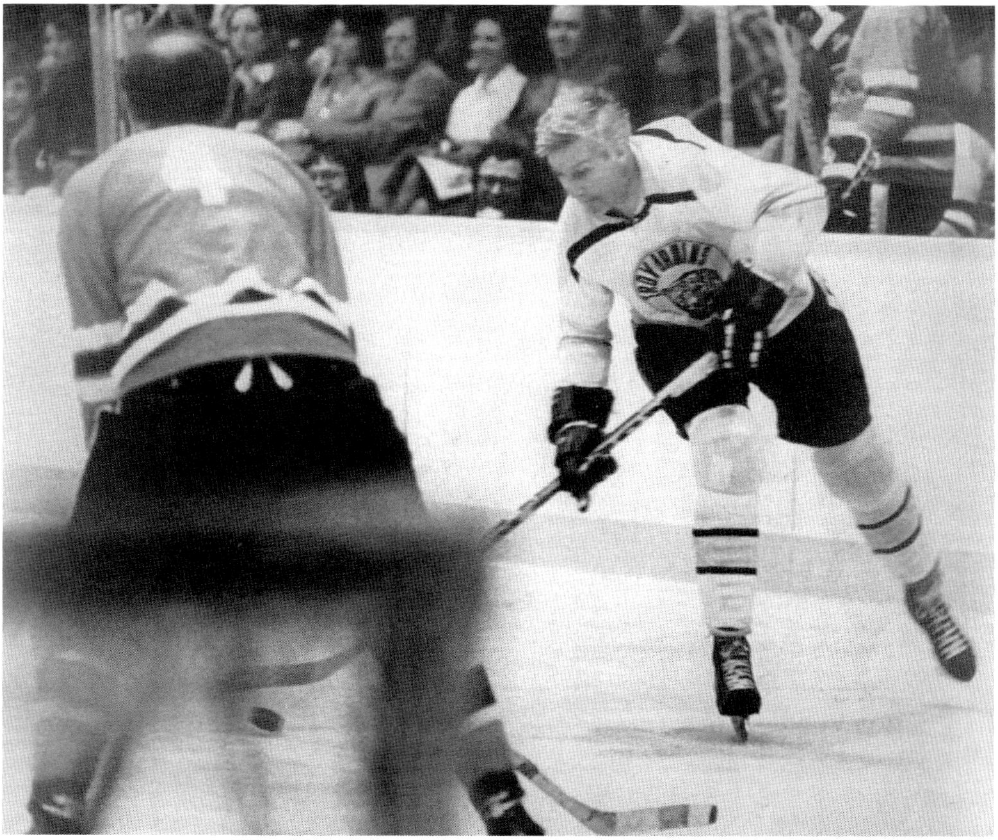

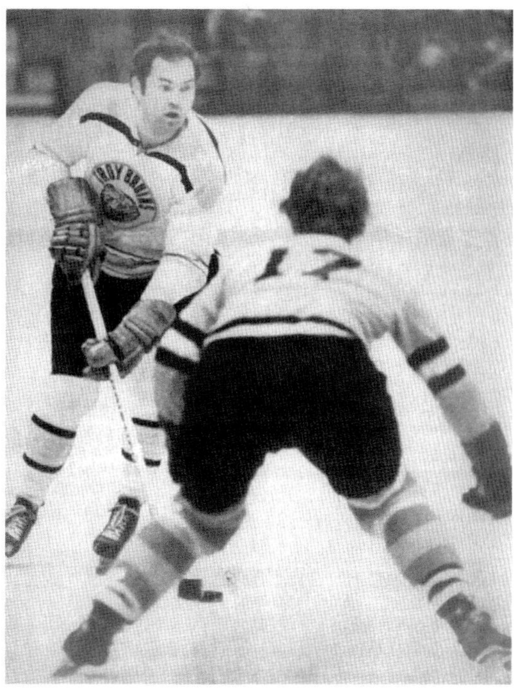

Over the years, former Dayton Gems and Troy Bruins players teamed up to play in old-timers games. These were usually played at Troy's Hobart Arena against old-timer teams from other cities. Bob Bailey (above) and Warren Back (right) often played with the Troy-Dayton team, which also featured many former Troy Bruins, like Bill Murphy. Other former Gems, including Pat Rupp, Ian Mackintosh, and Ron Meier, played in the games as well. (Both, courtesy of Bob Speck.)

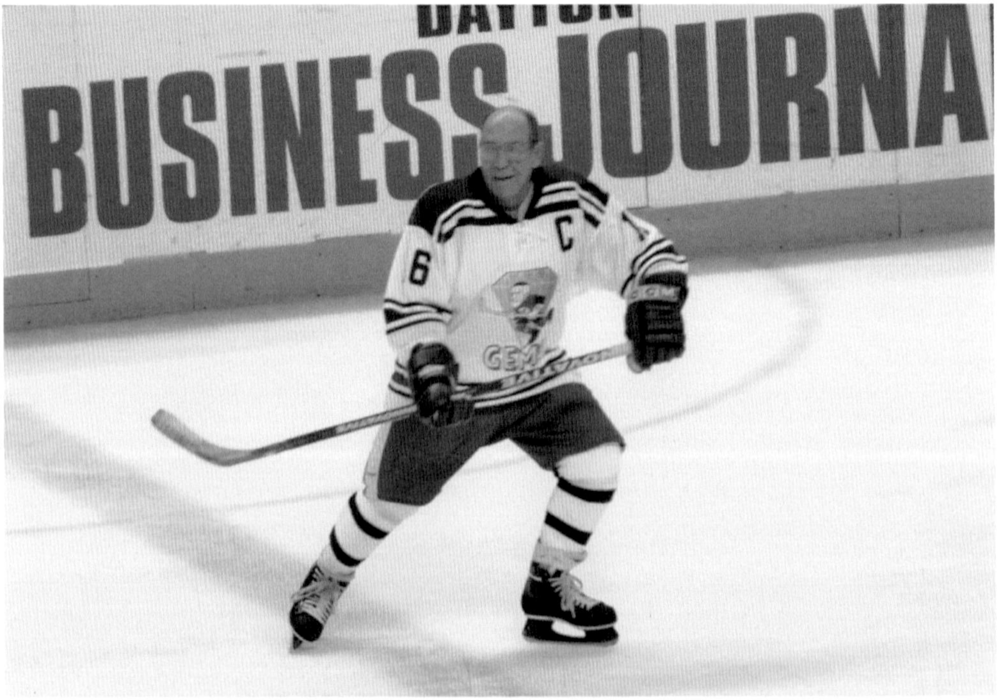

Former Dayton Gems Guy Trottier (above) and Don Westbrooke (below) play with other ex-Gems and Dayton Bombers in an old-timers game on January 6, 2006, at the Nutter Center. They skated against a team of former Detroit Red Wings. The Red Wings beat the Dayton team 8-1. Dayton players wore jerseys resembling the first Gems sweaters. (Courtesy of Max Surikov.)

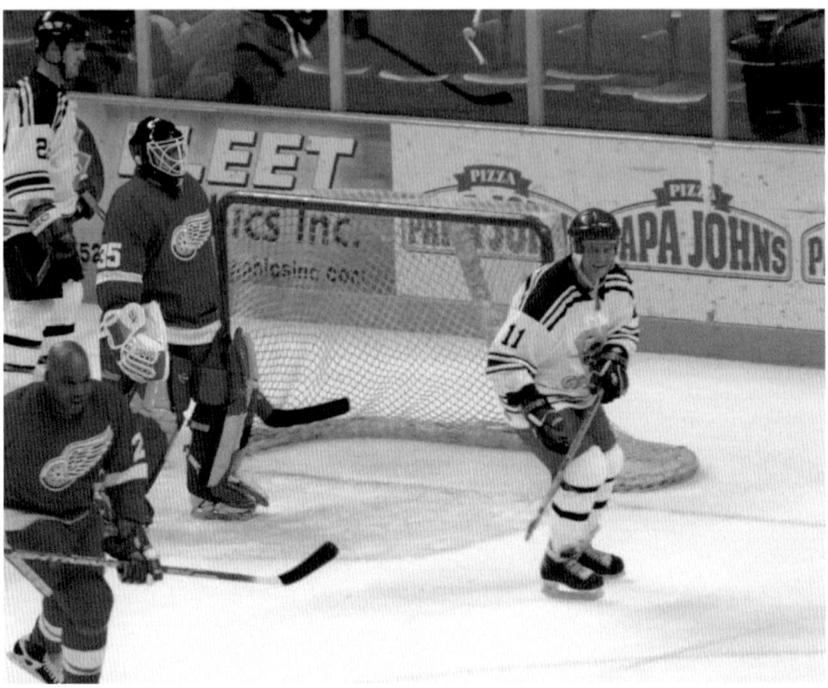

3

Let's Count 'em Down
The Dayton Bombers

By December 1990, it had been more than a decade since professional hockey was on the Dayton sports scene. What hockey fans there were when the Gems folded in 1980 found other things to occupy their winter months. Some followed University of Dayton basketball more closely. Others became fans of the Dayton Dynamo, an indoor soccer team that played in the late 1980s and early 1990s. Some still followed hockey on ESPN.

On Sunday, December 9, 1990, a story in the *Dayton Daily News* reported that two businessmen, Bud Gingher and Arnie Johnson, were seeking to locate an East Coast Hockey League (ECHL) franchise in Dayton, to begin play at Hara Arena in the fall of 1991. The ECHL was a developmental league, located in cities mostly in Virginia and North Carolina (the Cincinnati Cyclones joined the league in 1990). The commissioner of the ECHL was Pat Kelly, a friend of Gingher's who had played with the Troy Bruins during the 1958–1959 season. It was Kelly who traded Pat Rupp to the Gems in 1965 when he was coach of the Jersey Devils.

While the prospect of hockey returning to Dayton was exciting to many, there was also a good deal of uncertainty and doubt. Given the way the Gems had ended—with dwindling attendance and huge operating losses—many questioned whether hockey could successfully return to Dayton. In addition, a poor local economy existed at the time. Nevertheless, Gingher and Johnson felt it was time for hockey's resurrection in Dayton.

To gauge interest, the ECHL scheduled an exhibition game for February 20, 1991, at Hara Arena between the Cincinnati Cyclones and Knoxville Cherokees. Toward the end, the Gems were struggling to get 2,000 fans for home games. A similar turnout for the exhibition game would certainly doom Gingher and Johnson's plans and perhaps seal the fate for hockey in the area for years to come.

By the afternoon of February 20, nearly 4,000 tickets had been sold for the game. A few hours later, the game was completely sold out, to the delight of the new owners and area hockey fans. A Hara Arena crowd of 5,593 watched Knoxville win 9-4. But the only numbers that mattered were those in the seats. The crowd exploded during the game's second period, when it was announced that "hockey will return to Dayton." With those words, the Dayton Bombers were born.

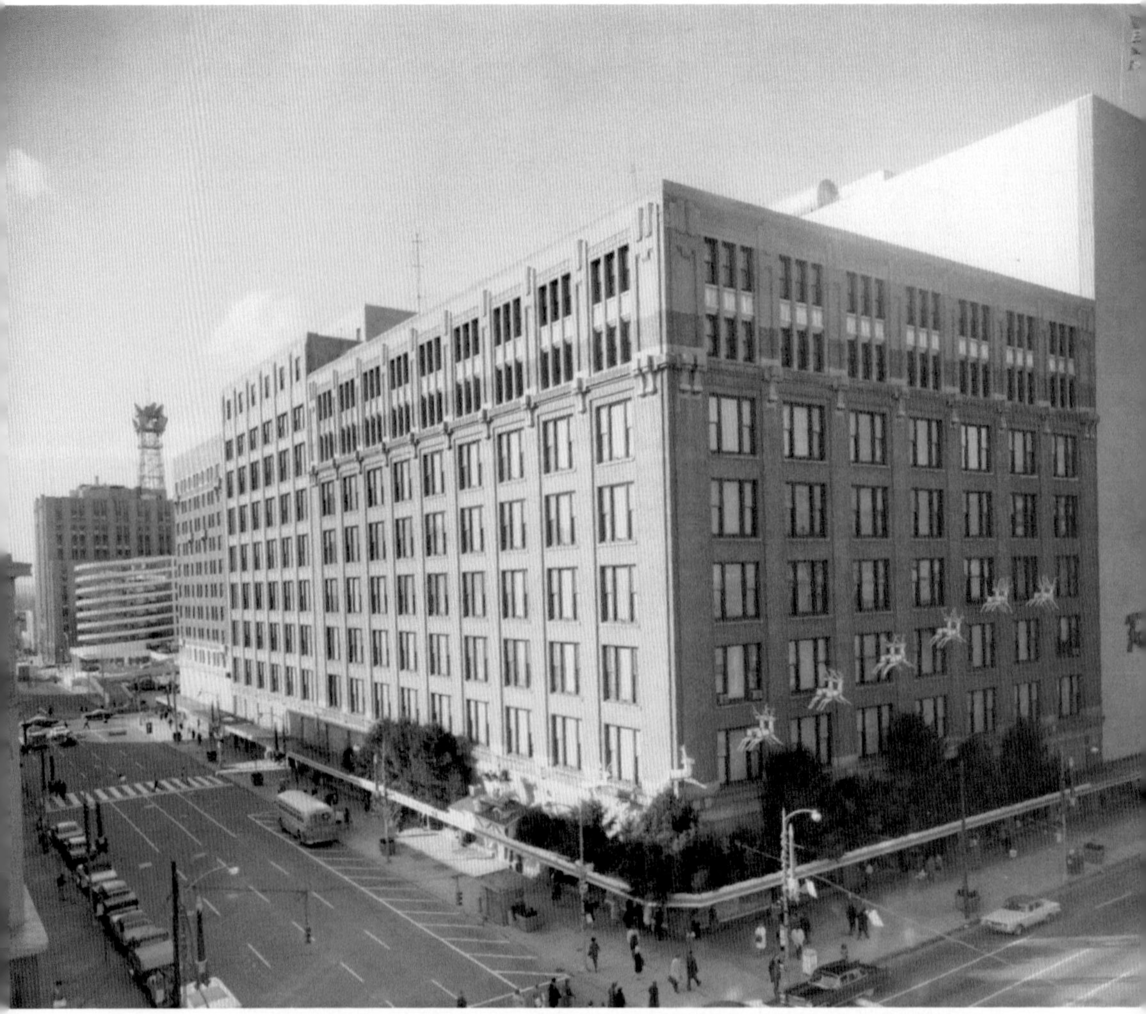

Like the rest of the country, Dayton struggled economically in the early 1990s. This was most evident in Dayton, as Lazarus department store (formerly Rike's) closed its historic downtown location (pictured) and Carlson Marketing moved its operations to Minneapolis, taking with it hundreds of jobs. (Courtesy of Wright State Special Collections.)

Bud Gingher and Arnie Johnson were college friends from their time at Bradley University. Gingher was part of a group that kept hockey alive in Peoria when the IHL Peoria Prancers were on the verge of folding in 1984. Gingher wanted to own a hockey team, and along with Johnson, paid $100,000 for a franchise in the ECHL. Gingher (below) and Johnson (right) looked at several cities in the Midwest, including Troy, which was denied by the league. The two decided on Dayton as the home for their team. The name of the new team would be the Bombers. (Right, courtesy of Gregg Wurtzler; below, courtesy of Wright State Special Collections.)

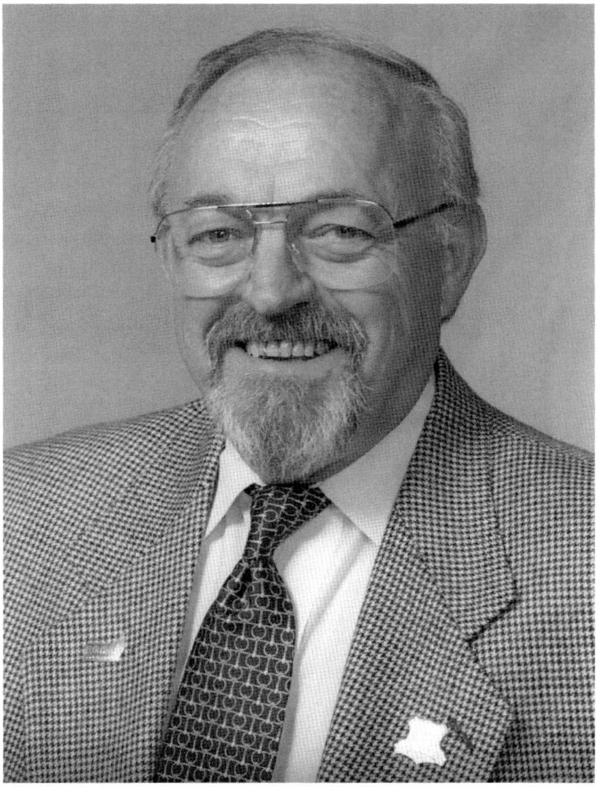

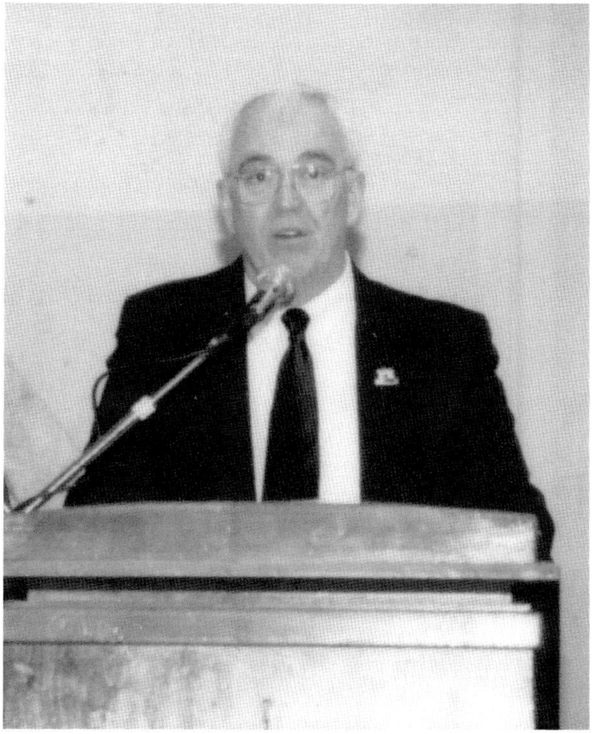

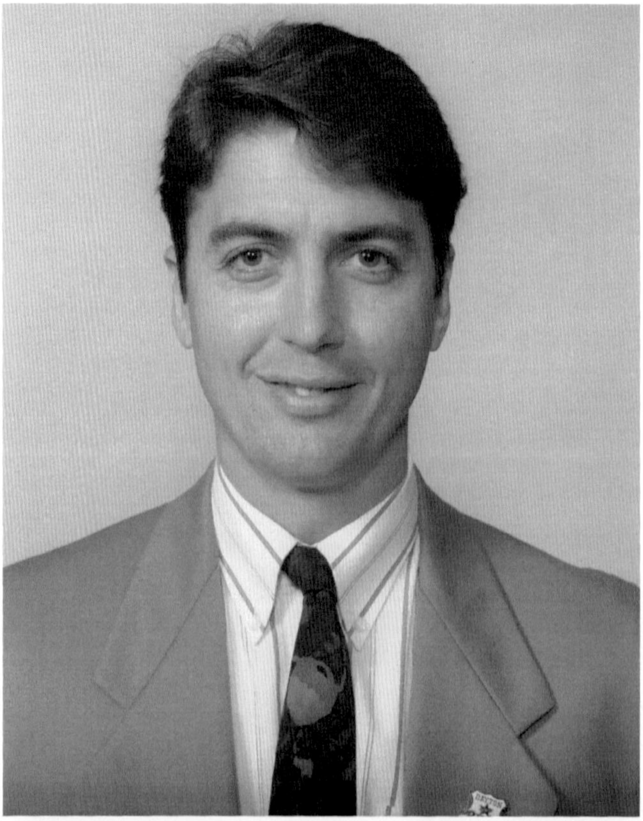

When Dayton entered the ECHL in 1991, Claude Noel (pictured) saw a great opportunity and moved north from Roanoke, Virginia, where he coached the year before. The soft-spoken Noel's hockey career included stops with the IHL Toledo Goaldiggers, where he was the 1982–1983 league MVP, and the NHL Washington Capitals. He guided the Bombers for their first two seasons, compiling a 65-49-12 record. Noel rose in the ranks of the NHL, coaching the Columbus Blue Jackets and Winnipeg Jets. (Courtesy of Gregg Wurtzler.)

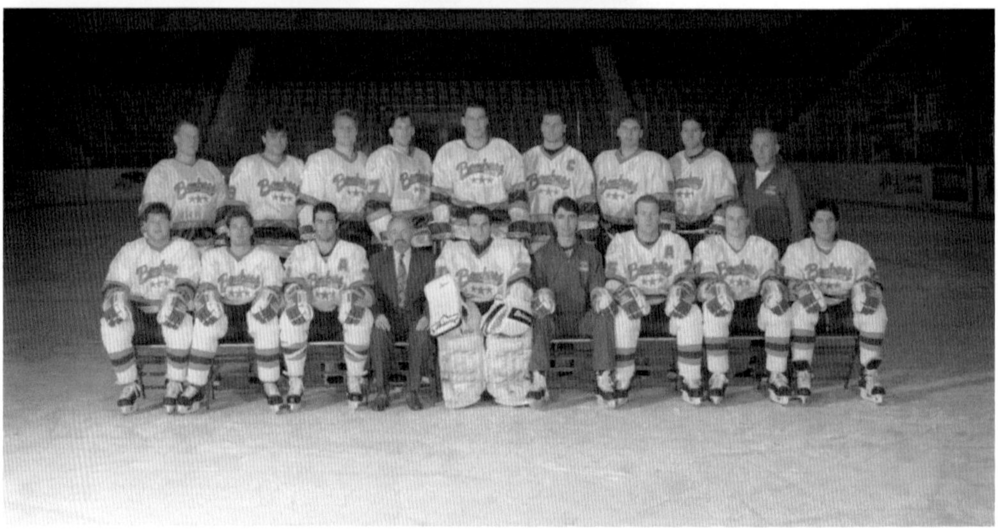

Only 20 or so players participated when Claude Noel opened the first Bombers training camp in October 1991. Fortunately, Noel was able to piece together a pretty good team, with a core that included defenseman Paul Marshall, goalie Rod Hauk, and forwards Darren Colbourne, Derek Crawford, and Mike Reier. The team was hobbled by call-ups, but finished with a 32-26-6 record and made the playoffs for the first of 11 consecutive years. (Courtesy of Gregg Wurtzler.)

Longtime Dayton radio personality Steve Kirk filled the role of Bombers public-address announcer during the Hara Arena years. "Kirkie" was best known for rousing the home crowd with "Let's count 'em down" following a Bombers goal—and the crowd would accompany the sound of explosions by counting the total number of Bombers goals. (Courtesy of Gregg Wurtzler.)

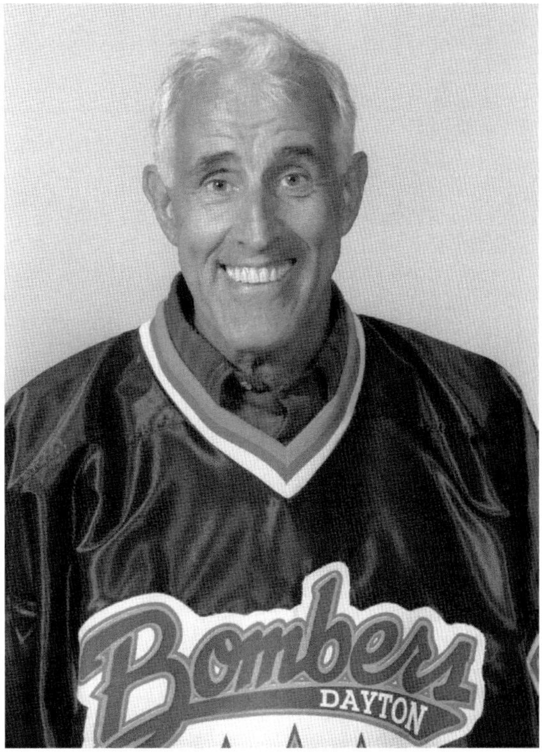

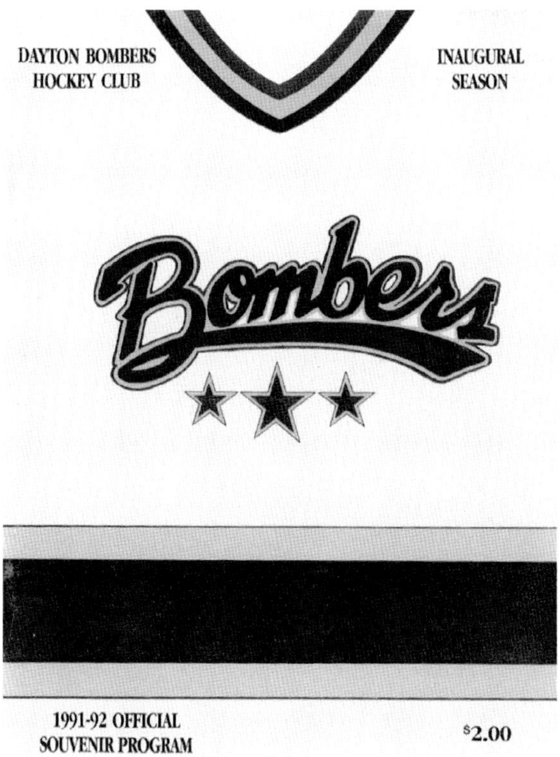

The Bombers' first game was at home versus the Raleigh Icecaps on October 25, 1991. An opening-night Hara Arena crowd of 4,152 watched the Bombers pound Raleigh 11-2. Jackson Penney scored four goals for the Bombers that night, and Darren Colbourne added a hat trick. (Author's collection.)

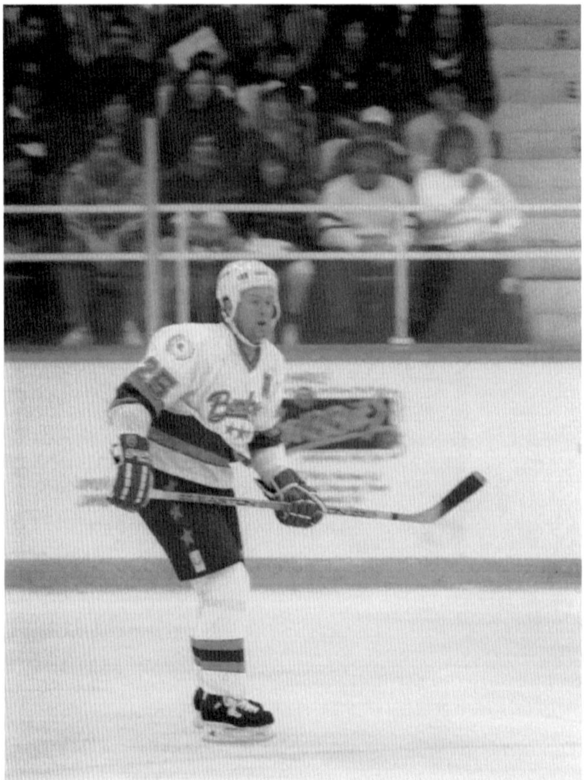

Darren Colbourne was the Bombers star scorer their first season. Colbourne scored 69 goals—the most any Bombers player would score in a season—and added 50 assists for 119 points, also a Bombers record. His goal-scoring prowess earned him the nickname "Deadeye." Colbourne was named the ECHL Rookie of the Year for the 1991–1992 season. He was the only Bomber to ever win the award. (Courtesy of Gregg Wurtzler.)

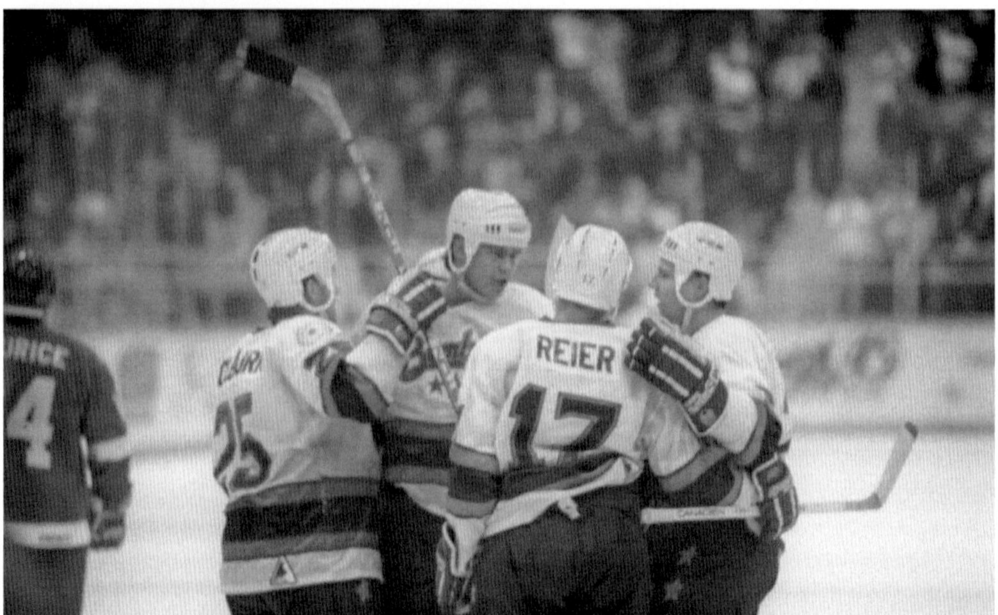

Darren Colbourne, Mike Reier, and Derek Crawford made up the Bombers' top line in the team's first year. The three combined for 129 of the team's 305 goals. Reier's 75 assists that year were second-most by a Bomber in a season, after Tom Nemeth's 82. (Courtesy of Gregg Wurtzler.)

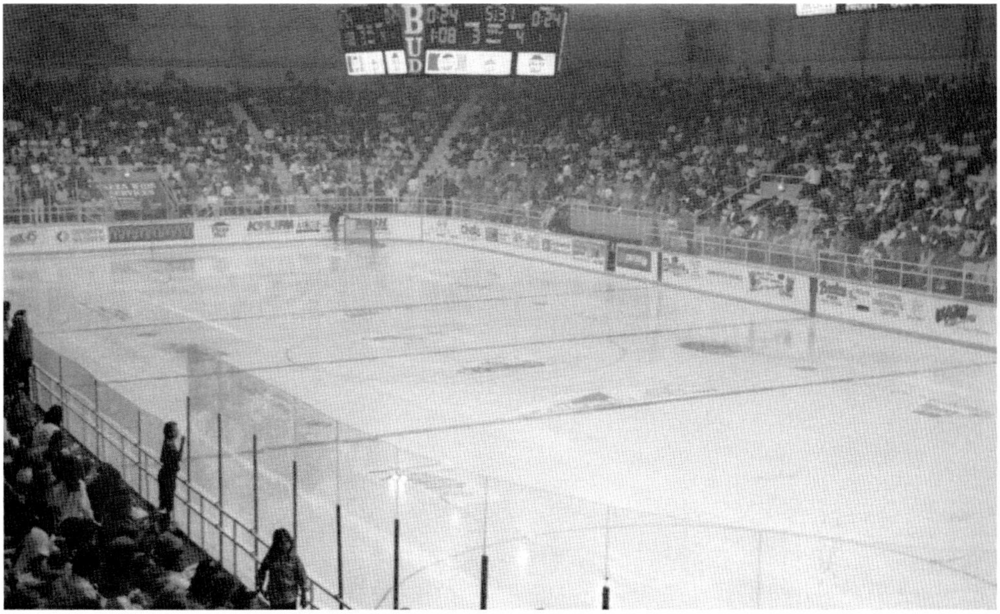

It did not take long for big crowds to turn out at Hara Arena to watch the Bombers. In their first year, the team had a total of 22 games with crowds over 4,000; twelve of those games drew crowds of 5,000 or more. That season also saw three sellouts. The team averaged over 4,100 fans a game the first season. (Courtesy of Gregg Wurtzler.)

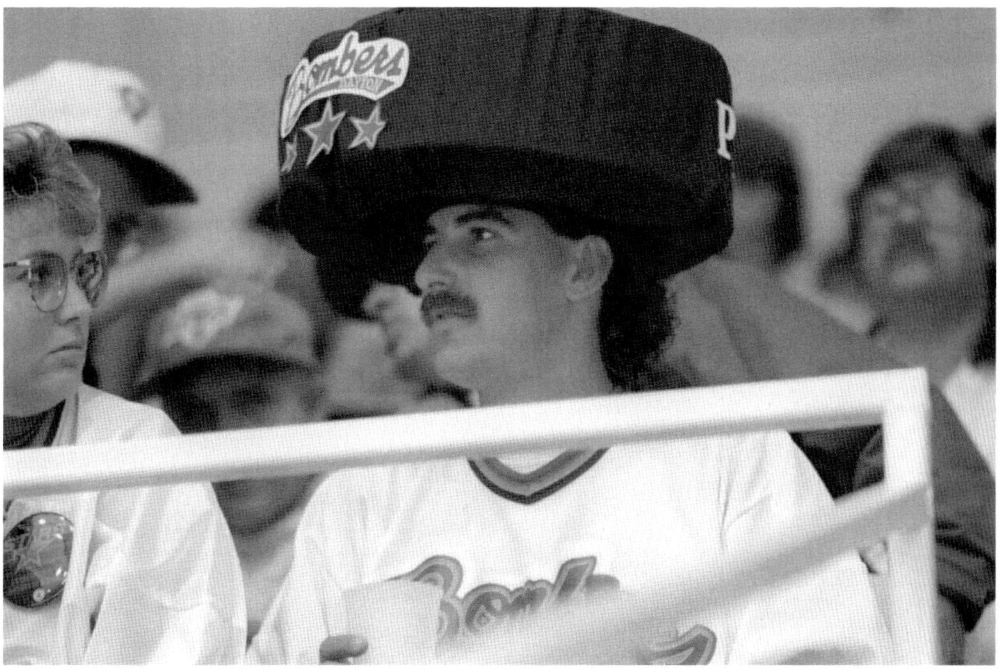

Aside from watching the action on the ice, fans enjoyed scanning the crowd at Bombers games. There were usually more than a few fans decked out in Bombers gear or donning some kind of fun costume to show their team pride. (Courtesy of Gregg Wurtzler.)

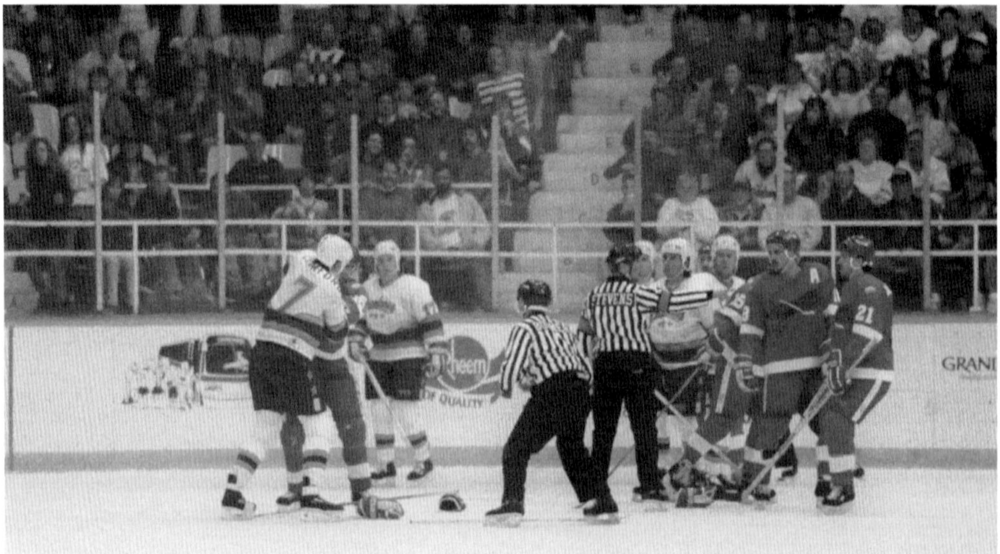

At the same time that Dayton came into the ECHL in 1991, so did the Toledo Storm and Columbus Chill, reigniting the fierce intercity rivalries that had started in the 1970s. The Storm (above) were an immediate success in the ECHL, winning three straight division titles (1992–1994) and back-to-back playoff championships (1993 and 1994). Bombers fans flocked to see the Storm—12 of the 29 Bomber sellouts from 1991 to 1995 were Storm games. The Chill were coached by NHL veteran Terry Ruskowski. He put tough, physical teams on the ice, reminiscent of the 1970s Columbus Owls. At one time, the Chill sold out the Ohio State Fairgrounds Coliseum for 83 consecutive games. Though successful at the gate, the Chill suspended operations in 1999 as Columbus awaited the arrival of the NHL Blue Jackets in 2000. (Both, courtesy of Gregg Wurtzler.)

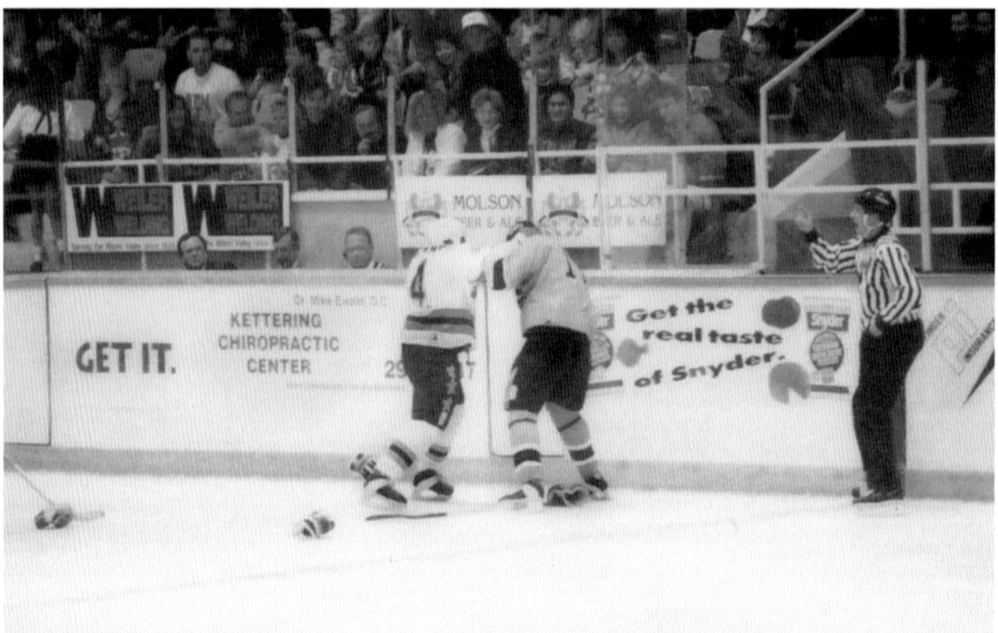

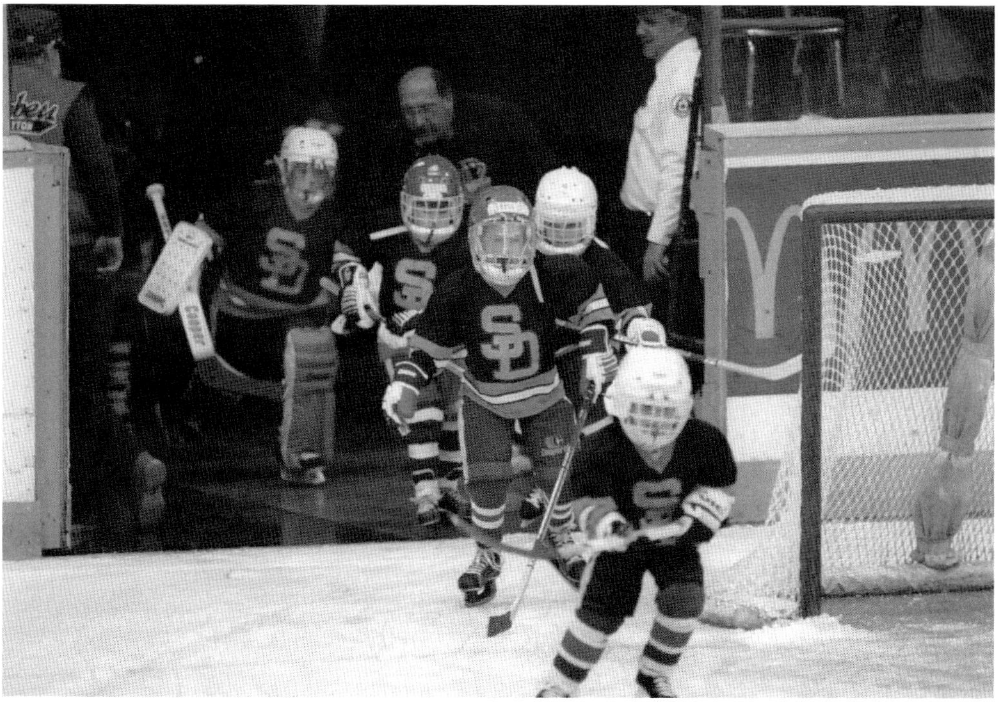

Between periods at Bombers' games, fans enjoyed more than just watching the Zamboni resurface the ice. The first intermission usually featured something fun to watch: a youth hockey game or an on-ice fan activity. The second intermission always included "Chuck-a-Puck," in which fans tried to win a prize by hurling foam pucks from the stands to a bull's-eye target on the ice while the song "You Dropped a Bomb on Me" played over the sound system. When the Zamboni did its work, fans would listen and sing along to "The Zamboni Song" or "The Good Old Hockey Game." (Both, courtesy of Gregg Wurtzler.)

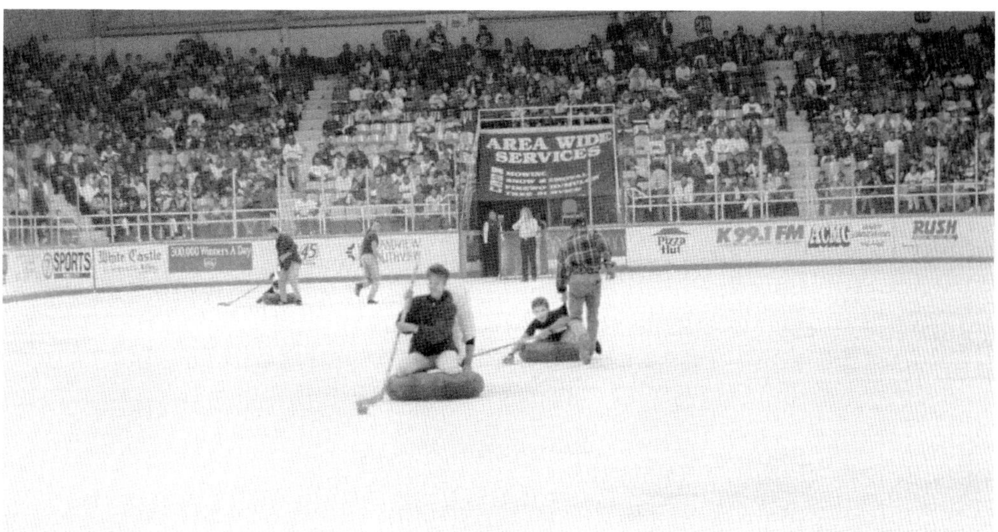

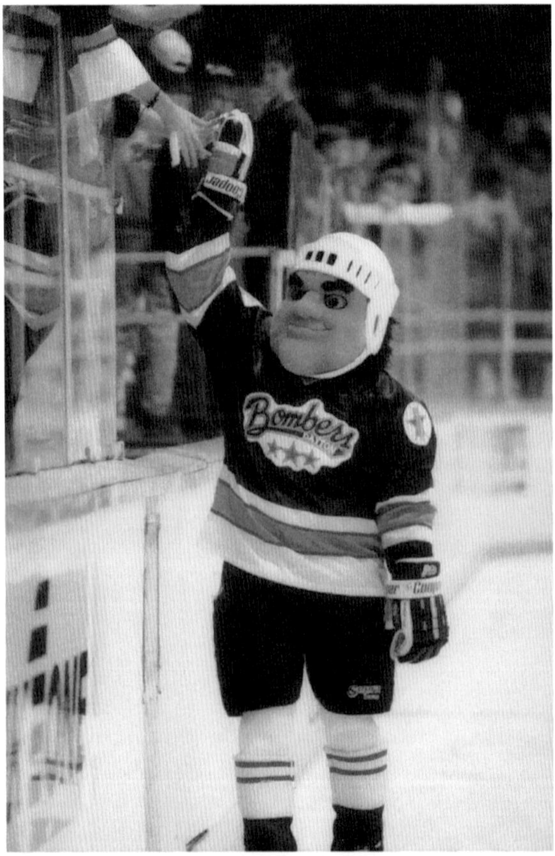

With the new team came a new mascot. "Adam Bomber" entertained the home crowds from 1991 to 1997. (Courtesy of Melissia Taziar.)

Defenseman Tom Nemeth had a cannon of a slap shot. Nemeth did two stints with the Bombers, the first from 1992 to 1994. In the 1993–1994 season, he collected 98 points on 16 goals and an incredible 82 assists. The 98 points and 82 assists still stand as ECHL records for a defenseman. The 82 assists are second to Bob Bailey's 87 as most by a Dayton hockey player in a season. He was named the 1993–1994 ECHL Defenseman of the Year. (Courtesy of Gregg Wurtzler.)

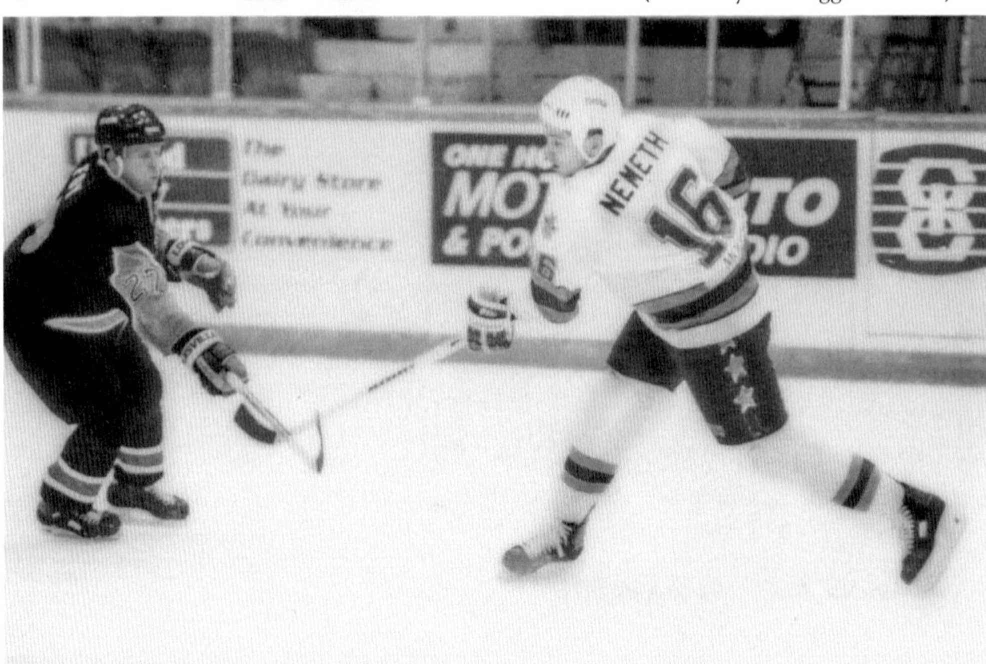

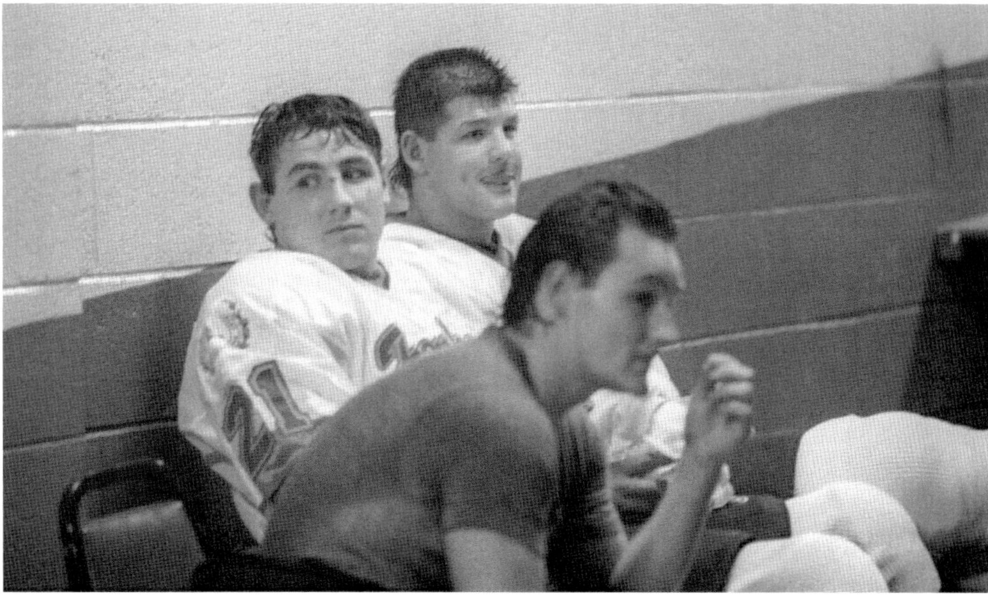

Shown here between periods of a Dayton Bombers game during the 1992–1993 season are, from front to back, Darwin McPherson, Darren Langdon, and Ray Edwards. (Courtesy of Gregg Wurtzler.)

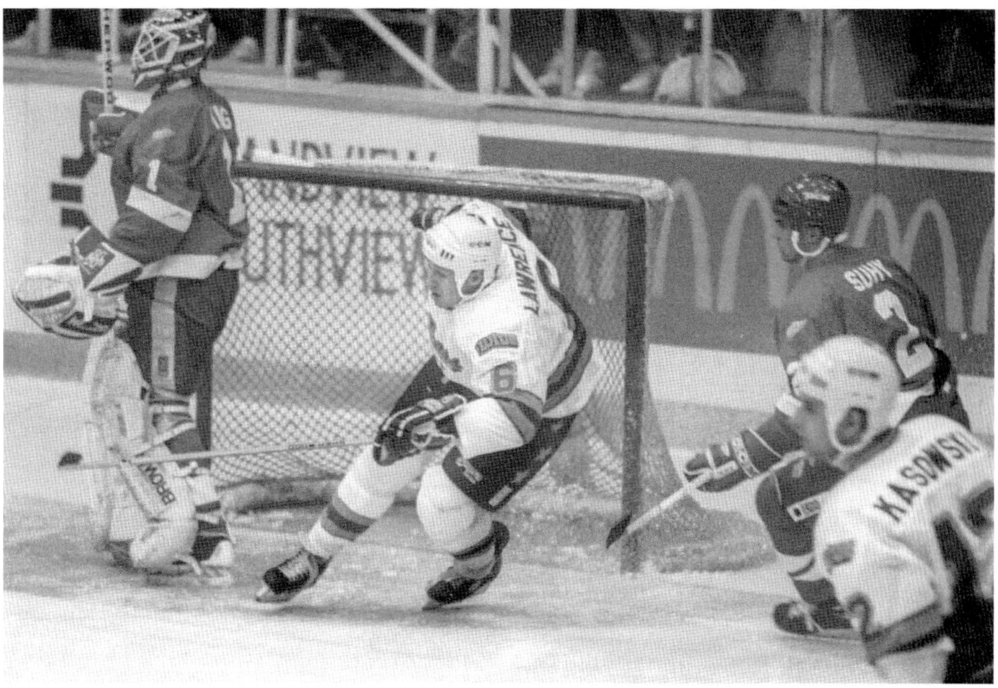

Bombers coach Claude Noel knew that Mark Lawrence would not stay long in Dayton—and he did not. The forward played only 20 games with the 1992–1993 Dayton Bombers, scoring eight goals and 14 assists before being promoted to the IHL Kalamazoo Wings. On February 4, 1995, Lawrence became the first Dayton Bomber to rise to the NHL, when he played with the Dallas Stars in a 7-4 loss to St. Louis. (Courtesy of Gregg Wurtzler.)

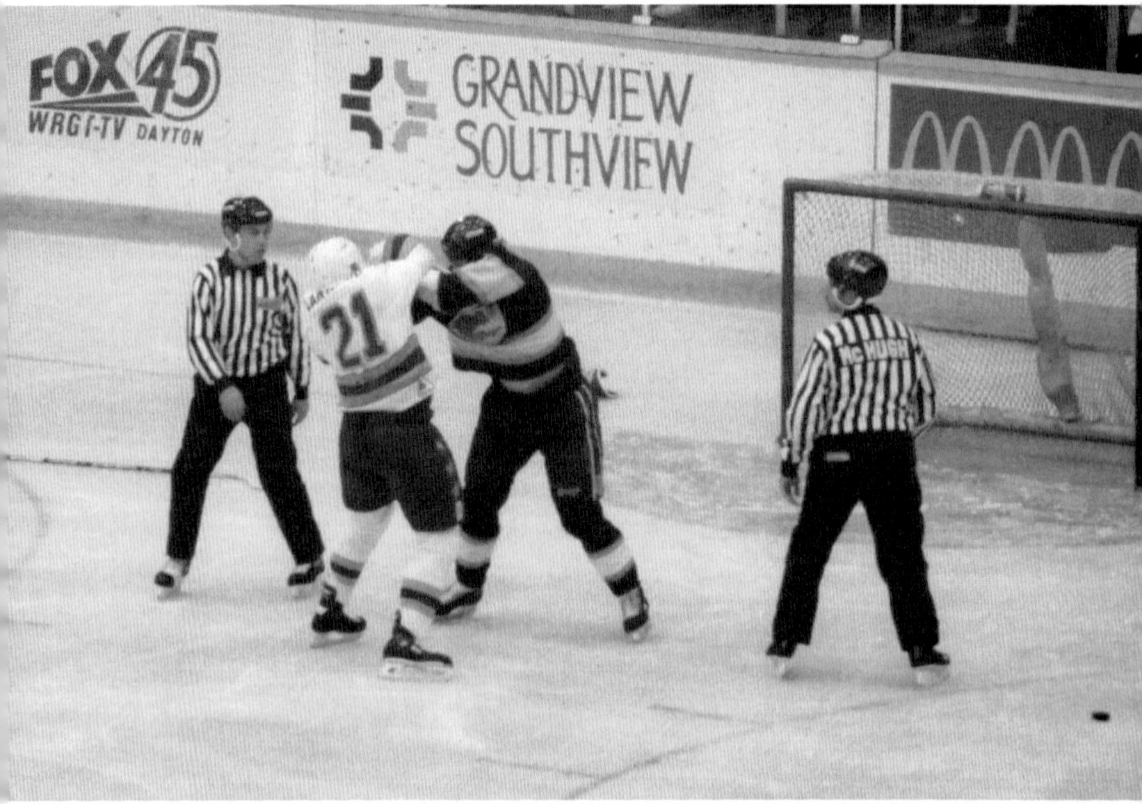

According to Claude Noel, it was former Dayton Gem and tough guy Bill Riley who told Noel about Darren Langdon. Along with Dayton Gems Gordie Lane and Stan Jonathan, Darren Langdon is probably the best fighter to ever wear a Dayton hockey uniform. Langdon amassed 429 penalty minutes—a Bombers record—during the 1992–1993 season. Most of his penalties came about through fisticuffs. But, like Lane and Jonathan, he could play hockey, too. Langdon scored 23 goals that year for Dayton. And, like the former Gems, Langdon had a long career in the NHL, beginning with the New York Rangers in 1995. In all, Langdon played in 521 NHL games—the most of any Dayton Bomber. He played with the Rangers (a teammate of Wayne Gretzky), Carolina, Vancouver, Montreal, and New Jersey. (Courtesy of Gregg Wurtzler.)

The Dayton Bombers hired Jim Playfair for his first head-coaching job. He took the place of Claude Noel. Demanding hard work and effort from his players, Playfair coached the Bombers from 1993 to 1996 and was named the 1994–1995 ECHL Coach of the Year, guiding the team to a franchise-best 42-17-9 record. Playfair became head coach of the Calgary Flames for the 2006–2007 season, leading the team to the Stanley Cup playoffs. (Courtesy of Gregg Wurtzler.)

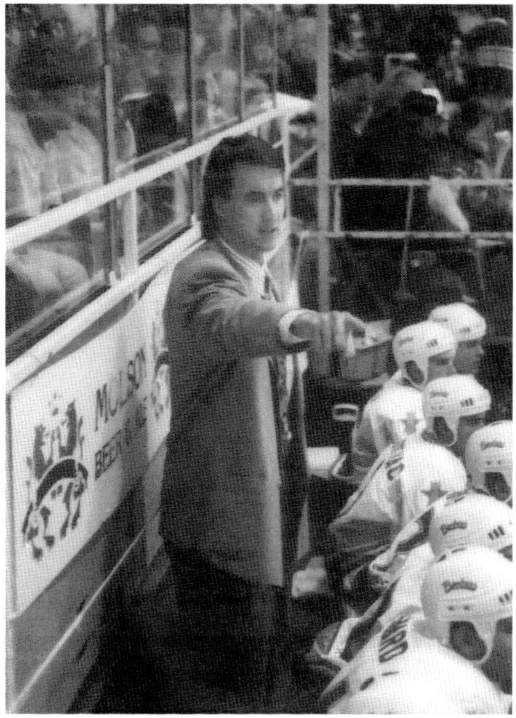

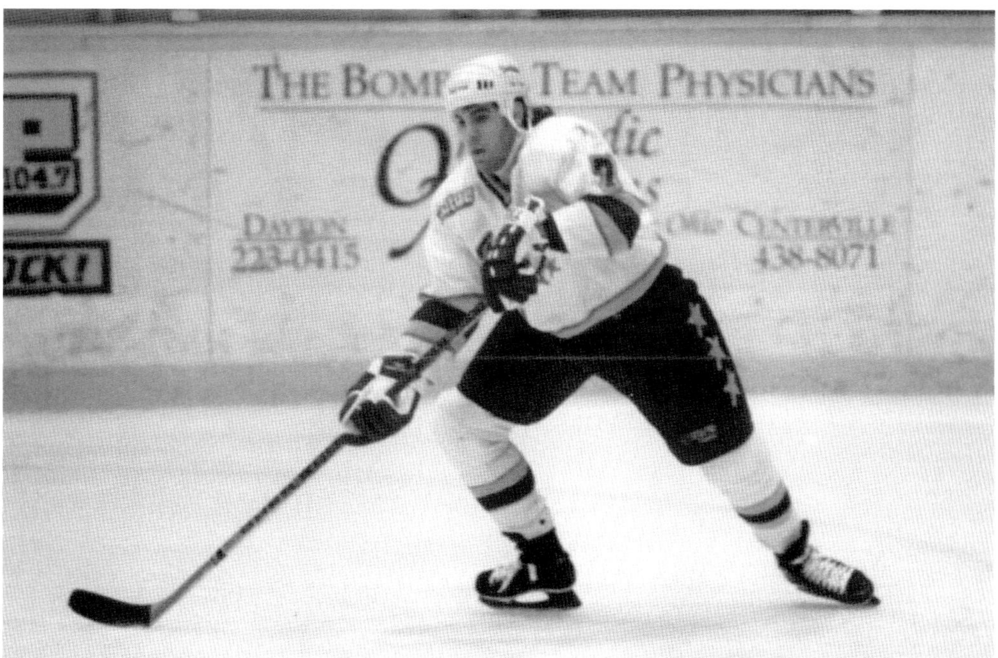

Craig Charron was as gifted a centerman and stick-handler that ever played for the Dayton Bombers. "Sureshot" Charron led the 1994–1995 Bombers in scoring with 82 points while playing in just 48 games. He was the nephew of 1980 US Olympic hockey team goalie Jim Craig. Sadly, Charron died of cancer in 2010 at the age of 42. (Courtesy of Melissia Taziar.)

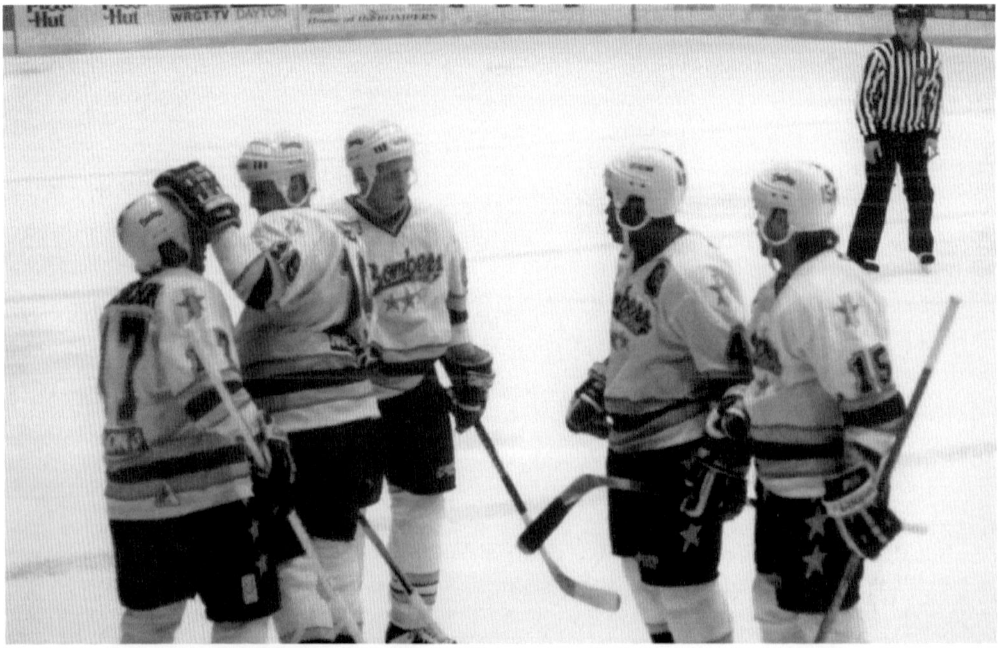

The 1994–1995 Bombers finished with a record of 42-17-9, the best of the team's first four years. The Bombers opened the season with eight consecutive victories, a record that still stands. The squad had a number of players who would make it to the NHL, including Brandon Smith, Sean Gagnon, and Pascal Trepanier. (Courtesy of Melissia Taziar.)

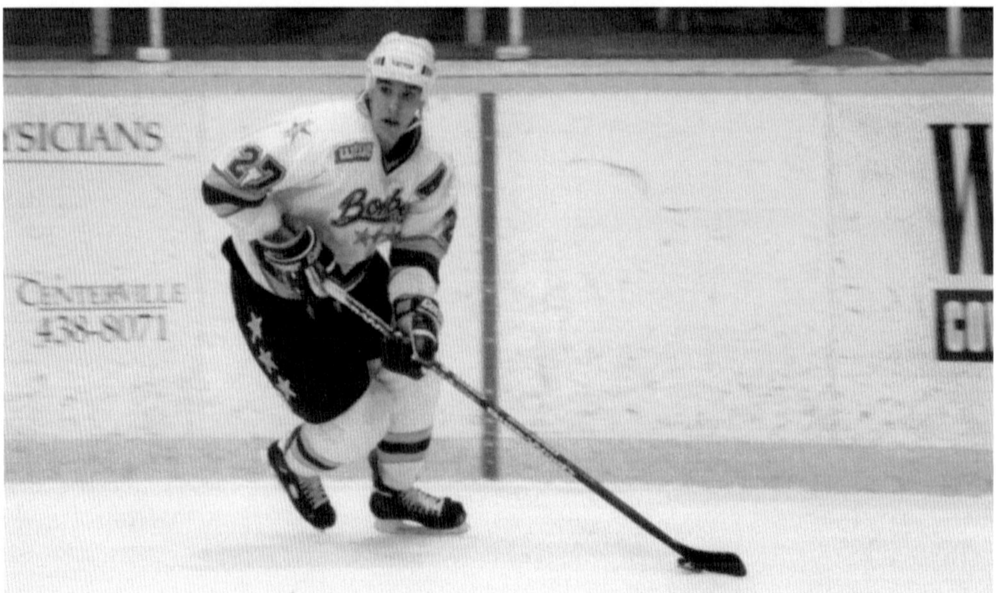

Brandon Smith was a standout defenseman for the 1994–1995 Dayton Bombers. He scored 16 goals and 49 assists in his only year as a Bomber. Smith was a first-team ECHL all-star and was named the 1994–1995 ECHL Defenseman of the Year. His talent took him to the NHL, where he played with the Boston Bruins and the New York Islanders. (Courtesy of Melissia Taziar.)

Pascal Trepanier had a big slap shot and was skilled at the lost art of the hip check. The hard-hitting defenseman played 36 games with the 1994–1995 Dayton Bombers. Trepanier enjoyed one of the longer careers of Dayton Bombers who made it to the NHL, playing in 229 games with the Colorado Avalanche, Anaheim Mighty Ducks, and Nashville Predators. (Courtesy of Melissia Taziar.)

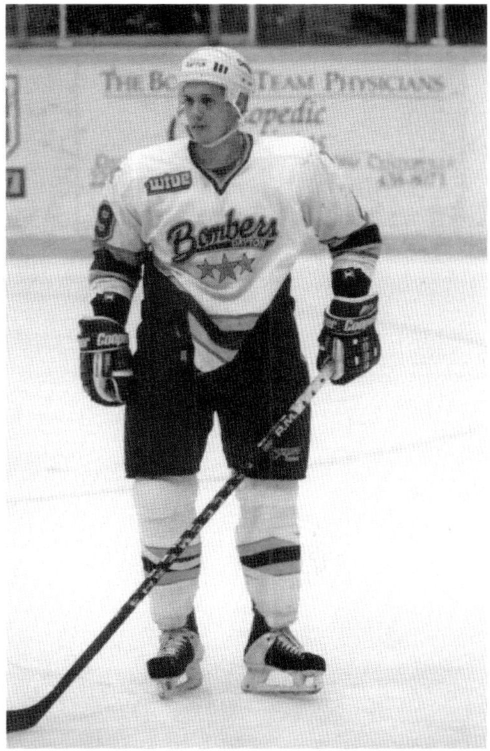

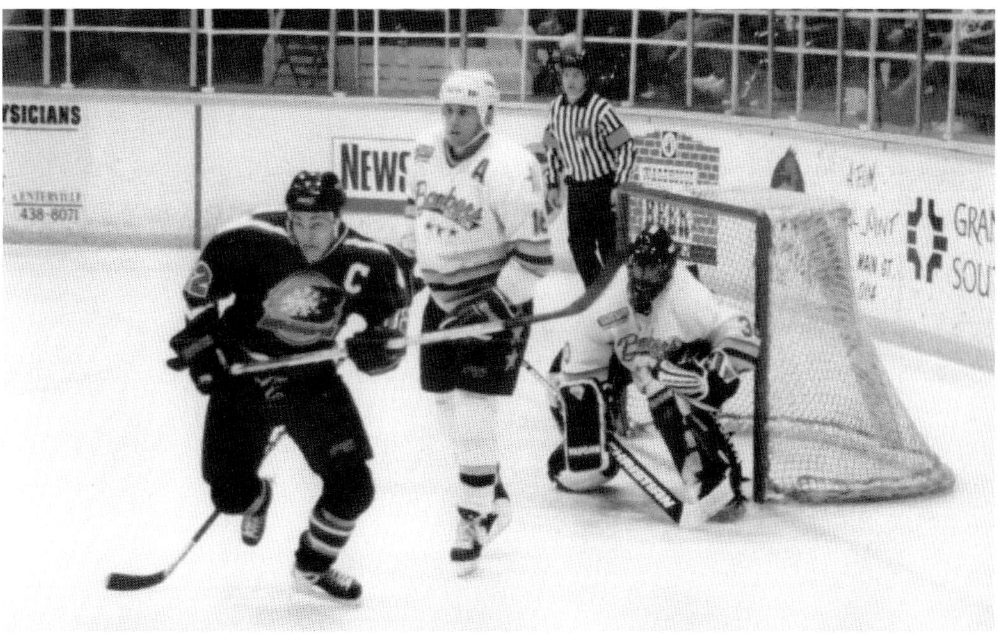

After three years of frustration, the Bombers finally won a playoff series, defeating the Huntington Blizzard in the first round of the 1995 Riley Cup playoffs. To that point, the Bombers had failed to win a playoff series, compiling a dismal record of 1-8 in the postseason. (Courtesy of Melissia Taziar.)

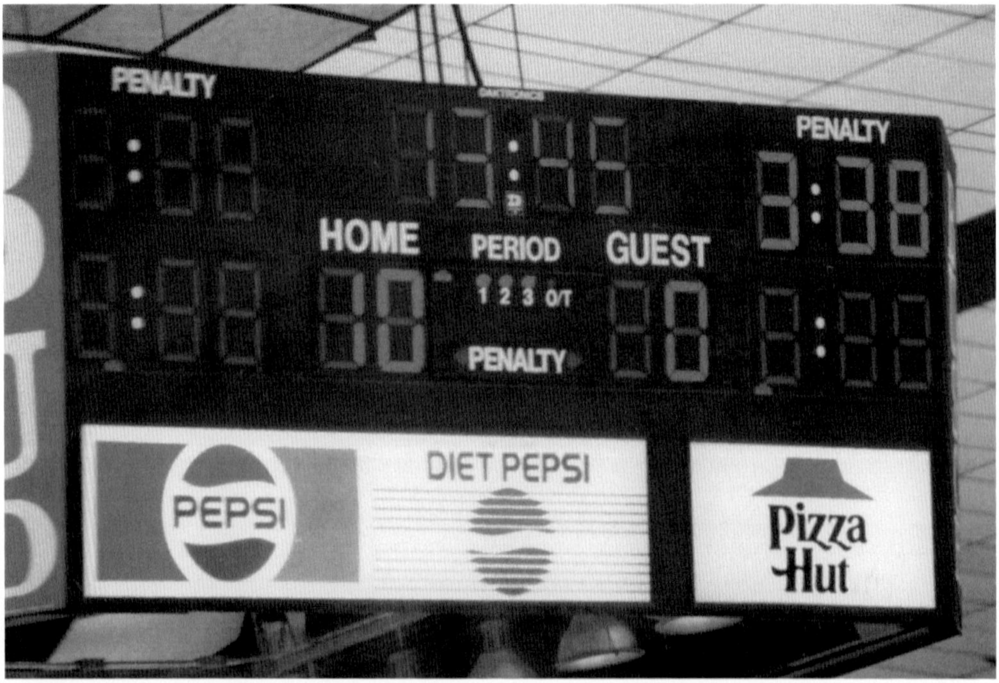

In round two of the 1995 ECHL playoffs, the Bombers met the Greensboro Monarchs in a best-of-five series. It became one of the most memorable playoff series in Bombers history. In game one, on April 2, 1995, at Hara Arena, the Bombers pounded the Monarchs 11-0, setting records for most goals in a playoff game and biggest margin of victory in a playoff game. Both records still stand. Greensboro won the next day to even the series. (Courtesy of Melissia Taziar.)

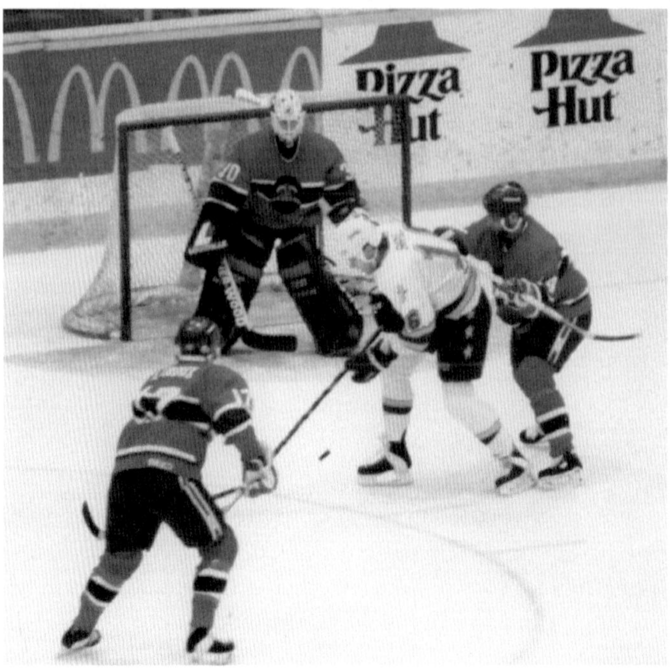

Games three and four were overtime contests, with each team winning one. The Bombers won game four 6-5 in Greensboro to avoid elimination. The deciding game five was played in Dayton on Saturday, April 9, 1995. The game was sold out early in the day. Owner Bud Gingher said that if Hara Arena held 8,000 seats, all would have been filled for the last game of the series. (Courtesy of Melissia Taziar.)

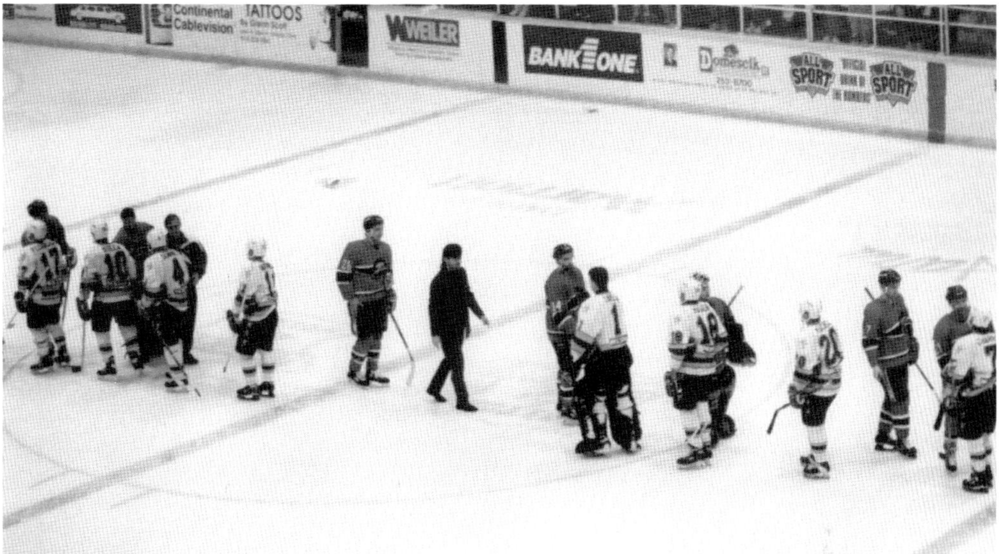

In the contest, the Bombers jumped ahead to a 2-1 lead, but the Monarchs tied the score and then jumped ahead 4-2 going into the third period. The Bombers cut the lead to 4-3. The teams traded goals late, but the Bombers fell 5-4 to Greensboro to end one of their more successful seasons ever. (Courtesy of Melissia Taziar.)

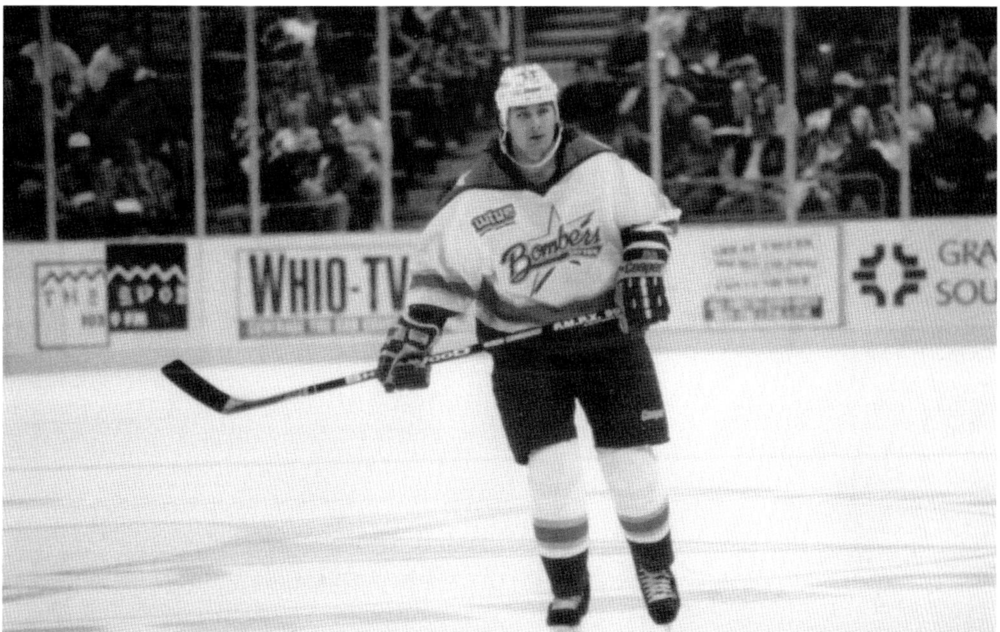

Colin Miller was the center on the Bombers number-one line from 1995 to 1999. Miller was a crafty center who rarely lost a face-off. In four seasons with the Bombers, Miller totaled 275 points on 83 goals and 192 assists. He returned as an assistant coach during the 2005–2006 Bomber season. (Courtesy of Melissia Taziar.)

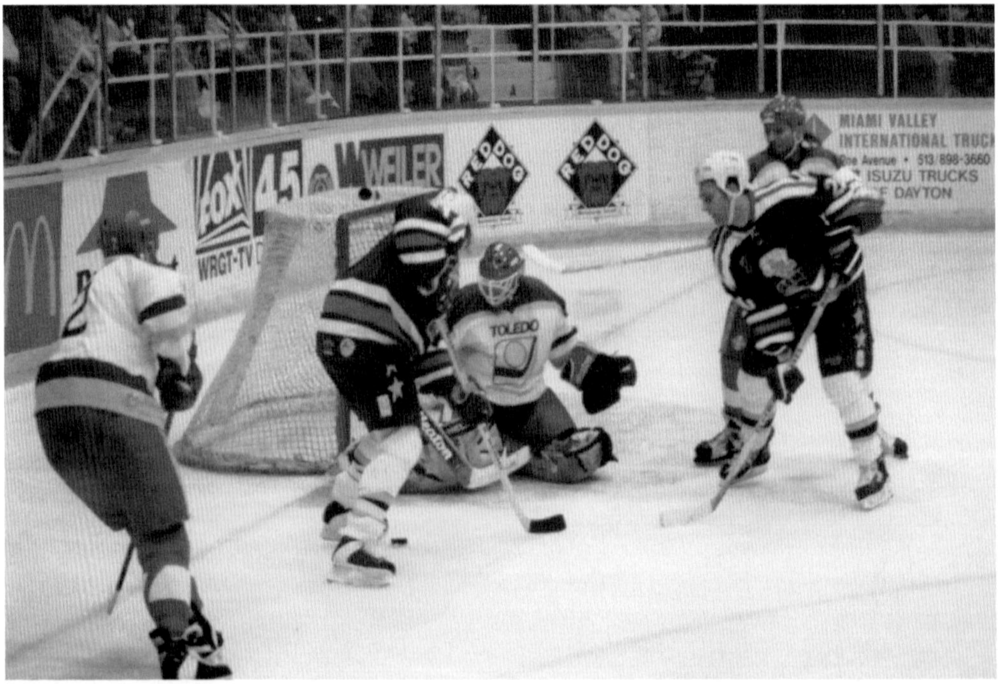

It was almost like a Dayton and Toledo game from 1975—without 10¢ beer night—when the Bombers and Storm played a game at Hara Arena on November 4, 1995. That night, the Bombers donned replica blue Gems road jerseys from their early days, while the Storm wore white, green, and gold Toledo Goaldigger home tops. The Bombers won the contest 6-4 before a packed house of 5,550. (Courtesy of Melissia Taziar.)

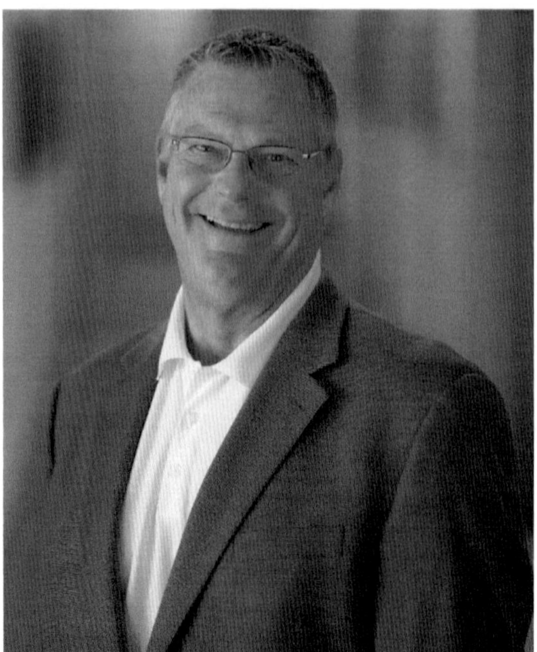

John Siehl began working as an usher at Hara Arena during Gems games in 1965. By 1982, he had become general manager of Hara. He assumed the same role at the newly opened E.J. Nutter Center on the Wright State University campus in 1990. He was the facility's executive director in early 1996, when Bombers owners Bud Gingher and Arnie Johnson called about possibly moving the team to the 9,950-seat Nutter Center, which was built without ice-making equipment. (Courtesy of John Siehl.)

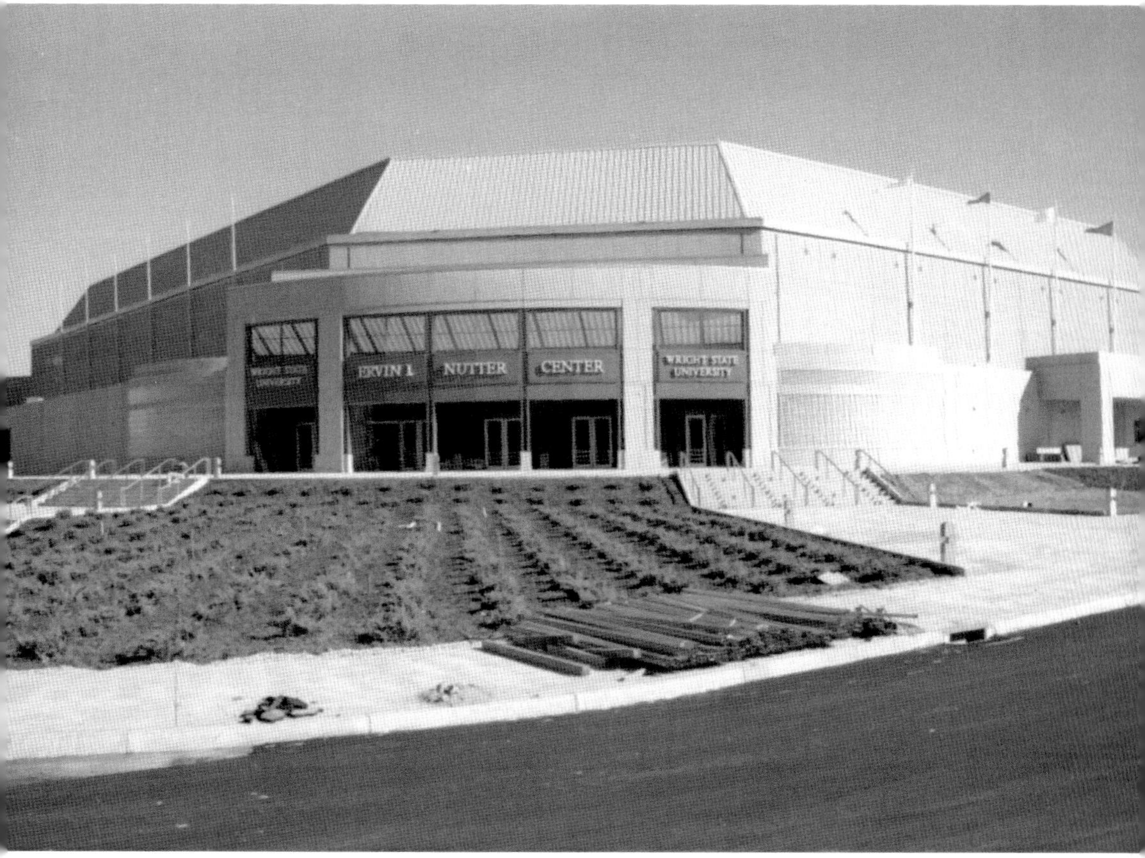

In March 1996, the Bombers and Greene County, Ohio, reached an agreement that would finance the installation of ice at the Nutter Center, allowing the Bombers to move from Hara Arena. The county would sell $1.5 million in industrial bonds, which the Bombers would repay over the next 10 years. A $1 service charge per hockey ticket would go to repaying the loan. In addition to the move to the Nutter Center, the Bombers also planned the construction of a second building on the campus that would serve as the team's practice facility and to host games for hockey leagues of all levels. That part of the plan never materialized. (Courtesy of Wright State Special Collections.)

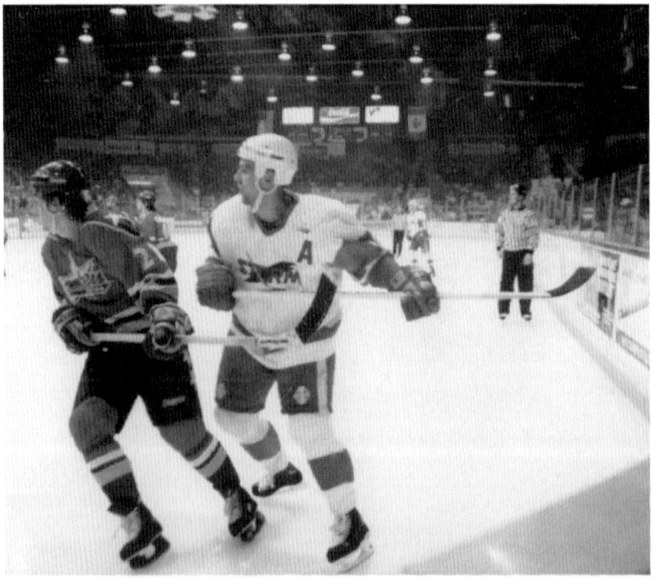

Built in 1947, the Toledo Sports Arena was home to many hockey teams in its 60-year existence, including the Bombers' archrival Toledo Storm. The Sports Arena was a small facility seating around 5,200 and had a reduced ice surface measuring 185 feet by 85 feet. Not only did the fans sit close to the ice, but the short visiting players' bench meant that some opposing players sat among the Toledo fans. (Courtesy of Melissia Taziar.)

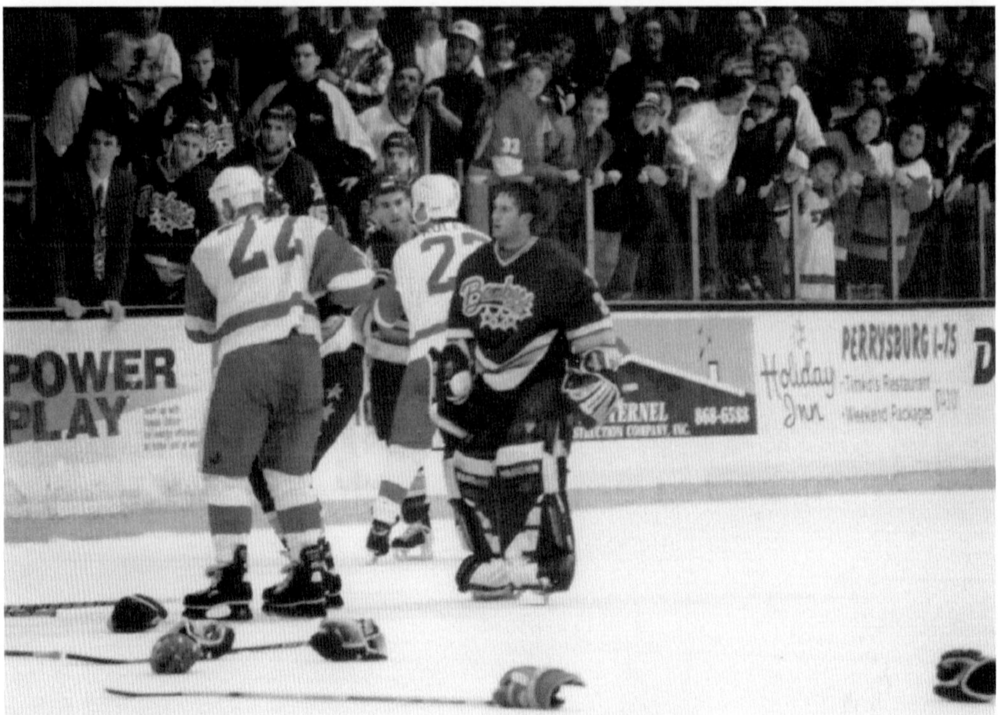

Toledo teams were always physical, and Toledo fans were hostile to the visiting team. When fights occurred (like this one between the Bombers and Storm), it was not unusual for the opposing player to get an earful from the Toledo fans or perhaps a beer shower. On occasion, a folding chair might get tossed onto the ice from an unruly fan. Like Hara Arena, the Toledo Sports Arena was one of a kind. (Courtesy of Melissia Taziar.)

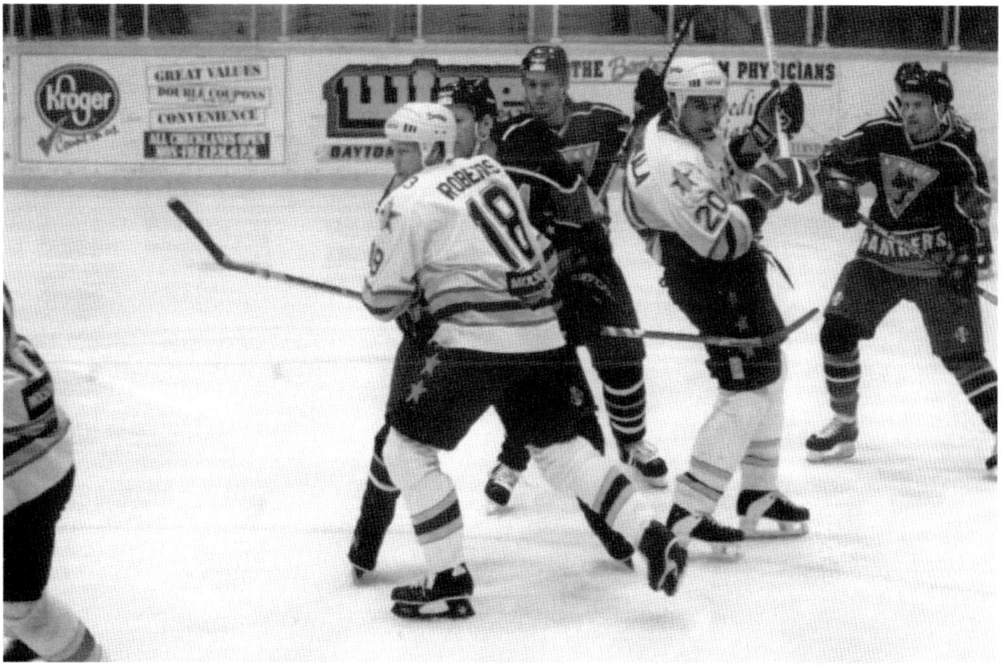

On March 14, 1996, a crowd of 4,020 watched Dayton beat the Erie Panthers 2-1 in the team's last regular-season game at Hara Arena. Though home attendance dropped by nearly 1,000 fans a game from the year before, team owners were confident that the move across town would increase fan support. (Courtesy of Melissia Taziar.)

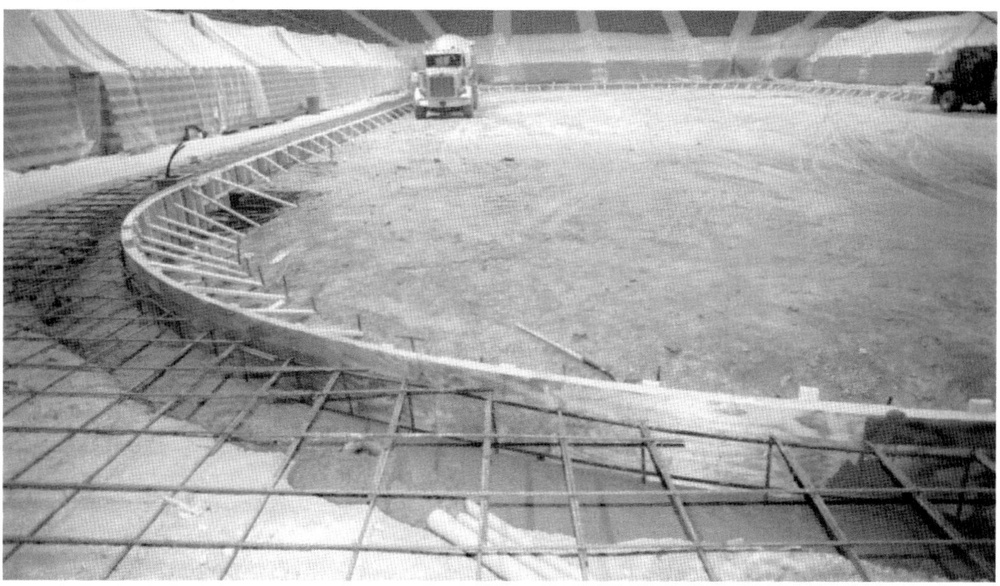

In the summer of 1996—after a KISS rock concert, according to John Siehl—construction crews began digging up the floor of the Nutter Center so that the refrigeration unit could be installed. Crews completed the work in time for the Bombers to open camp in their new home in early October. (Courtesy of Wright State Special Collections.)

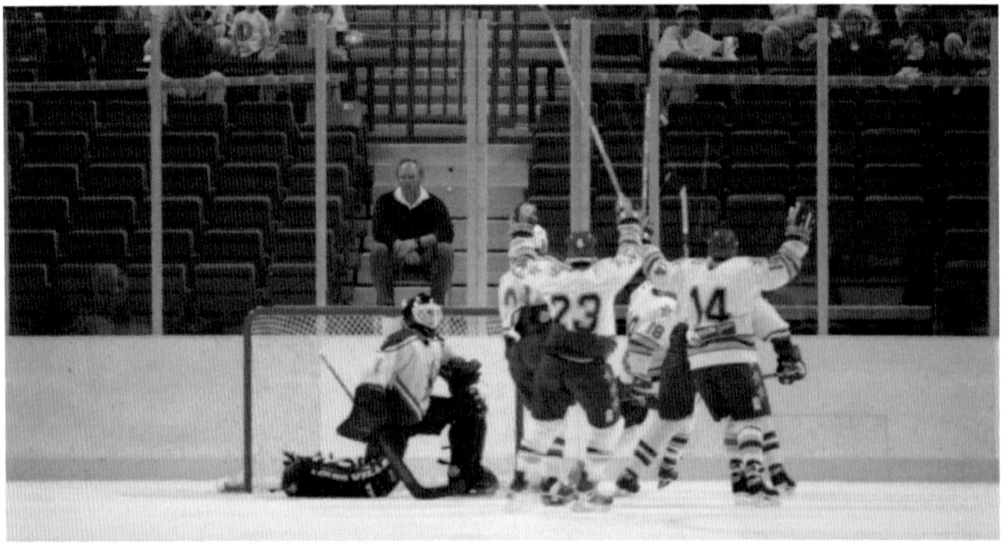

A crowd of around 2,000 turned out on October 9, 1996, to watch the first Bombers game at the Nutter Center, an exhibition game against the Peoria Rivermen. Peoria won the game 5-3. (Courtesy of Wright State Special Collections.)

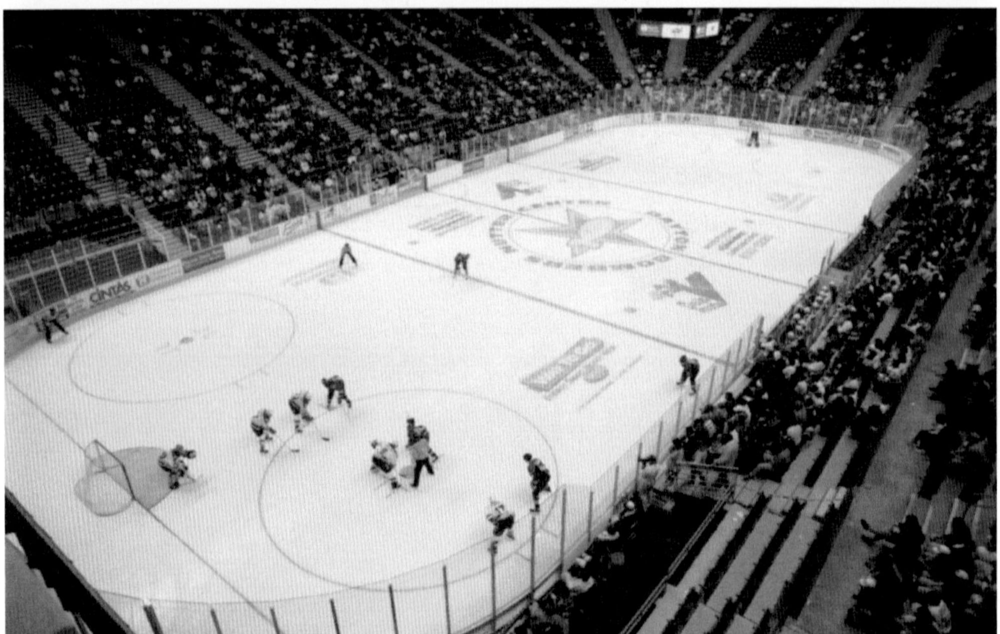

The Dayton Bombers officially christened their new home at the Nutter Center on the afternoon of October 20, 1996, taking on the Peoria Rivermen. The pregame festivities included a stirring rendition of "The Star-Spangled Banner" by Wayne Messmer, who performed the anthem before Chicago Blackhawks games. A Dayton hockey record crowd of 6,250 turned out to see the Bombers in their new home—nearly 700 more than the capacity of Hara Arena. (Courtesy of Wright State Special Collections.)

Colin Miller (8) mixes it up against Peoria in the first game at the Nutter Center. Dayton's John Emmons scored 41 seconds into the game to give the home team an early lead, but the Rivermen dominated the rest of the game, winning 6-1 and spoiling the day at the Bombers' new home. (Courtesy of Wright State Special Collections.)

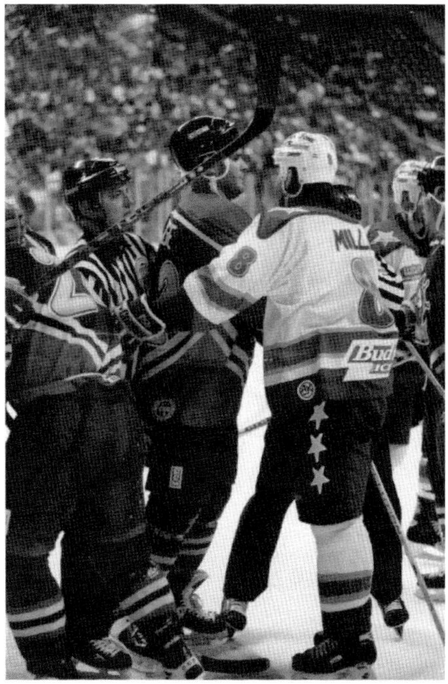

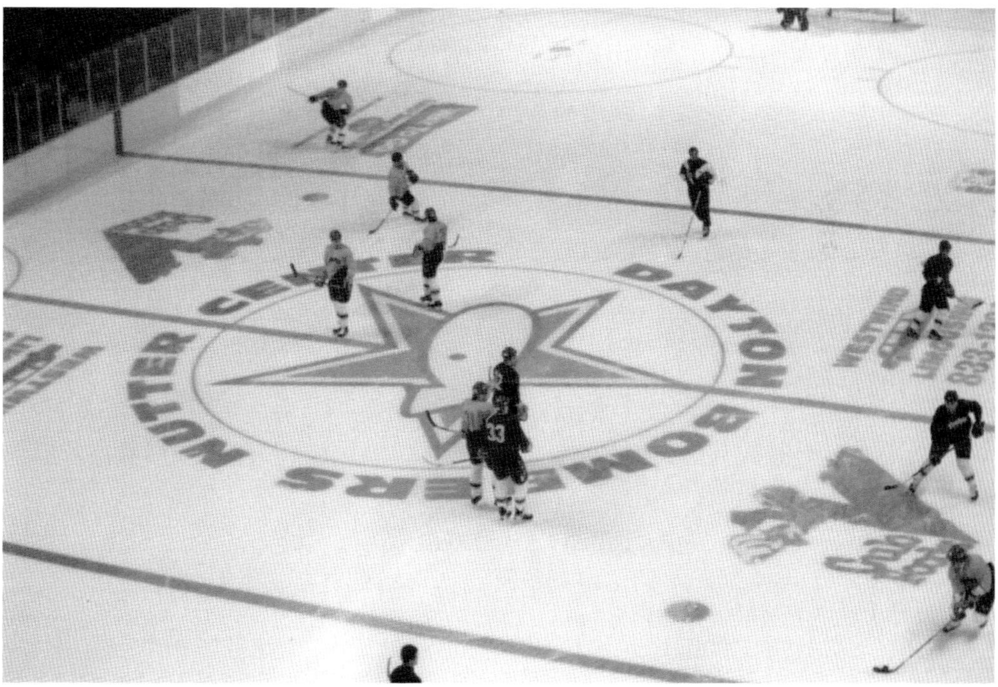

The rink dimensions at the Nutter Center were a regulation 200 feet by 85 feet, compared with Hara Arena, which measured 195 feet by 84 feet. At Hara, Bombers teams were bigger and more physical to take advantage of the smaller rink size. With the Nutter Center as home ice, Bombers teams became, if not smaller, much faster, to take advantage of the larger rink. (Courtesy of Melissia Taziar.)

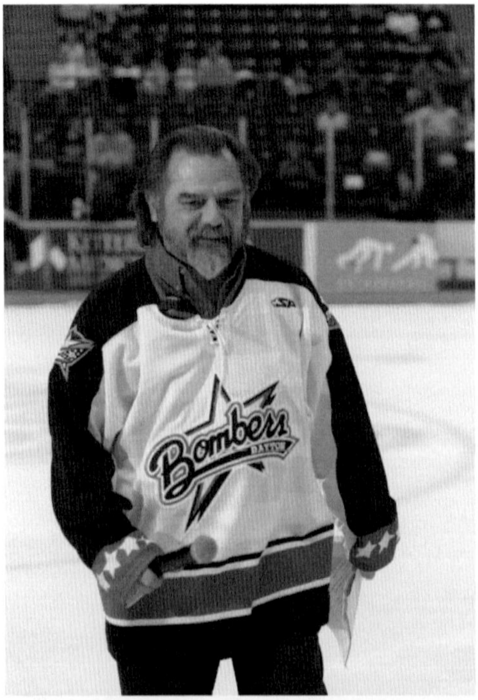

Dayton radio personality Bill Kirby served as PA announcer for the Bombers' first year at the Nutter Center and then played "Game Night MC" for the remaining years, interacting with the crowd throughout the game. "I knew nothing about hockey," Kirby recalled. "But Bud Gingher said 'It's just like baseball, just a few more rules'. So I got a couple of books on hockey and kind of learned as I went." (Courtesy of Max Surikov.)

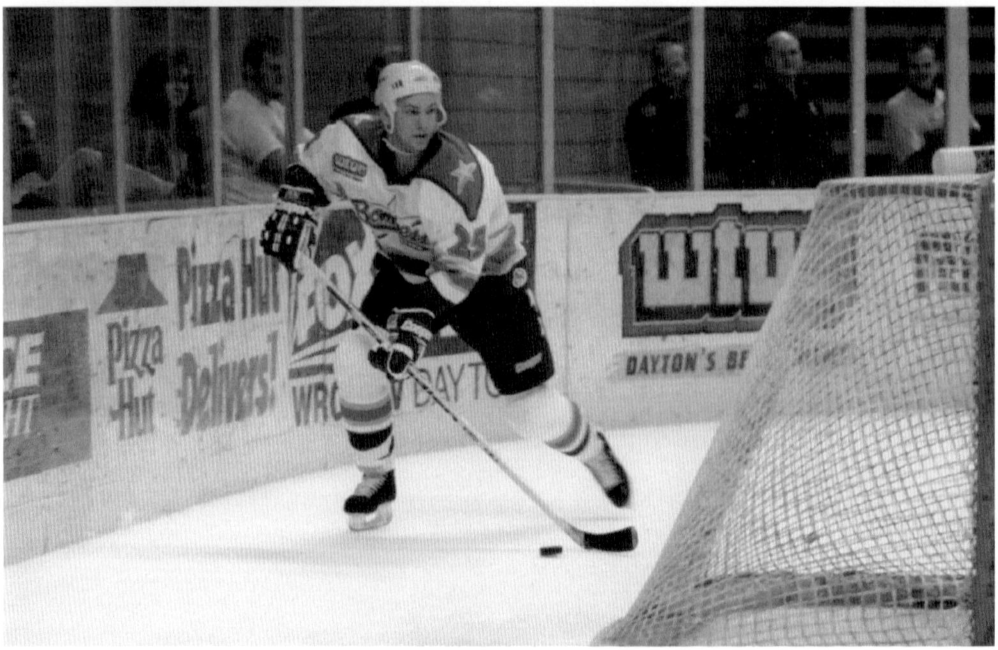

Tom Nemeth returned to the Bombers late in 1996 and remained with the team until 2003, anchoring the power play most of the time. Nemeth is the Bombers' all-time leader in games played (440), assists (334), and points (448). He is second to Sid Garant in career points by a Dayton hockey player. He was ECHL Defenseman of the Year three times and was inducted into the ECHL Hall of Fame in 2009. (Courtesy of Melissia Taziar.)

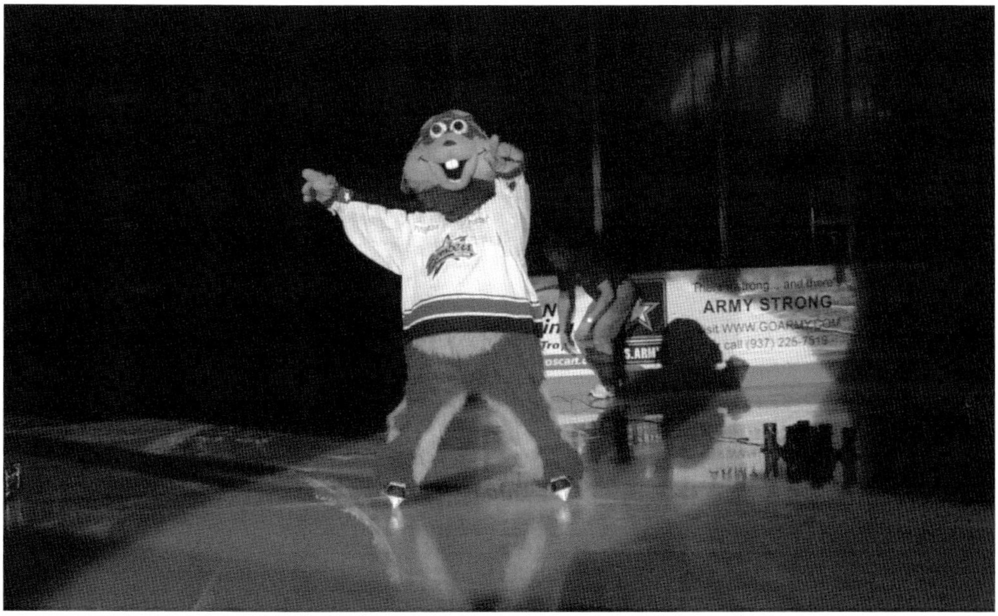

With the move to the Nutter Center, the Bombers also looked to rebrand the team by creating a new mascot. "Bucky the Flying Squirrel" was introduced to Bomber fans on opening night 1997, sliding down a cable from the upper concourse to the ice 60 feet below—a squirrel zip line of sorts. It was the only time the cable was used for a Bucky entrance. (Courtesy of Max Surikov.)

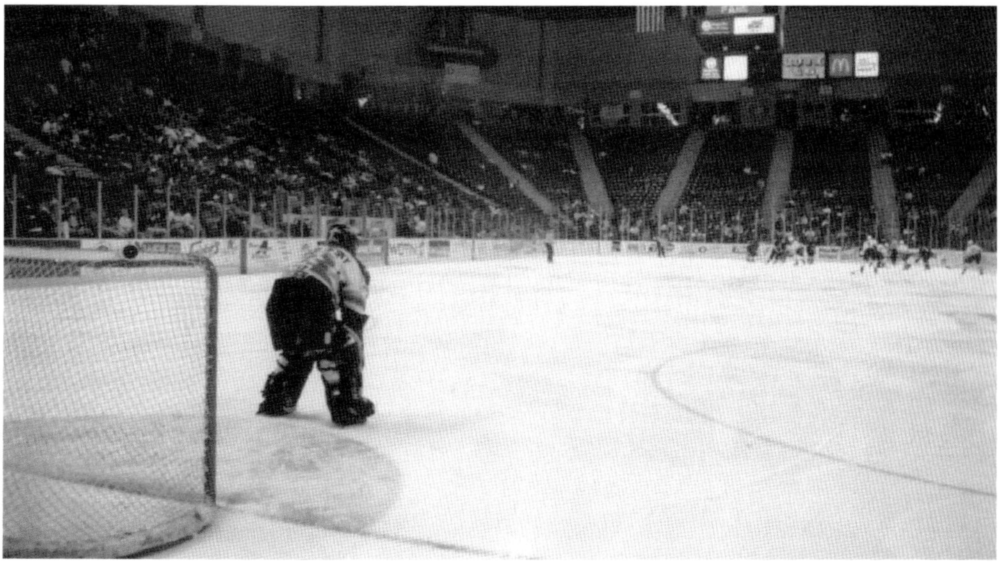

Goaltender Derek Herlofsky watches during a Bombers game at the Nutter Center during the 1996–1997 season. Whether because of the competition with the Dayton Ice Bandits or for other reasons, Bombers attendance the first year in the Nutter Center fell to 3,183 a game—the lowest of their first six years. Attendance picked up by over 1,000 a game the season after the Bandits folded. The 4,528 game average during the 1998–1999 season would be tops during the team's existence. (Courtesy of Melissia Taziar.)

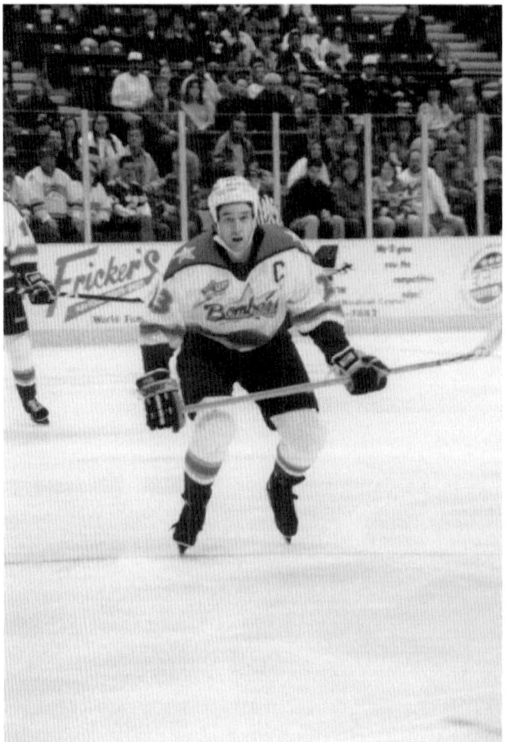

John Emmons had a one-season stay with the Bombers on his way to the NHL. During the 1996–1997 season, he scored 20 goals and had 37 assists. Emmons broke into the NHL with the Ottawa Senators during the 1999–2000 season. In all, he played in 85 NHL games with Ottawa, Tampa Bay, and Boston. (Courtesy of Melissia Taziar.)

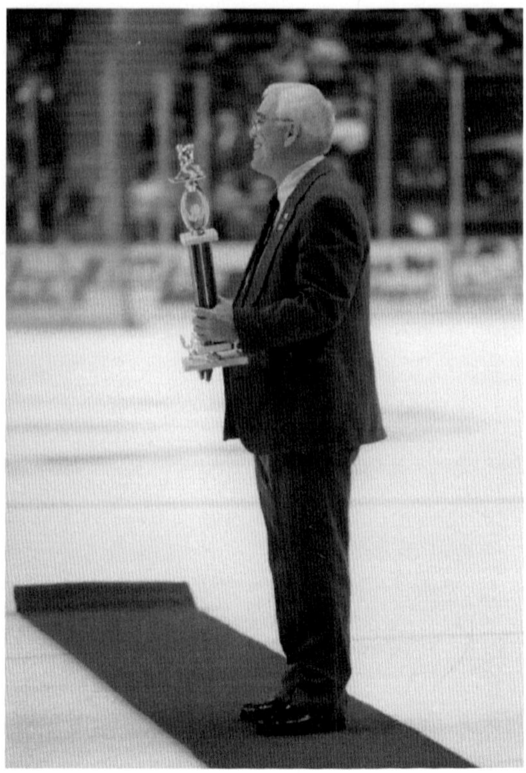

In July 1998, Bud Gingher (pictured) and Arnie Johnson sold the Bombers after seven years as owners. In the first two years at the Nutter Center, the team lost over $500,000, mostly due to paying back the debt on the Nutter Center ice. Over the next 11 years, the team had three different owners, who all faced the same issue of paying off the ice debt while trying to make the team profitable. (Courtesy of Melissia Taziar.)

Like the Dayton Gems, the Bombers had a few trades that were lopsided in their favor. One such acquisition was when the Bombers obtained Jamie Ling from the Chesapeake Icebreakers for "a thousand dollars," according to Ling. Ling played college hockey at Notre Dame and led the Irish in scoring each of his four years. Upon coming to Dayton, he led the Bombers in scoring in each of the next four years (1998–2002), tallying 333 points over that period. He was an ECHL all-star three times and was the recipient of the ECHL Sportsmanship Award three times (1999–2001). He totaled 383 points as a Bomber, second to Tom Nemeth's 448. Ling was inducted into the Dayton Hockey Hall of Fame in 2005. (Courtesy of Melissia Taziar.)

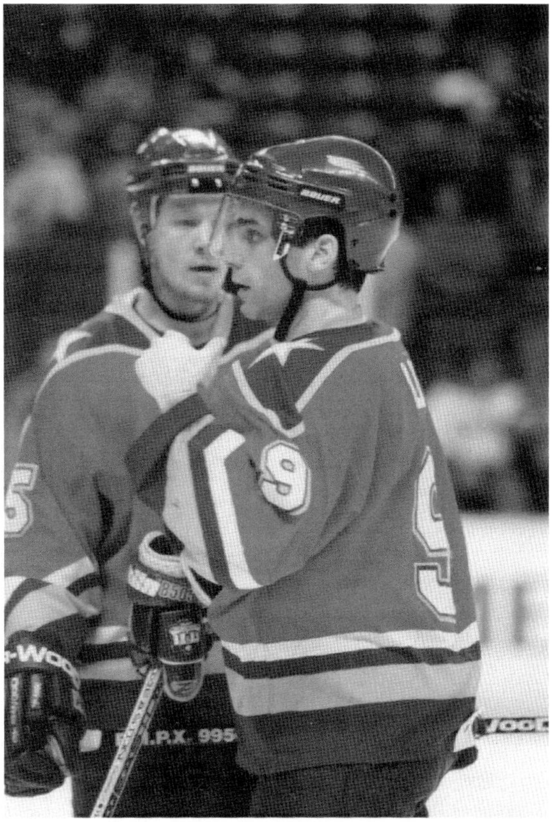

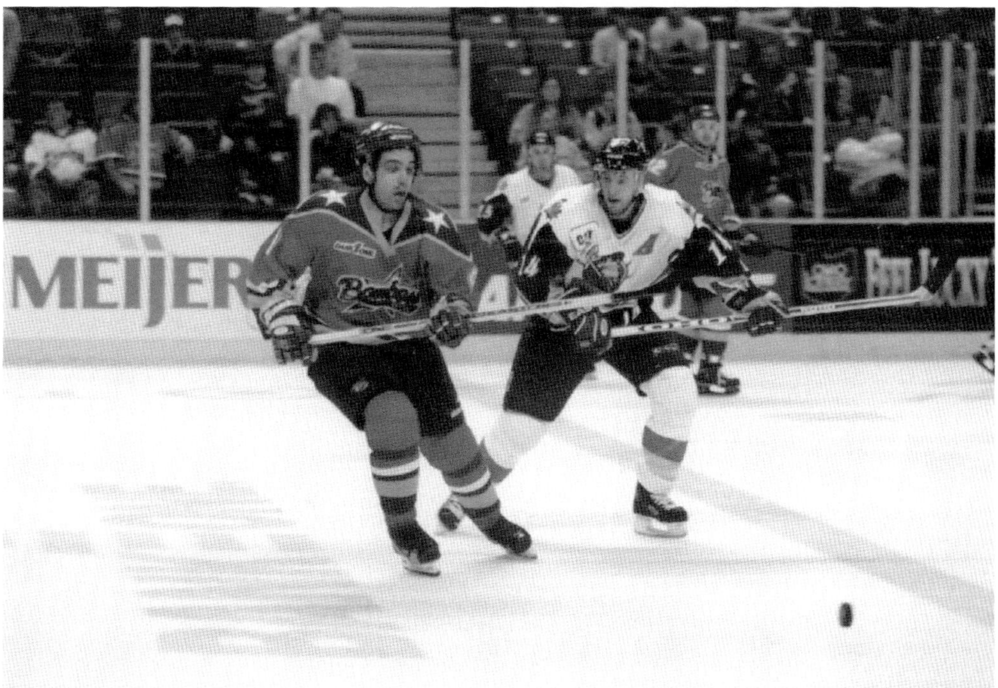

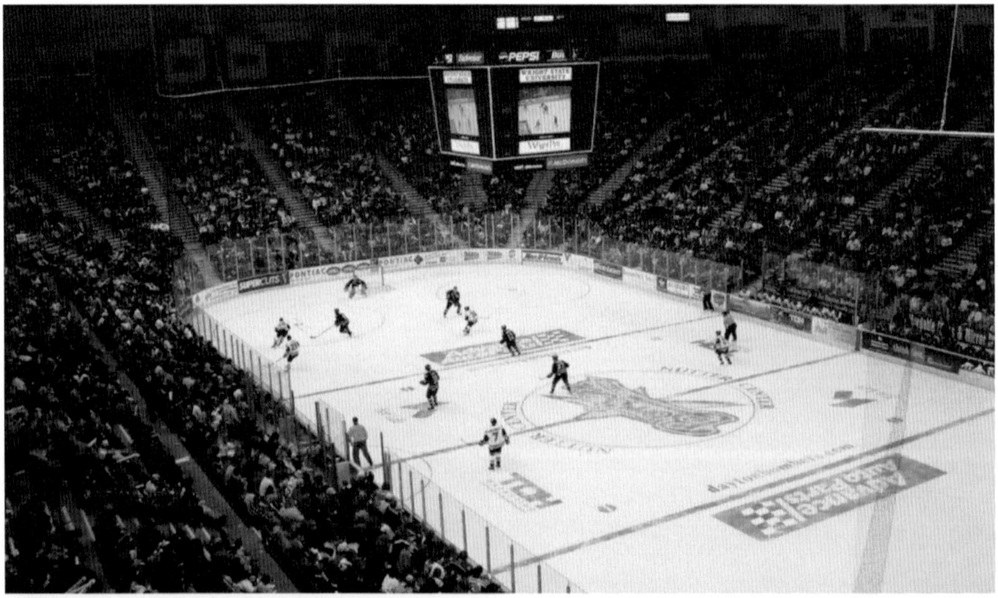

When the NHL's Hartford Whalers announced they were leaving Connecticut in the spring of 1997, the team considered Columbus, Ohio, and Raleigh, North Carolina, as possible locations. Had the Whalers chosen Ohio, the Nutter Center likely would have become the team's temporary home until an arena could be built in Columbus. However, North Carolina was selected, and the Hartford Whalers became the Carolina Hurricanes. (Courtesy of Nikki Jahns.)

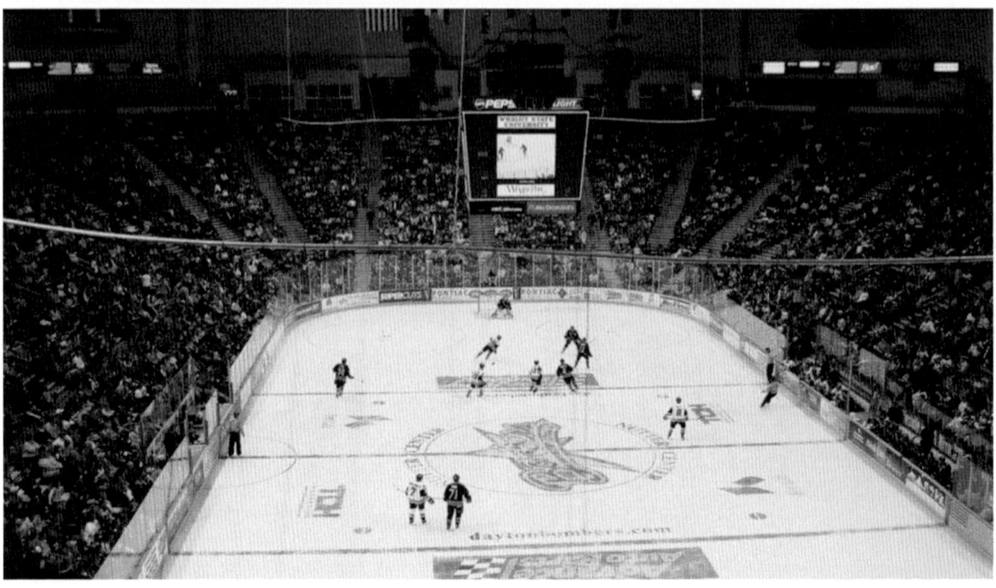

On January 23, 2004, a record Dayton hockey crowd of 10,057 jammed inside the Nutter Center to see the Bombers take on the Peoria Rivermen. But, many fans were actually there to see and meet Dale Earnhardt Jr. or have their photograph taken with his car. "Junior" was on hand that night as the Bombers lost to Peoria 3-1. Peoria was in town the next night, and the Bombers won 4-2. Without Earnhardt, the crowd was 4,936—still a pretty good turnout. (Courtesy of Nikki Jahns.)

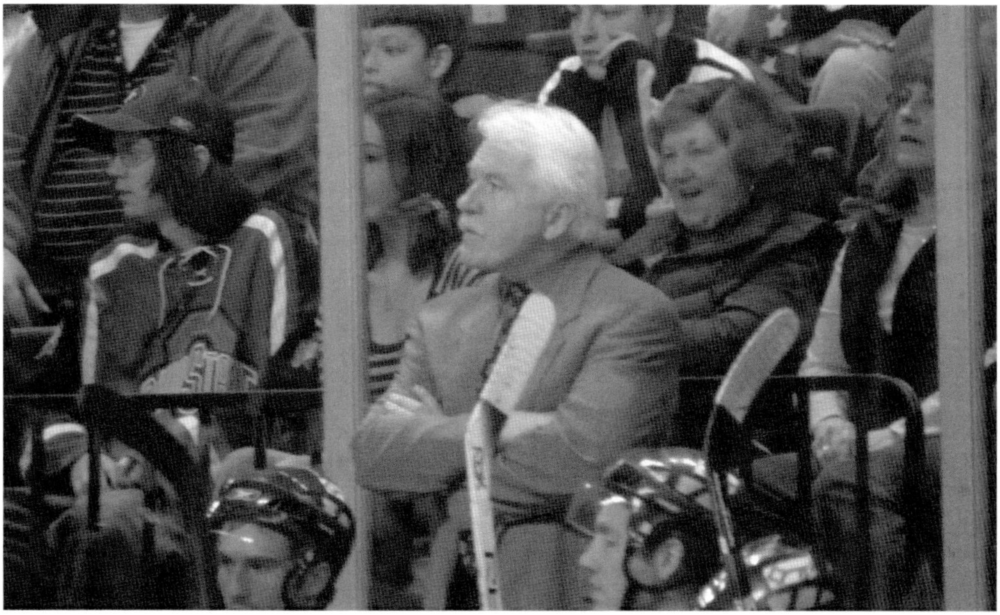

On July 21, 2004, Costa Papista and Don MacAdam (pictured) became the fourth owners of the Dayton Bombers, saving the franchise from going out of business. Papista focused on getting people into the Nutter Center, while MacAdam, once a Detroit assistant, became coach. MacAdam led the 2006–2007 Bombers to the Kelly Cup finals, where they lost to Idaho. (Courtesy of Nikki Jahns.)

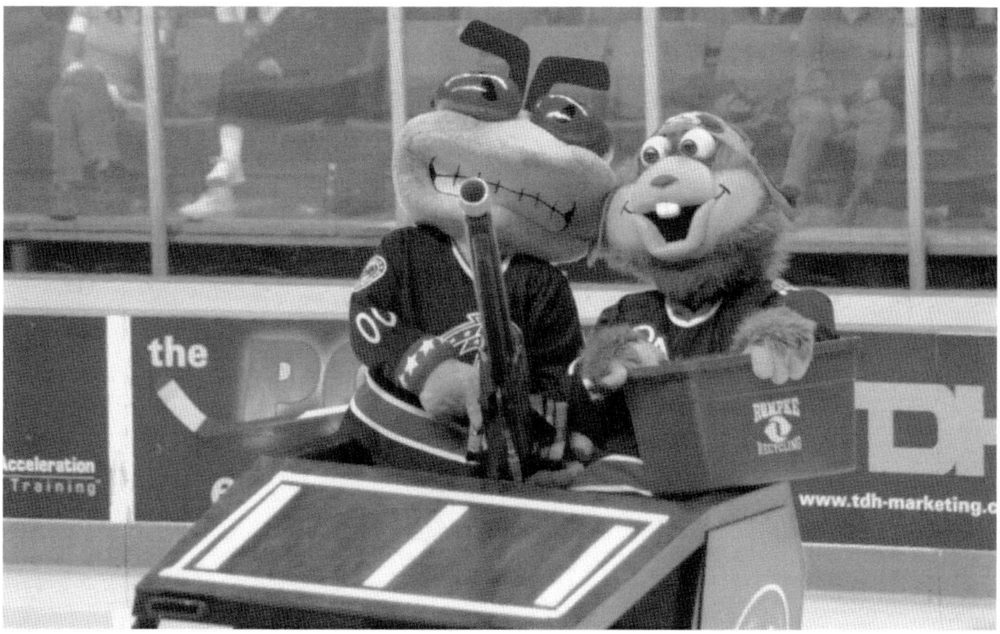

Bucky the Squirrel and Columbus Blue Jacket mascot "Stinger" hang out between periods of a Bombers home game. The Bombers became a farm team of the Blue Jackets when Columbus entered the NHL in 2000. A number of Bombers rose to the parent team, including Kristian Tollefsen and Dan LaCosta. (Courtesy of Max Surikov.)

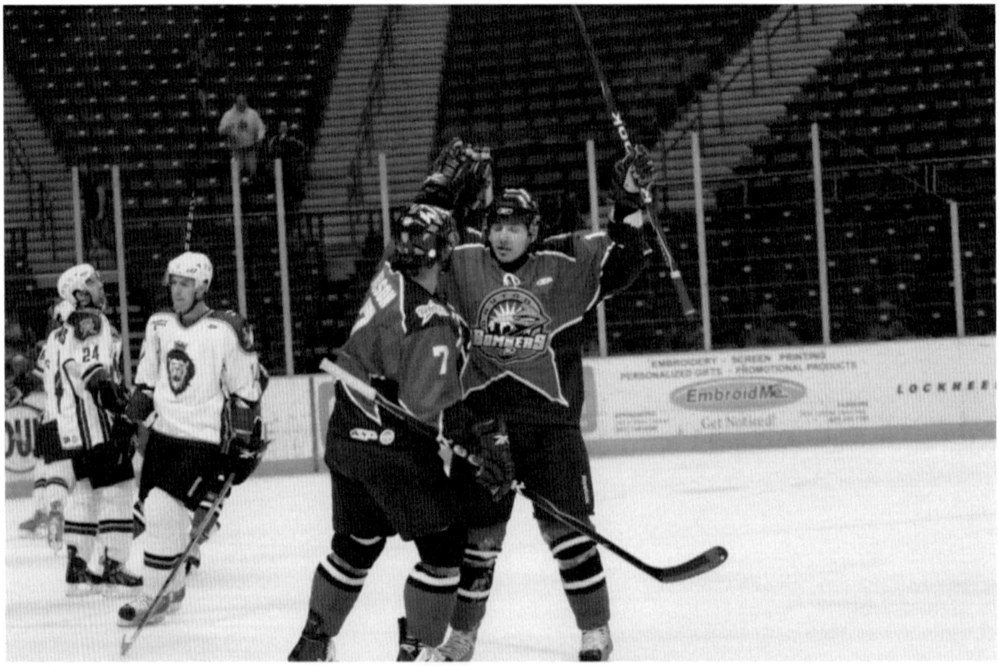

Throughout the Nutter Center years, at no time were the attendance struggles more obvious than during weeknight contests. While announced crowds were often above 2,000, the actual number of fans in attendance was often much less. Occasionally, some sections in the Nutter Center were completely empty, making the 10,000-seat home rink seem cavernous. (Courtesy of Max Surikov.)

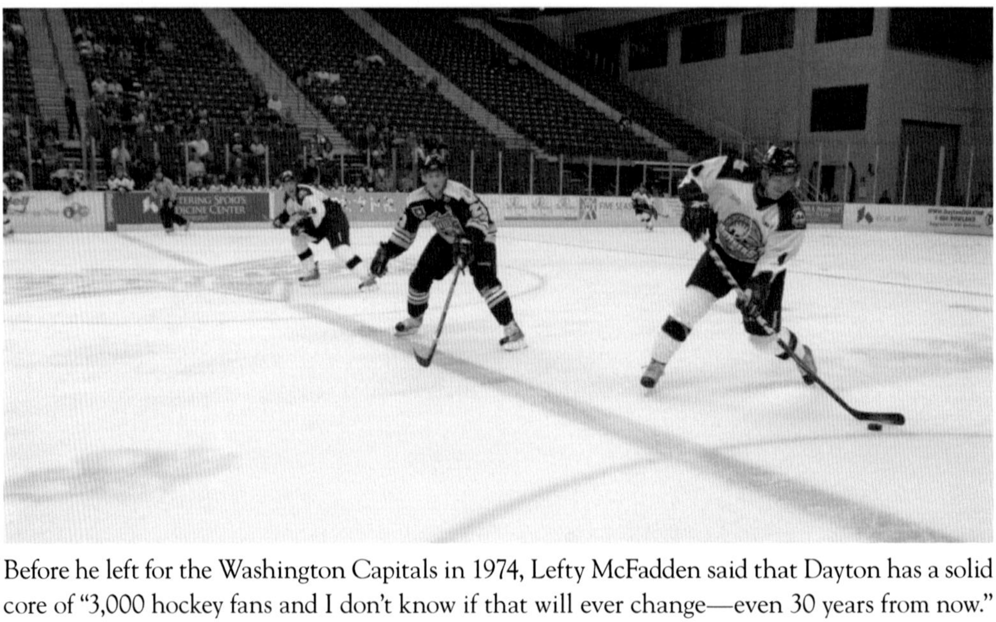

Before he left for the Washington Capitals in 1974, Lefty McFadden said that Dayton has a solid core of "3,000 hockey fans and I don't know if that will ever change—even 30 years from now." Almost prophetically, in the last seven years of the Bombers' existence, attendance never surpassed 3,700 fans a game. (Courtesy of Max Surikov.)

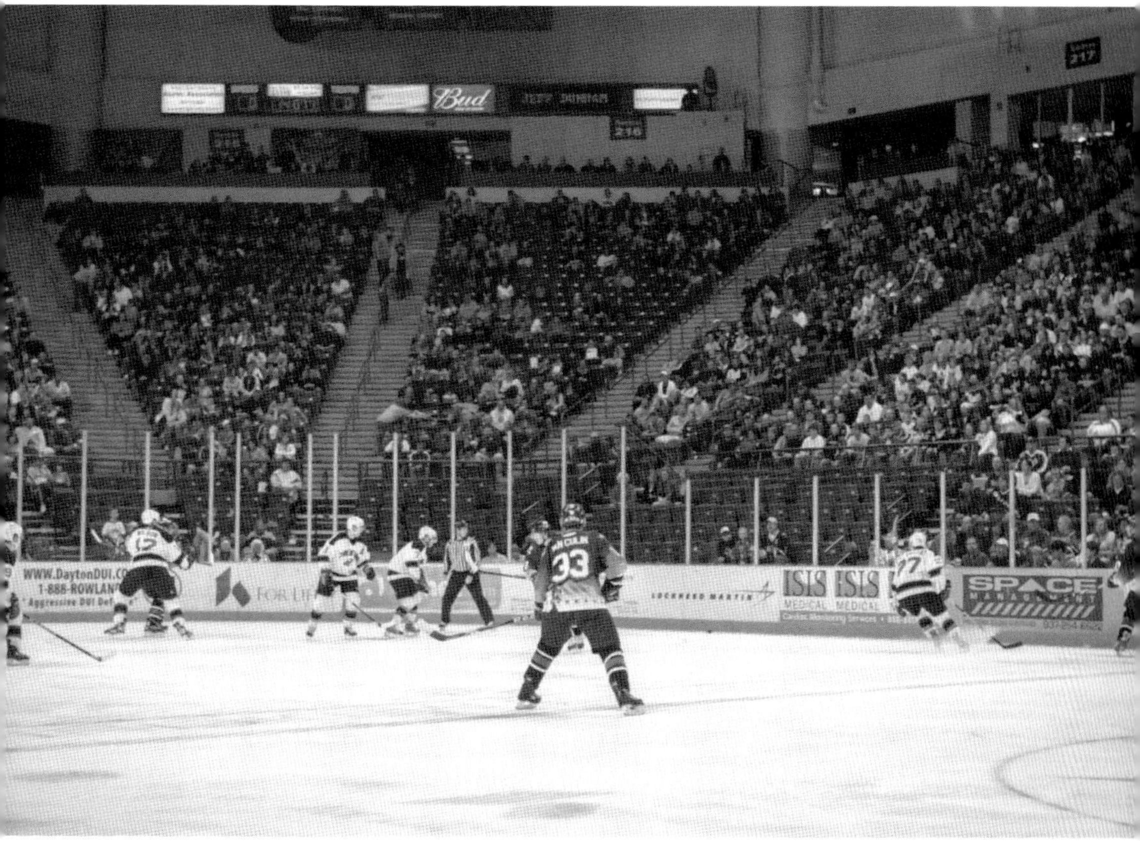

A season-high crowd of 8,108 turned out at the Nutter Center on March 28, 2009, to watch the Bombers play their last game there. The Bombers lost 3-1 to the Trenton Devils. A few days later, it was announced that the Bombers would not return to the ice for the 2009–2010 season. Over the next few months, owner Costa Papista attempted to secure new investors, with limited success. A number of factors came into play, most notably the lack of profitability the franchise had while at the Nutter Center. In late June 2009, Papista returned the team's league membership to the ECHL, ending the 18-year run of the Dayton Bombers. (Courtesy of Max Surikov.)

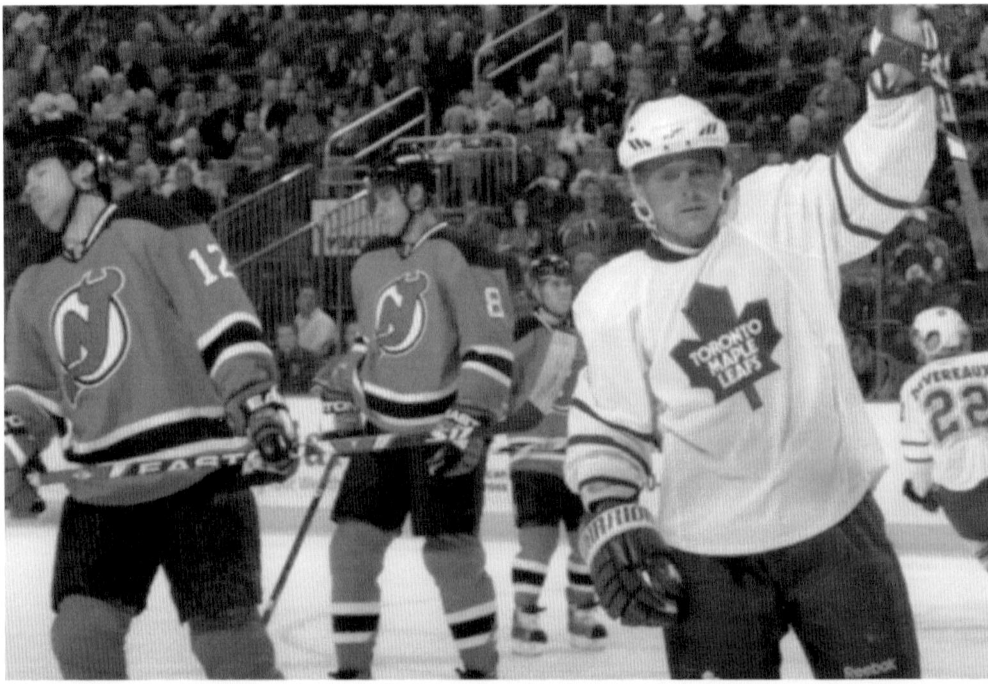

Jeff Hamilton never played hockey professionally in Dayton. He grew up in Englewood and played his youth hockey a few miles away at Hara Arena and Winterland ice arena. Hamilton went to Yale, where he became the school's all-time leading scorer. He went on to play in the NHL with the New York Islanders, Chicago Blackhawks, Carolina Hurricanes, and Toronto Maple Leafs, playing in 157 games and scoring 32 goals. (Courtesy of Dr. Michael Hamilton.)

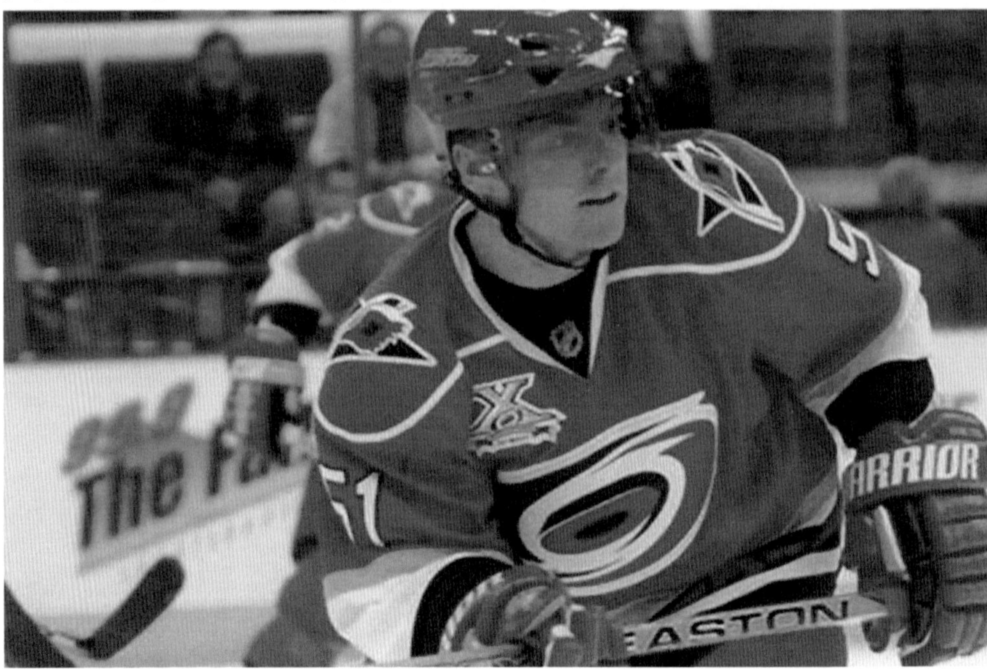

4

And the Others

From the Owls to the Demons

In addition to the Bruins, Gems, and Bombers, several other teams have played hockey in Dayton. There was one team that never played a game, but had it done so, it would have altered the history of Dayton hockey—and maybe even the city itself.

In October 1971, the World Hockey Association (WHA) was founded as a competitor to the NHL. Dayton—along with nine other cities, including Chicago, Los Angeles, and Miami—was given a charter franchise to start play in the fall of 1972. The Dayton franchise was led by architect Paul Deneau. The league estimated that each team would need to average 8,500 fans a game to break even. With no local facility to accommodate that number, Deneau proposed the construction of a 14,000-seat downtown arena across from the new Dayton Convention Center.

With the Gems still playing at Hara Arena, many felt that the area could not support two teams and that the Gems would have to be bought out by the WHA team—which would be named the Aeros—and then either moved or dissolved. In either case, Lefty McFadden believed the original Gems stockholders would need to receive fair compensation by Deneau for their investments.

By late December 1971, the City of Dayton agreed to fund the new arena and was considering putting temporary ice and 6,000 seats in the convention center as an interim home for the Aeros. With support for the arena and a temporary home in place, only the issue of the Gems' future remained. The Aeros presented Gems stockholders with a buyout offer, which was rejected. With the Gems' decision to stay, sentiment toward the Aeros began to change quickly. Soon after, the City of Dayton pulled its support for the arena and the convention center plans.

Unfazed, Deneau named NHL veteran Bill Dineen as the Aeros first coach. The WHA draft was held soon after. But investors began to pull out, and no funding was found for the new arena. In late March 1972, Deneau moved the team to Houston. The team became the Houston Aeros. Gordie Howe and his sons Mark and Marty would play there together in the mid-1970s. Dayton's opportunity for a big-league hockey franchise and downtown arena—which the city still does not have—was gone.

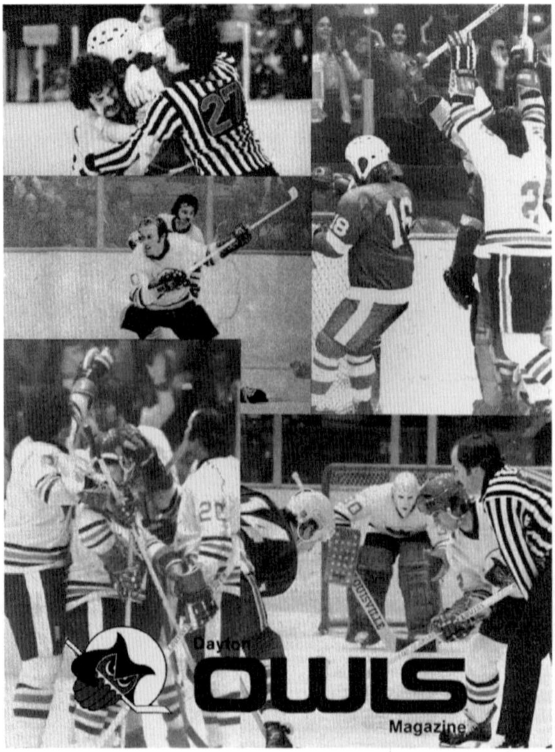

In August 1977, after the Gems had suspended operations, the Columbus Owls announced they would leave Columbus and move to Dayton to play at Hara Arena. Suddenly, Dayton fans would have to root for a team that, just a few months before, was one of the Gems' most bitter rivals. (Author's collection.)

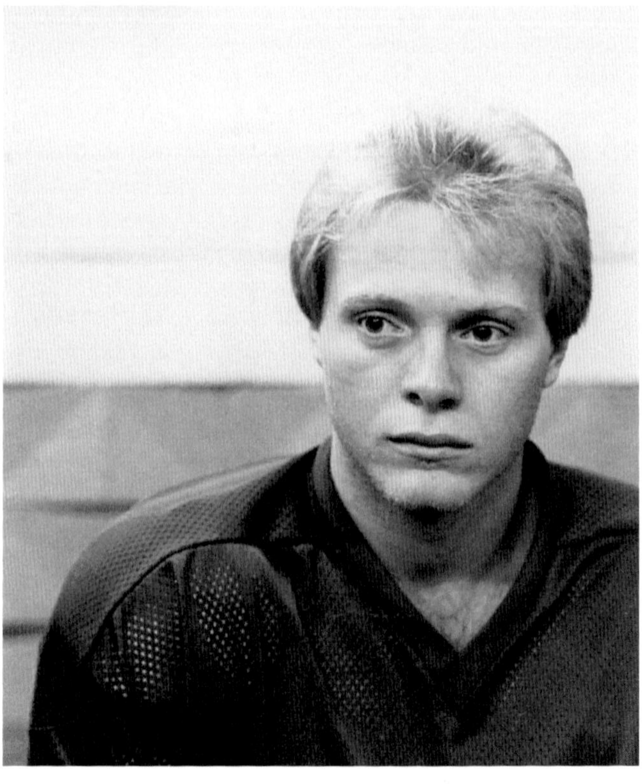

Prior to playing with the Dayton Owls, Guido Tenisi had a role in the hockey movie *Slapshot*, which starred Paul Newman and featured the Hanson brothers. Tenisi played the part of Charlestown Chief Billy Charlesbois, a player as interested in his good looks as he was in playing hockey. (Courtesy of Wright State Special Collections.)

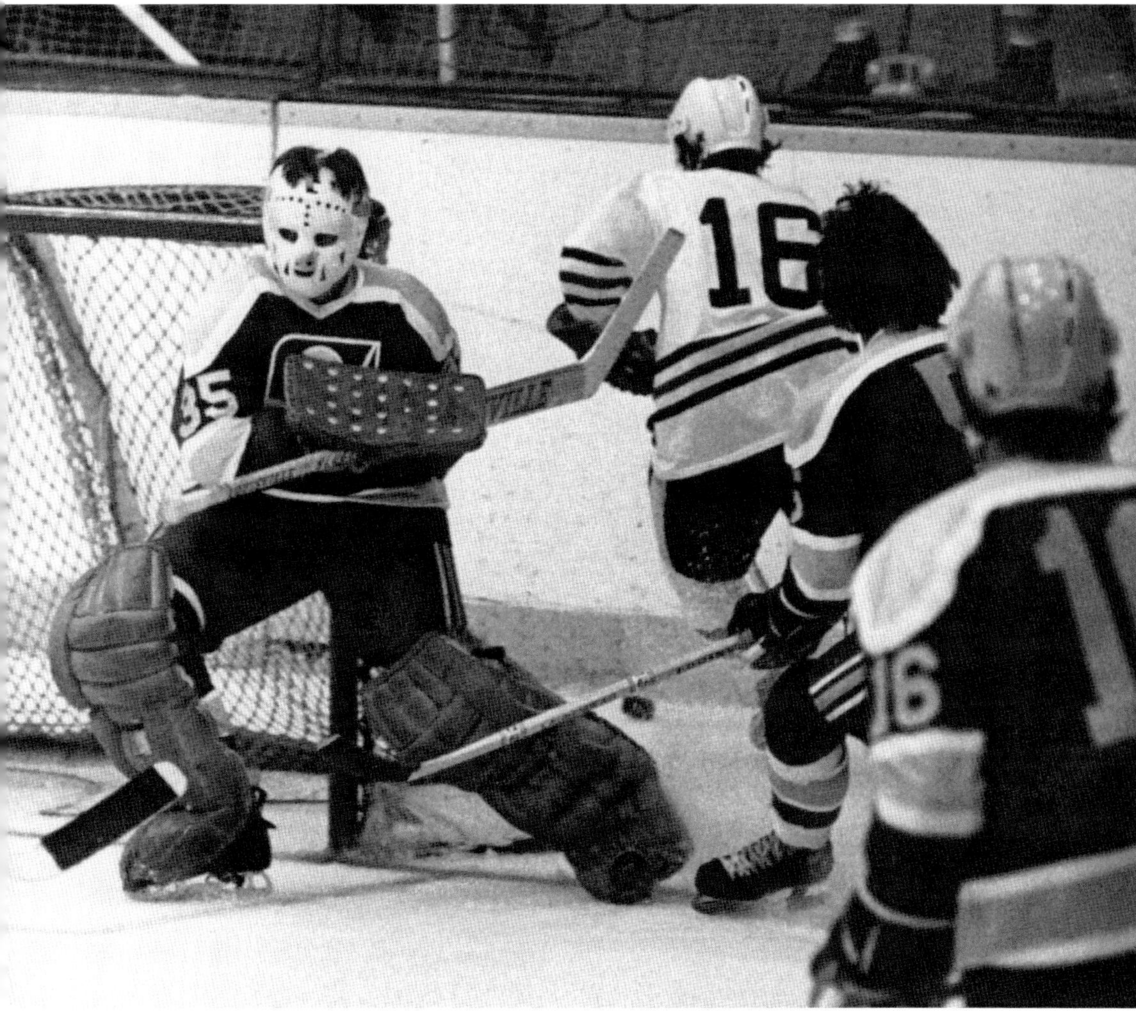

The Owls played the Toledo Goaldiggers in their first home game at Hara Arena on October 22, 1977. A crowd of 2,351—not much better than the Gems had drawn the year before—showed up to watch the Owls lose 3-1. Home attendance continued to be poor for the next few months. Finally, facing potential losses of several hundred thousand dollars, owner Al Savill moved the Owls to Grand Rapids in December 1977. (Courtesy of Wright State Special Collections.)

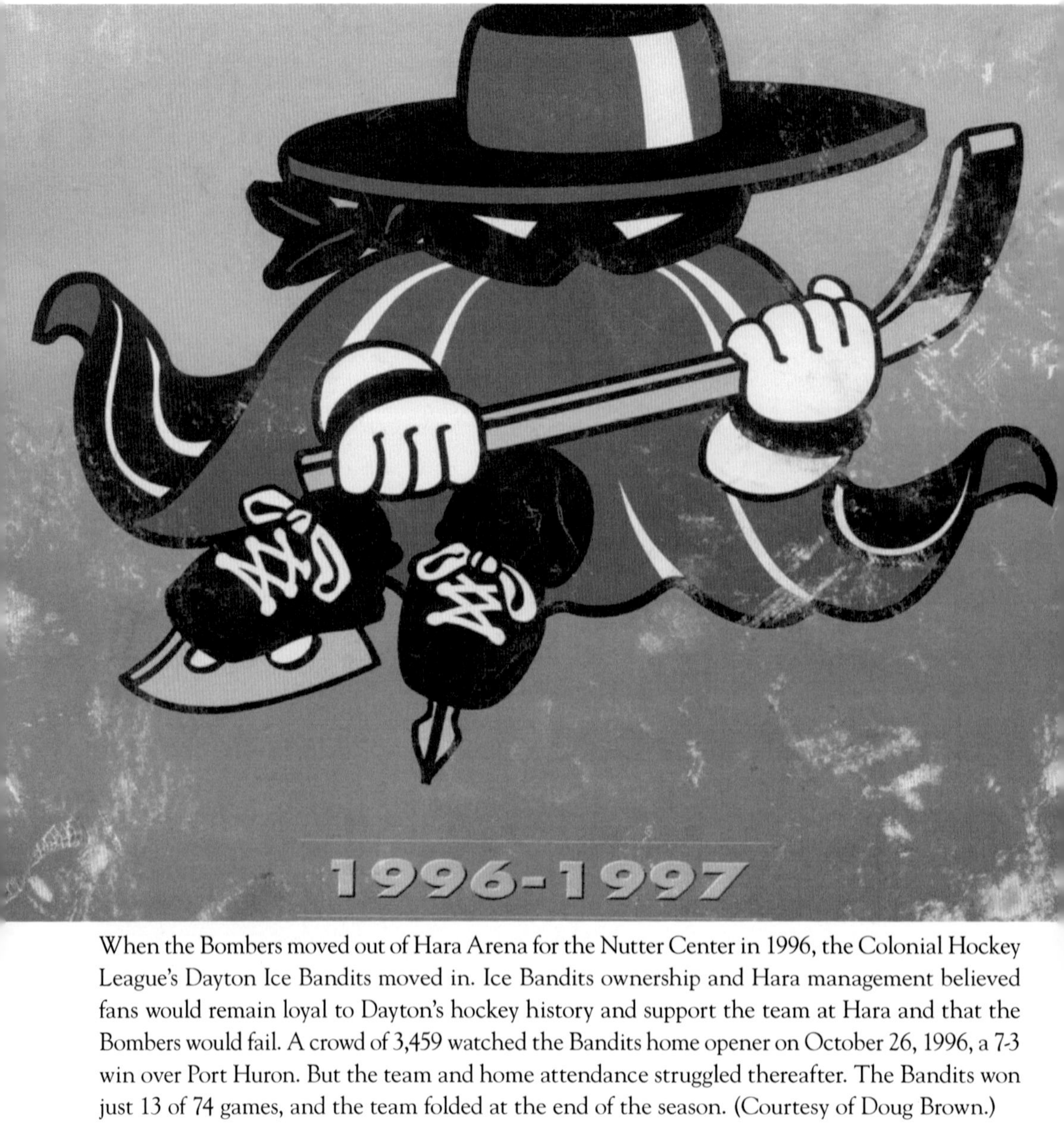

When the Bombers moved out of Hara Arena for the Nutter Center in 1996, the Colonial Hockey League's Dayton Ice Bandits moved in. Ice Bandits ownership and Hara management believed fans would remain loyal to Dayton's hockey history and support the team at Hara and that the Bombers would fail. A crowd of 3,459 watched the Bandits home opener on October 26, 1996, a 7-3 win over Port Huron. But the team and home attendance struggled thereafter. The Bandits won just 13 of 74 games, and the team folded at the end of the season. (Courtesy of Doug Brown.)

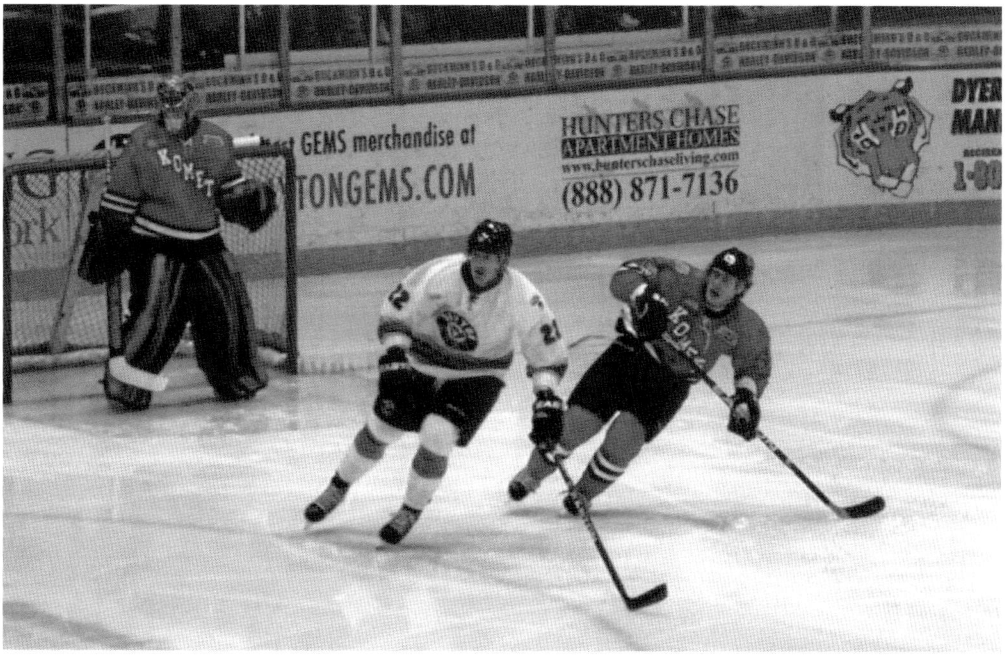

Not long after the Bombers announced they would not return, Fort Wayne businessmen Rich Brunner and Ryan Yarrick announced that they intended to revive the Dayton Gems to play in the new International Hockey League beginning in the fall of 2009. The original IHL had ceased operations in 2001, but it was revived in 2007 as a single-A league. Former IHL cities including Fort Wayne, Muskegon, and Flint would play in the new league. (Courtesy of Chris A. Photography.)

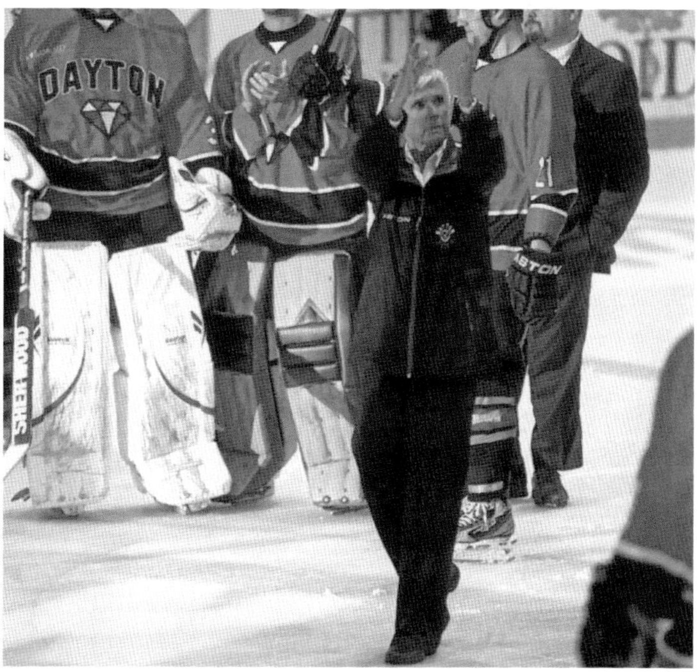

Just two months into the 2009–2010 season, the IHL removed Ryan Yarrick and Rich Brunner as owners. A group of local owners that included Rob Garfield, Dr. Paul Nitz, and Kathy Rupp (pictured), wife of the late Pat Rupp, who played goal with the original Gems, took control of the team. (Courtesy of Chris A. Photography.)

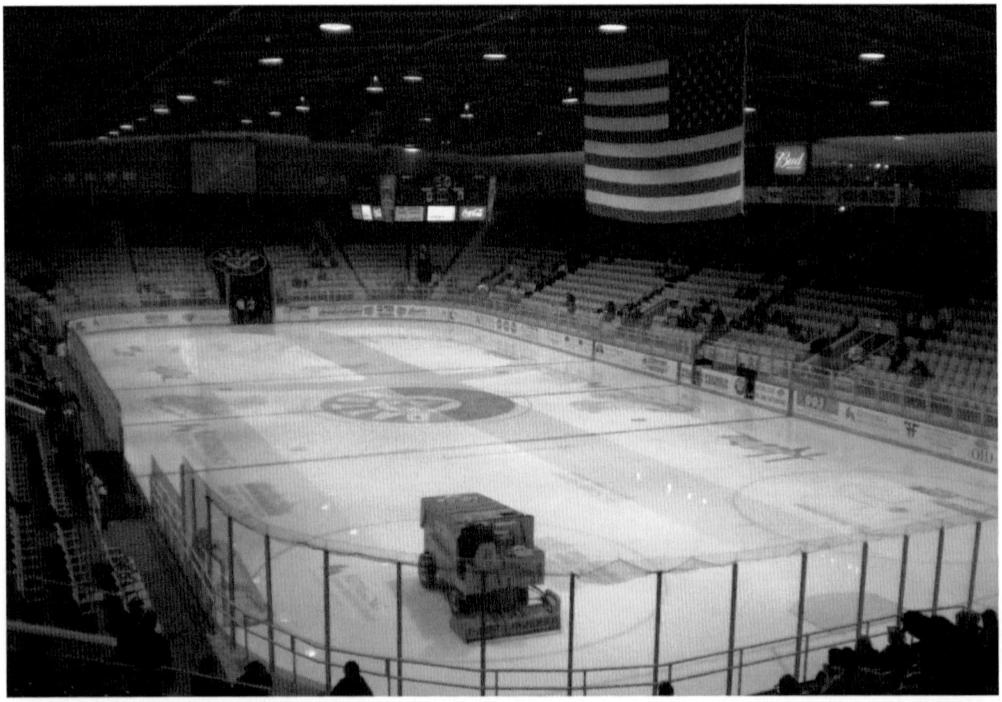

The "new" Gems played at Hara Arena, not the Nutter Center. The team and owners worked hard to rekindle the atmosphere the original Gems created at Hara in the 1960s and 1970s. (Courtesy of Stadium Journey/Konrad Klank)

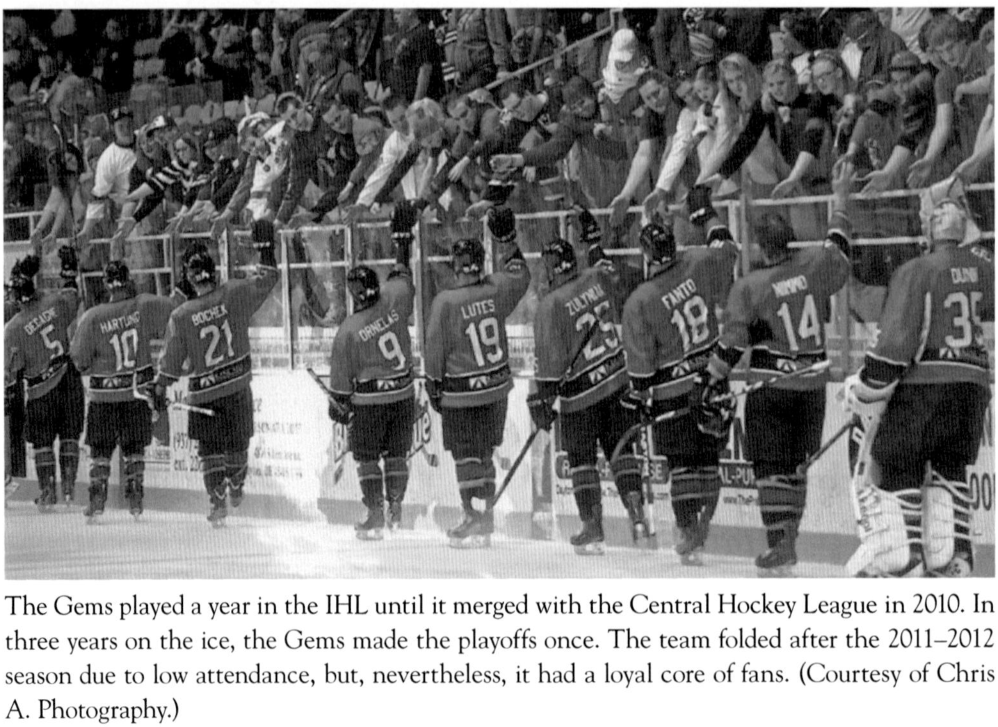

The Gems played a year in the IHL until it merged with the Central Hockey League in 2010. In three years on the ice, the Gems made the playoffs once. The team folded after the 2011–2012 season due to low attendance, but, nevertheless, it had a loyal core of fans. (Courtesy of Chris A. Photography.)

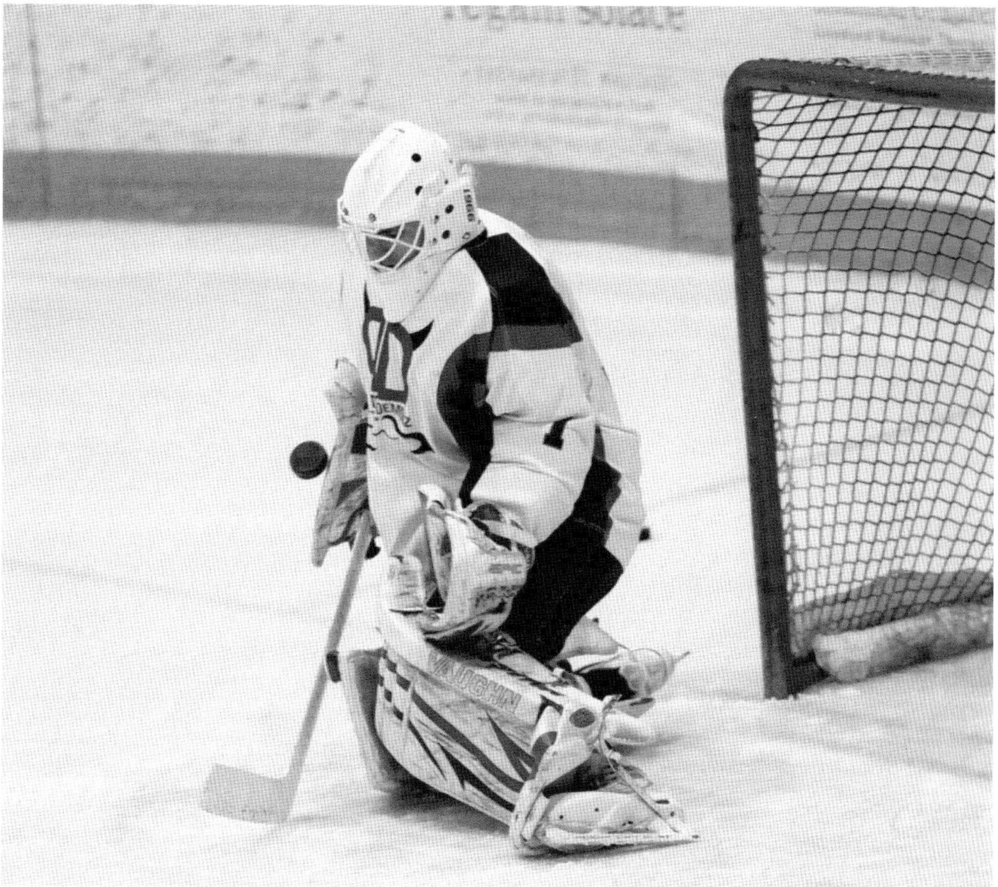

The Dayton Demonz took up residency at Hara Arena following the Gems' exit in 2012. The Demonz compete in the Federal Hockey League—the name of the fictitious league in the movie *Slapshot*. The Demonz won the 2014 Federal League playoff championship. (Both, courtesy of Mike Clare.)

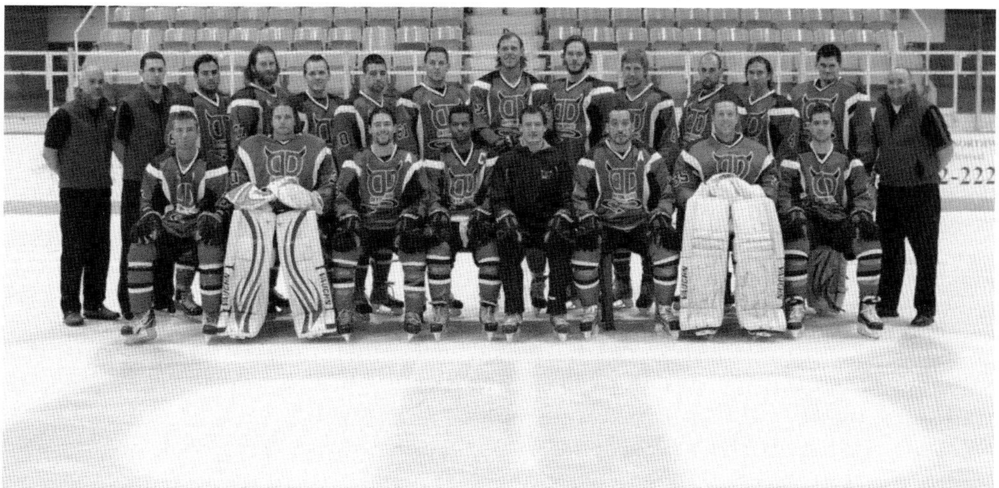

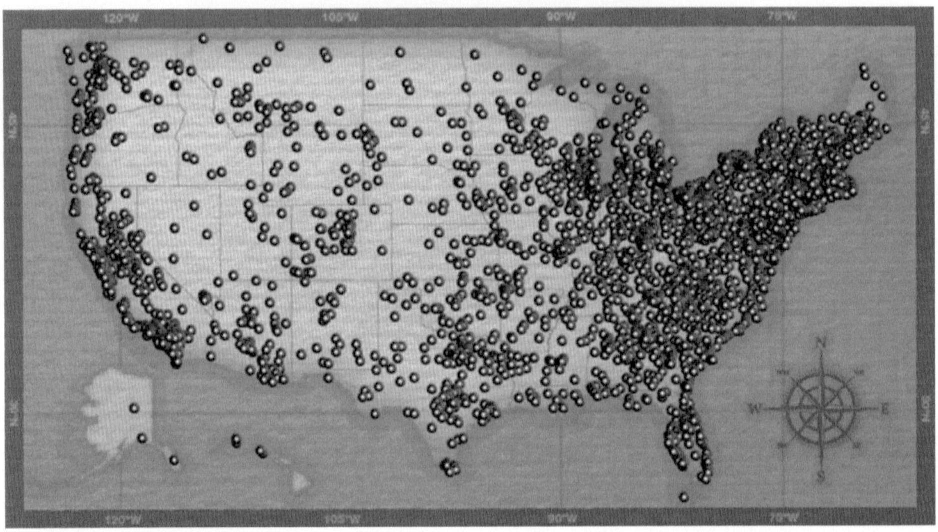